QUEST FOR A
STABLE
AFGHANISTAN

Praise for the Book

The international military aid and development assistance in Afghanistan have been largely ineffective and wasteful in fixing the war-torn country. In *Quest for a Stable Afghanistan*, Sujeet provides an intimate and detailed account of how the haggard and faulty policies of the West have put Afghanistan on the brink of a deeper and increasingly worrisome crisis. The author has a history and temperament of calling a spade a spade.

—Mohammad Ehsan Zia
Country Director Afghanistan, US Institute of Peace and
Former Minister, Rural Rehabilitation and Development,
Government of Afghanistan

Having spent more than a decade in Afghanistan, Sujeet is brutally honest about the current state of affairs in that country. His razor-sharp analysis of the failure of the West, especially the US, in stabilizing Afghanistan is noteworthy. He has not spared Pakistan either for fomenting trouble inside Afghanistan. Overall, very insightful and worth reading.

—Mansoor Faizy
Editor-in-Chief, *Afghanistan Times*

A must-read for the US political leadership, Afghan politicians, international strategic community and anyone who is interested in knowing about what went wrong in Afghanistan. It is evident from the flair, authority and the depth of writing that the author has intimately witnessed the developments in Afghanistan over the last two decades.

—Hussain Marefat
Chairperson, Afghanistan Group of Newspapers

QUEST FOR A STABLE AFGHANISTAN

A VIEW FROM GROUND ZERO

SUJEET SARKAR

RUPA

Published by
Rupa Publications India Pvt. Ltd 2021
7/16, Ansari Road, Daryaganj
New Delhi 110002

Sales Centres:
Allahabad Bengaluru Chennai
Hyderabad Jaipur Kathmandu
Kolkata Mumbai

ISBN: 978-93-91256-35-7

Second impression 2021

10 9 8 7 6 5 4 3 2

The moral right of the author has been asserted.

Printed at Sanat Printers, Sonipat

Dedicated to my team members and friends
who lost their lives towards creating a better Afghanistan.

~

Contents

~

As strongly predicted in the book, the Taliban captured Kabul on 15 August 2021, when India was engrossed in celebrating its 75th Independence Day. The embattled Afghan president Ashraf Ghani fled the country on Sunday (15 August) with his entourage of ministers and advisors to an undisclosed destination, leaving behind tales of destruction and shattered hopes of seeing a progressive and stable Afghanistan. Many experts believe that it is a return to the Stone Age, and the death of democracy forever, while the rest fear that the Taliban rule will unleash extreme oppression and loss of liberty and freedom of women forever. As foreigners and locals are caught in a stampede to leave the beleaguered nation, the world is watching if Taliban 2.0 would be any different from Taliban 1.0.

~

Introduction

In 2001, the United States (US) orchestrated an express overthrow of the Taliban regime as an aftermath of the September 11 attacks. This was inevitable after the former US President George W. Bush's numerous calls to the Taliban regime to hand over Osama bin Laden, the main architect of the 9/11 attack, failed to elicit an affirmative response. By refusing to capitulate to the military might of the US, the Taliban were preparing for a long and protracted war. This resulted in massive US troops rallying with the latest military arms and equipment all over Afghanistan, with a special focus on the hostile southern provinces. The predator unmanned aerial vehicles, armed with drone missiles, were employed in large numbers to target militants hiding in inhospitable mountainous terrains and the safe sanctuaries of the Afghanistan-Pakistan border.

After the collapse of the Taliban regime, the objective of the war on terror was expanded to weed out al-Qaeda and Taliban militants, and irreversibly degrade their capabilities to strike and control Afghanistan again.

After more than 19 years of relentless war and over

$2 trillion spent, it is now becoming increasingly clear that the Taliban are far from being vanquished.[1] In fact, according to US intelligence reports, they have grown more lethal and organized in the course of this war. From their traditional bastion of the southern region of Afghanistan, the Taliban have wormed into the relatively stable provinces of the northern region. They are further congregating on the outskirts of Kabul and attacking the capital at their free will. Fifty out of Afghanistan's 370 districts lie under the direct control of Taliban.[2] The writ of the fragile Ashraf Ghani 2.0 government is being openly challenged.

With the war showing no sign of ending, the Pentagon is smoking the peace pipe with the same Taliban that it had set out to eliminate. In fact, at this juncture, the US is both fighting and talking peace with the Taliban. There is a greater realization in Washington that the war in Afghanistan is unwinnable and is going to leave the Taliban in a much stronger position than they were in 2001. The peace deal is the only face-saver for the US exit from Afghanistan. Former US president Donald Trump had signed a peace agreement with the Taliban on 29 February 2020, after cancelling the same in the first week of September 2019. This on-again, off-again peace process, now running over a decade, shows no sign of conclusion; and anyway, it seems, in this entire process the Taliban are set to gain more leverage at the peace table.

The peace deals will remain academic, unless the intra-Afghan peace dialogue concludes to the satisfaction of both the Taliban and the incumbent government of Afghanistan.

---

[1] Almuktar, Sarah, 'What did the US get for $2 Trillion in Afghanistan?' *The New York Times*, 9 December 2019.

[2] Robertson, Nic, Mohammed Tawfeeq and Richard Roth, '50 of Afghanistan 370 districts have fallen to Taliban since May: UN,' CNN, 22 June 2021.

The nascent but pivotal intra-Afghan political dialogue has failed to gather momentum for one reason or the other, with each party blaming the other for the standstill. While the Taliban claim that the Ghani government bedevils the peace process with the delay in releasing their fighters languishing in various jails of Afghanistan, the Afghan government demands 'demonstrable evidence' from the Taliban about their sincerity and commitment to the peace process. The deadlock between the Taliban and President Ghani's administration has exacerbated the violence and terrorist attacks to a historic high. Since the US-led invasion in 2001, Afghanistan has never been as insecure as it is now. Civilian casualty has reached an unprecedented high, even from the crude matrix of Afghanistan, which has a legacy of civil strife and terrorism. The Afghanistan Independent Human Rights Commission has, in its 2020 Annual Report, stated that around 11,000 civilians, including 2,696 children, have suffered casualties in the ongoing conflicts during the last year.

The money machine

Poppy remains the axis of evil and continues to poison Afghanistan. Poppy production has an inescapable link with the rise of terrorism, with the Taliban reportedly making anything between $220 and $250 million per year from the extended value chain of poppy within Afghanistan. With the help of this money, the militant organization continues to fill its coffers and fund its overt aggression through fresh recruits of fighters and procurement of the latest range of military equipment. The poppy money lubricates the entire Taliban machinery with a regular and adequate flow of resources, giving the group an extended motivation to fight for the overthrowing of the US-supported government in Kabul. The international security assistance forces launched a massive poppy eradication programme to eliminate poppy from the minds and fields of the farmers, in order to choke the chief source of finance for the Taliban. However, the campaign has largely proven counterproductive and turned the poppy-growing farmers against their own government. In a way, the inept campaign made the farmers turn towards the Taliban for succour.

The faulty poppy eradication programme has inadvertently ceded the control of Afghanistan to the Taliban, with poppy production showing no sign of declining. According to the latest United Nations Office on Drugs and Crime (UNODC) data, poppy cultivation has increased from 74,000 hectares (2002), a year after the Taliban regime was toppled, to 2,63,000 (2018)—depicting an alarming three-fold rise. Though there was a slight fall in poppy cultivation (net sown area) in 2019, the yields were higher owing to better weather conditions and almost no plant disease, according to the latest UNODC data. Opium production has increased from 185 metric tonnes in 2001, the year that witnessed the toppling of the Taliban regime, to 5,500 metric tonnes in 2019, registering an alarming thirty-fold rise. This unprecedented rise in poppy cultivation, despite funneling billions of dollars, calls into question the approach and effectiveness of the West-sponsored counter narcotics intervention in Afghanistan.

The much-hyped state-building process too did not produce much to rejoice about. The vast resources and efforts channelled towards building the nascent institutions of the state to shape the future of the country seem to be faltering. Over more than $100 billion was deployed by the West to train and nurture the Afghan military and police forces alone.

However, despite decades of investment, the Afghan security forces continue to be sitting duck for the Taliban. As per conservative estimates, the average death toll of soldiers lies between 60 and 70 personnel per day. And this is only rising with every passing year. One needs to note here that the Afghan government doesn't release any official data of these battlefield deaths. But the growing losses are turning out to be a deterrent to fresh recruits in the armed forces.

Afghan security forces are perennially confronted with a plethora of challenges, including lack of numbers, training, mechanization, equipment and infiltration of Taliban supporters within the army. This is further compounded by a high attrition rate due to a combination of desertion and casualty. One of the major goals of the Americans has been to upgrade the training of the Afghan troops. Most of the American spending on reconstruction has gone to a fund that supports the capacity-building of the Afghan security forces. But nobody in Afghanistan—neither the American military nor President Ghani's top advisers—is of the opinion that the Afghan military forces could support themselves and withstand the onslaught of the Taliban.

Corruption continues to riddle every state institution and puts a spanner on the efforts of the government to provide good governance. As per the Corruption Perception Index 2020, released by the Transparency International, Afghanistan stands as the fifteenth most corrupt country in the world.[3] Though this is a marked improvement from the ranking of 2019, which placed Afghanistan as the tenth most corrupt country, it is still far from being acceptable. State building

---

[3]Atakpal, Haseeba, 'Afghanistan among fifteen most corrupt countries: Watchdog,' Tolonews, 29 January 2021, https://tolonews.com/afghanistan-169610, accessed 2 July 2021.

and development interventions in Afghanistan are further jeopardized by an ever-engulfing conflict-induced insecurity, adversely impacting the lives and the welfare of ordinary Afghans and their access to public services in many districts that are directly under the influence of the Taliban. The State seems to surrender its democratic gains with an unfailing regularity. The sharp drop in voting percentages and the rising complaints pertaining to election frauds have severely dented the legitimacy of the recently concluded presidential election.

Ghani, the President of Afghanistan, won a second term after securing 50.64 per cent of the votes, while his main rival, Abdullah Abdullah, won 39.52 per cent of the votes, in the September 2019 election. But Abdullah rejected the results, complaining about electoral fraud and fraudulent voting. After almost six months of bitter feud over presidency, post the presidential elections that bred dissent and rivalry, the warring leaders finally signed a deal on 17 May 2020, agreeing to share power. Abdullah will lead peace negotiations with the Taliban under the title of Chairman of the High Council for National Reconciliation, while Ghani remains the President of Afghanistan. The ministries and important portfolios were further distributed between the two factions.

Political games

Months of political bickering and simmering tension took away the impetus that was required to put to work the peace deal engineered by the US. The US swung to power diplomacy coupled with an aid cut, in making the warring leaders agree to another installment of unity government—unity Government 2.0. Though slightly different in their making and power distribution pattern from the first installment, the common factors that remain in play are indecision and policy paralysis because of the presence of two opposing political visions and ideologies wedded into an increasingly uncomfortable alliance. The legitimacy of the government is on a continual erosion. The ultimate sufferer is governance and by extension the citizens of Afghanistan.

Trump was desperate to exit Afghanistan and looked towards Pakistan to help him out, after blaming Islamabad squarely for aiding and abetting terrorism in Afghanistan through its covert support to the Taliban. This 180-degree turnaround depicts the US's limitation-cum-anticipated defeat in Afghanistan. Will the newly elected US president, Joe Biden, abide by the peace deal signed between Trump and the Taliban? Will President Biden rely on Pakistan to the degree his predecessor did to conclude the peace deal in Afghanistan? The extension of the Pakistan-centric approach may cool Washington's warming bilateral ties with India. India and Pakistan have already locked horns in a bitter proxy war in Kabul.

Nineteen years after the West, under the leadership of the US, went to war in Afghanistan, the Taliban are still gaining momentum, seizing territory, and killing Afghan security forces in record numbers. All said, the cost of over 19 years of war in Afghanistan will amount to more than $2 trillion! Still, why is Afghanistan looking more precarious than ever? Was the money well spent? What went wrong in Afghanistan? Will the peace process ever conclude? Will poppy production come down and cut off the lifeline of the Taliban? Will Pakistan, after decades of aiding the Taliban, alter its egregious but dividend-yielding strategy and arm-twist the Taliban to sign the peace deal? Will the US leave a far worse Afghanistan than it took over in 2001? Does a Taliban takeover of Kabul seem imminent? And above all, what is the future of Afghanistan?

There are endless questions. Like many others, I too subscribe to the dream of a stable and peaceful Afghanistan, and in this pursuit, I joined an international agency as a governance advisor, in 2005. During my professional stint, I closely witnessed the governance processes across all echelons of society—rural to urban areas, from the north to the militant-infested south, from the government to the governed and, more importantly, from the ordinary citizen to the power corridors of Kabul. Having worked in Afghanistan for over 14 years as an international advisor on governance, I thought of undertaking a fresh and incisive look into the Afghan crisis and analyse it threadbare.

Quest for a Stable Afghanistan aims to expose some of the faulty and haggard policies of the West at play and provide the balance sheet of the 'war on terror' from ground zero, for anyone interested in knowing what happened in this most dangerous theatre of war. Through an easy-to-understand narrative, the book also provides a daring outlook, denouncing several myths that colour the perception of this war-ravaged nation, and further elaborates on the critical challenges ahead of Afghanistan.

1

Poppy: The Axis of All Evils

Poppy fuels insurgency in Afghanistan, and so does its eradication. Despite soaking in billions of dollars, the poppy eradication campaign has only led to an obnoxious threefold rise in the product's cultivation. Without poppy, the war in Afghanistan would have been long over. So, what went wrong in the complex campaign against poppy?

Poppy is perceived as the axis of evil in Afghanistan. It is integral to the politics of Afghanistan and deeply entrenched in the conflict engulfing the nation over the last four decades. Afghanistan has earned the stench of a narco-state due to opium production and rampant drug trafficking, mainly related to this production. The country supplies about three-fourth of the world's opium and almost 90 per cent of the world's heroin. Poppy poisons the formal Afghan economy and fuels a burgeoning illicit economy. It accounts for more than one-third of the country's shadow gross domestic product (GDP). It is deeply rooted in the socio-economic fabric of the country, and by extension in its political arrangement and order too. It incentivizes corruption and criminality, and is a constant source of terror-funding inside the country. It does not spare the bureaucracy either. Poppy breeds corruption, and is corrosive to state-building in Afghanistan. The tumultuous history of Afghanistan over the last four decades, which includes the erstwhile Soviet occupation and the subsequent dislodging of the Russians from power by the US-backed covert war, the civil war, the rise, fall and renewed resistance of the Taliban, has one thing in common—poppy. The centrality of poppy in aiding instability and further determining the fate of successive regimes and foreign intervention is bewildering. And now, poppy seems to decide the fate of the US war on terror in Afghanistan.

The history of poppy dates back to the pre-Soviet occupation era in Afghanistan. Before the Soviet invasion in 1979, poppy was a marginal crop and was produced on a limited scale, mostly in the southern region of Afghanistan. As the Afghan government began to lose control over the provinces from 1979 onwards, the hinterlands of the country witnessed a severe security vacuum. The Mujahideen-turned-warlords started exploring several ways and means to generate cash for supporting their movement of resistance against the Soviet occupation. The warlords resorted to poppy for funding their war against the Soviet occupation. A system swiftly evolved, whereby, the warlords started encouraging large landowners and drug merchants to multiply poppy cultivation in their areas of command. They not only started providing protection to poppy cultivation, but also facilitated the shipments of opium.

It is worth mentioning the value chain of poppy here—poppy buds are harvested, made into opium and later even processed and refined into heroin. This practice of resource generation soon multiplied across the entire length and breadth of Afghanistan. It coincided with a phase when food inflation had skyrocketed. The rudimentary financial system had come to a grinding halt, straining the farming sector. The fragile livelihoods of the farmers were under severe duress, emanating from the war and the political uncertainty. The Mujahideen-backed drug lords began browbeating the farmers into growing poppy.

The open licence system enabled them to aggressively push the farmers towards poppy cultivation. As relentless warfare took its toll, Afghan farmers were coerced to grow poppy in order to generate quick-and-easy money for the Mujahideen to fund their war against the Soviet occupation. Farmers also resorted to poppy cultivation in bulk, since it turned in 'high profits' that covered rising food prices and provided them a secure livelihood, besides protecting them from the Mujahideen. The growing nexus of warlords and drug lords significantly gained from this new equation. Poppy was the crop of convenience for all and thus received a major fillip during this period.

The overall milieu was also conducive to opium cultivation. Caravans carrying arms supplied by the US's Central Intelligence Agency (CIA) into Afghanistan for arming the resistance often returned to Pakistan loaded with opium; at times, the matter got reported by several US-based newspapers during that period. Charles Cogan, a former director of the CIA's Afghan operation, later spelt out the agency's choices. 'Our main mission was to do as much damage as possible to the Soviets,' he told an interviewer in 1995. 'We didn't really have the resources or the time to devote to an investigation of the drug trade. I don't think that we need to apologize for this... there was a serious fallout in term of drugs. But the main objective was accomplished. The Soviets left Afghanistan.'[1] The Inter-Services Intelligence (ISI) generals of Pakistan became an integral part of this thriving poppy ecosystem, proliferating the cross-border opium traffic and profusely gaining from it. By then, a powerful and well-organized drug cartel had started operating on both the sides of the Pakistan-Afghanistan border.

The US military turned a blind eye, fearing that any action against this new poppy-based ecosystem would distract the fighters from their end goal of defeating the Soviet forces in Afghanistan. In fact, one reason why the US strategy succeeded was that the surrogate war launched by the CIA did not disrupt the way its Afghan allies used the country's swelling drug traffic to sustain their decade-long struggle. The CIA also brushed aside the deep engagement of the ISI in fanning cross-border smuggling of poppy, fearing that any intervention would rub its allies the wrong way. When Soviet forces began to pull out, the US reduced the military aid, leading to a severe resource crunch in Afghanistan. It needs to be mentioned here that the CIA provided the Mujahideen guerrillas with an estimated $3 billion in aid, including arms. These funds, along with the revenues from an ever-swelling opium production, sustained the successful resistance against the Soviet occupation.

When Washington shifted its attention from Afghanistan to other foreign policy hotspots in Africa and the Persian Gulf, it failed to set up a power-sharing arrangement or kick-start a process of long-term financial reconstruction. Afghanistan

---

[1] The *guardian.com*, UK, quoted the said interview in the 9 January 2018 edition of the newspaper.

slipped into a protracted phase of lawlessness and civil strife. The Mujahideen leaders, competing for a stake in the new Kabul government, turned their guns against one another, jostling for more power and authority. The civil war divided the country and Kabul itself into warring fiefdoms. As the Mujahideen guerrillas-turned-warlords gained ground, they began to create their own liberated zones within Afghanistan. Such zones and the regional warlords continued to use poppy as a means to generate revenues. This time, they needed poppy revenues to ride their political aspirations. They combined arms and opium in a countrywide struggle for power. This was the need of the hour not only to protect their regions, but also to capture and control more regions within the country. The situation resulted in the complete integration of narcotic and opium money with the politics of the beleaguered country.

The opiate of the masses

Opium production and trafficking were also institutionalized to provide secure and lucrative incomes for the population, under the Mujahid control. Collecting taxes from peasants who grew opium poppies constituted the lion's share of their core income. A system swiftly developed where poppy was a crop of choice and convenience for both the warlords as well as the farmers. The orchards gradually carpeted into poppy fields. Afghan farmers raised the only crop that ensured instant and supernormal profits—opium poppy. Having multiplied twentyfold during the covert-war era of the 1980s, the opium harvest would more than double again during the civil war of the 1990s.

In this extended period of unrest, the rise of poppy is best understood as a response to severe damage from two decades of destructive warfare. With the return of some three million refugees to a war-ravaged land, the opium fields turned out to be a godsend to the employment-generation zones, requiring nine times as many labourers to cultivate wheat, the country's traditional staple. The formal economy, which was largely urban-centric, was crippled by now and in no position to replace the labour-intensive, rural-based opium poppy economy.

The massive expansion of poppy cultivation also needs to be understood from the farmer's perspective. Poppy was not a crop of choice for most Afghan farmers. With the passing years, Afghan farmers were not in a position to desist from growing it, either. Like other countries, the farmers of Afghanistan too want to make the most from their meagre land holdings to reverse their economic misery. Agriculture in conjunction with livestock remains the mainstay of the rural economy. The agriculture sector of Afghanistan is plagued with many problems, including a non-existent agriculture infrastructure coupled with poor access to the market. Continual fragmentation of arable land due to steep population growth has stagnated agriculture production and generated large-scale unemployment and under-employment in the primary sector. Opium grows on low-quality land and is resilient to the harsh climate of Afghanistan. The production is labour-intensive, accommodating the ever-growing family members of the farmers. For most rural households, the only alternate source of income is to send their sons to join the Afghan security forces, including the army. But that is far riskier than growing poppy under the patronage of warlords or government-linked power brokers.

Recurrent phases of war and insecurity have significantly damaged the livelihoods of ordinary Afghans. Their ongoing plight coupled with a prolonged phase of insecurity have gradually turned a large number of farmers towards poppy cultivation, with the hope of liberating themselves from the vicious cycle of low income and high debt. Poppy is estimated to yield approximately eight times more income per hectare than wheat, and it requires less water and fewer inputs. There are no other options that can remotely match poppy in terms of profit. Opium also operates like a spot and future market, with traders providing credit for production. The organized poppy merchants have accumulated capital rapidly enough to be able to provide poor poppy farmers with much-needed cash advances, which could go up to half of their annual income. The credit serves as a lifeline and remains integral to the survival of many impoverished farmers. A well-known advantage of opium cultivation for farmers is that traders come directly to the villages to buy the produce. It also serves as a means of savings and collateral for instant credit. There is simply nothing that produces more jobs and profit, or could do so in the foreseeable future, than the cultivation of opium poppy. Poppy remains the best bet for thousands of Afghans to escape poverty.

The Taliban, largely comprising radical Muslim clerics and students from the Pashtun belt of southern and eastern Afghanistan, emerged in 1994 as one of the prominent factions in the Afghan civil war. They finally succeeded in capturing almost 75 per cent of the country and ruled during 1996–2001. The Taliban were no different in their approach and outreach to poppy. The diabolic intentions of the Taliban found a perfect solution in the drug. Poppy was continuously employed as a means to fill the coffers of the Taliban in their quest to arm themselves to expand and establish their rule across Afghanistan. The informal tax generated from poppy was also used to cover a major part of their administrative expenses.

Farmers were given open support to grow poppy. During the Taliban rule, Afghanistan saw a bumper opium crop of 4,500 metric tonnes in 1999. This phase also witnessed a sharp growth in the organized opium cross-border cartel with the assistance of a few ISI generals along with their Taliban counterparts. During the Taliban regime, the drug lords passed on a part of their profits to the Taliban, who kept accommodating the drug lords in the power structures in lieu of these financial gratifications. The lethal nexus grew to the extent where it began to blur the line between the Taliban and the drug lords. The Taliban co-opted the drug lords into the political and power structures of Afghanistan and the revenue from poppy kept funding their nefarious designs in Afghanistan. The legitimacy of the Taliban was getting established, and the farmers were not complaining either. The poppy lobby was getting stronger than ever. It started flaunting its political muscle and took complete command of the farmers in the rural hinterland of Afghanistan.

At their peak of power, the Taliban were overtly supporting poppy and opium transport with the state-run airlines, Ariana Airlines, almost turning into a 'narco-terror' charter service ferrying Islamic militants, weapons and heroin to the United Arab Emirates (UAE) and Pakistan. Mohammad Fedawi, President of Ariana Airlines during the Taliban takeover, later said that senior Taliban officials ordered him to hand out flight-crew passes to dozens of 'foreigners', including al-Qaeda members, who would be allowed to travel to whichever destination the airline serviced throughout the Indian subcontinent and the Middle East. 'Sometimes they would schedule special night flights to Kandahar and to the

Emirates, mainly Sharjah and Dubai,' Fedawi added. 'No one was allowed to see what the Taliban loaded on these planes in Afghanistan.'[2]

Escalating concern from various quarters that Ariana was transporting drugs, weapons and terrorists, led the United Nations (UN) to impose international flight sanctions on the Taliban in late 2000, barring international destinations for the airlines. Meanwhile, poppy had enabled the Taliban to further strengthen their grip and legitimacy in Afghanistan. In a milieu, where poppy has historically received backing through successive regimes—and given the pitiable conditions of the farmers, who are bent on making the most from their arable land—one should hardly be surprised at the sharp rise in poppy cultivation. These complex situations, and not just the profit alone, have fuelled poppy production in Afghanistan.

However, there was a drastic change of scenario in 2000. The same Taliban that went all out to increase poppy cultivation, vowed to eliminate poppy from Afghanistan during the last year of their rule. They ran the most successful poppy eradication campaign in the history of Afghanistan, as per the UNODC records. A subsequent UN crop survey of 10,030 villages found that this prohibition had reduced the harvest by 94 per cent. This sudden 180-degree turnaround by the Taliban completely stunned the international community. The supreme leader of the Taliban, Mullah Mohammed Omar, declared that growing poppy was un-Islamic. The Taliban enforced a ban on poppy farming via threats, forced eradication and public punishment of transgressors. A few errant farmers were also put behind bars. As per the records of the US military, there was a 99 per cent reduction in opium poppy farming in

---

[2]Gretchen Peters, *How Opium Profits the Taliban*, Peace Works, US Institute of Peace.

Taliban-controlled areas, eliminating almost three-quarters of the world's supply of heroin at the time.

The Taliban, who used to collect taxes on the movement of opium, lost significant revenue in their bid to eliminate poppy from Afghanistan. The Taliban's sudden penchant for opium eradication proved to be an act of economic hara-kiri that brought a fragile economy on the brink of a collapse. A 2001 UN survey found that the ban had 'resulted in a severe loss of income for an estimated 3.3 million people'[3]—about 15 per cent of the total population. It was a tectonic shift, given the fact that the Taliban used the illicit money-spinning poppy to ride their political aspirations in Afghanistan. The Taliban rationalized the poppy ban citing Islamic prohibitions against drugs, and this campaign on religious grounds made their followers and ordinary farmers hard to defy. The end of opium poppy cultivation in Afghanistan came at a huge cost to the farmers. The ban brought them to the brink of economic ruin in the final year of Taliban rule.

Afghan experts cited the poppy ban as a strategic ploy by the Taliban to get into the good books of the western countries and earn recognition by countries other than Pakistan, Saudi Arabia and the UAE. It was also aimed at earning a seat in the UN, which would have given their government broader international approval. Getting foreign aid was also an objective, though secondary, behind this well-thought-out move. The effort did not go in vain. The US announced a $43 million bounty as an emergency aid for the Afghan farmers. The UN too employed a team of experts to study the campaign

---

[3]McCoy, Alfred W. 'How the heroin trade explains the US-UK failure in Afghanistan,' *The Guardian*, 9 January 2018, https://www.theguardian.com/ news/2018/jan/09/how-the-heroin-trade-explains-the-us-uk-failure-in-afghanistan, accessed 18 June 2021.

in greater detail and derive learning insights to replicate the lesson in drug hotspots like Colombia, Peru, Bolivia, etc. However, just when the Taliban started gaining accolades for their campaign against poppy, the catastrophic terror incident of 9/11 too place. The US zeroed in on Afghanistan as the origin of the attack. The Taliban could have handed over Osama bin Laden, the chief architect of 9/11, to the US, in lieu of a lucrative reward and recognition. However, they decided against it due to their ideological leanings and shared aspirations. As a result, the allied forces of the US and the UK started air-striking the Taliban and the al-Qaeda targets on 7 October 2001. Within a span of a little over two months, the Taliban ceded control of the Kandahar-southern heart and their spiritual capital to the US forces.

Being at the helm of power for a little over four years, the Taliban's tryst with power was quite adventurous and were not willing to slip into the annals of history with the loser tag. The US forces did not contemplate a Taliban return after driving them out of Kandahar city. Much to the surprise of locals, only a small number of allied troops was posted on the outskirts of Kandahar city, creating a dangerous security void. This created a fecund ground for the Taliban camping in the remote and inhospitable parts of Kandahar to plan their revenge. The Taliban quietly began to regroup, and commanders started reaching out to one another after lying low for a few years. Mullah Omar reportedly contacted his deputies and appointed them to organize his fighters, pick up fresh recruits from Pakistani madrasas, locate weapons stashes and raise funds.

The Pakistan military, on the other hand, did not fully subscribe to or agree with President Pervez Musharraf's decision to side with the US in the war on terror. And some of the disgruntled ISI generals extended their support in arming and training the Taliban in secret camps around Waziristan. Later, President Musharraf too appeared to be on board with the idea to gain leverage in Afghanistan through the Taliban. This was part of Pakistan's larger deceit and duplicity game in Afghanistan. Overtly, it would appear to be on the side of the US, but covertly supported the Taliban by offering them safe havens and trainings inside Pakistan.

The drug smugglers were in a tearing hurry to oblige the Taliban by arranging funds to help revitalize the exiled movement. Local media reported that many commanders raised money by selling off old stock of poppy stashed in their hideaway. The Taliban did not waste any time in reaching out to drug lords and traffickers in arming their resistance against the US invasion. Soon, the poppy tax net was widened to include large landowners growing poppy. The more the Taliban were getting hold in Afghanistan, the more poppy carpeted the Afghan countryside. Once again poppy moved to the centre stage in defining the future of Afghanistan. What made the Taliban resort to poppy—the same poppy that was abandoned by them in 2000? The Taliban constructed a new narrative around poppy—consumption of opium was forbidden, as was the manufacturing of heroin, but production of and trading in opium were not. With this new narrative, they ruthlessly exploited the poppy chain to turn it into a lethal and mean force. Poppy made the Taliban switch from a self-acclaimed, ideology-based organization to an organized drug cartel that was hell-bent on making the most to fund their war against the US. This was the beginning of a new phase of turmoil for Afghanistan.

Since the 2001 US-led invasion of Afghanistan, poppy has been silently playing a critical destabilizing role, both in corrupting the Afghan government and in bankrolling the resurgence of the Taliban. The poppy-aided Taliban resistance to overthrow the US-backed Afghan government gained serious momentum. The Taliban have systematically tapped into the supply chain at each stage of the narcotics trade. They profit from the opium trade by taxing the poppy-growing farmers, nondescript low-cost primary opium-processing factories, and further, the smugglers engaged in transporting opium out of the borders of Afghanistan for international consumption. The 'tax' is levied on account of providing security and protection to all stakeholders engaged in the entire poppy value chain in areas under the Taliban's control within Afghanistan. The Taliban also assisted the smugglers in facilitating the movement of poppy from Afghanistan primarily to Pakistan, Iran and Russia, against a protection fee.

The Taliban commanders, from the district level up to the top leadership, have left no stone unturned to expand their involvement through the drug trade. They have significantly gained from the constantly increasing poppy cultivation in Afghanistan. According to conservative estimates, the Taliban reportedly make anything between $200 and $250 million per year from the poppy cultivation and its extended value chain. The money is channelled for purchasing sophisticated arms and recruiting a new crop of young guerrilla fighters from the villages to bolster the Taliban's bench strength and cover up for the casualties in the ongoing war. These funds further play a key role in financing the operational costs of the Taliban and many of their affiliates. The Taliban are not alone to benefit from poppy. The profits from poppy and its lengthy value chain including heroin, fund the web of terrorist groups like the Islamic State, al-Qaeda, etc. The highly organized drug cartel and the local criminal gangs too make a significant chunk of money from the poppy production and consequent processing, including trade. This by extension corrupts the warlords, police, politicians and the Afghan bureaucracy, to a large extent. The lure of easy and lucrative money that revolves around this crop massively corrupts the state machinery and undermines all efforts of improving governance.

It is not that the US military think tank at the Pentagon was ignorant of the damage that poppy could do to the rebuilding and reconstruction of Afghanistan. The officials were also aware that poppy could foil the American dream and give a lifeline to the Taliban for their revival. On 11 October 2001, exactly four days after Operation Enduring Freedom wreaked havoc for the Taliban, President Bush explored the possibility of hitting drug labs and opium storage areas but failed to act due to the fear of 'collateral damage'. The UK military too suggested bombing the drug targets. However, the fear of a revolt by the local Afghan commanders fighting for the US to dislodge the Taliban, put the proposal on the back-burner. The US viewed narcotics as a 'lesser evil' to the bigger challenge of irreversibly damaging the Taliban, at hand.

After dismantling the Taliban from Afghanistan, the US military and its long-standing ally decided to eradicate poppy completely, because it was viewed as the root cause of all evils in Afghanistan. They knew that if they had to irreversibly defeat the Taliban, poppy needed to be defeated first. Targeting opium production in Afghanistan was critical for varied reasons: opium fuels an illicit economy, incentivizes corruption and criminality, and is used to fund terrorism. Zeroing in on poppy would arrest the threat and the spread of the drug menace in western countries too. The US policy driver further assumed that an attack on poppy would frustrate the Taliban and trigger a revolt among its cadre base, which was largely oiled by the profits from poppy. Around 60 per cent of the Taliban's finances came from the narcotics trade, thus it was anticipated that an attack on the drug trafficking network would choke the insurgents' revenues. It was assumed that the eradication of poppy would also damage the backbone of the powerful drug lords, in addition to stemming the flow of traditional funding for the Taliban to spread unrest and terrorism. Distantly did they realize that after 18 years of relentless military operations their war against poppy would eventually end up fuelling a record opium production and a stronger Taliban than ever before.

A comprehensive poppy eradication programme was developed by various think tanks primarily under the guidance of its all-weather ally, the UK. The strategy relied on substitution of crops for opium, stepped-up interdiction efforts, targeting narcotics kingpins for arrest, financial rewards for provinces that slash poppy cultivation along with manual eradication of standing poppy crops with adequate compensation. Special anti-narcotic forces were constituted and deployed across the poppy-infested provinces of Afghanistan, to manually eradicate standing poppy crops directly at the field.

Even though the strategy was diverse and multipronged, the counter narcotic forces heavily relied on the usage of brute power to destroy standing poppy crop. The method of manual opium eradication, such as the use of sticks by the local officials to break the stems of the poppy flower, was not fully successful. The eradication team was attacked when they tried to venture into areas under the stronghold of the Taliban, particularly southern Afghanistan. Regardless of who controlled the land, the eradication teams were vulnerable to corruption. There were reports of corruption at the ground level due to lack of proper performance metrics for officials engaged in this daredevil act. Some crop damage was reported from various parts of Afghanistan.

The biggest sufferers of this state-led attack against poppy were the farmers of Afghanistan, especially the small and marginal ones. The livelihoods of the farmers were broken irreversibly by this ill-conceived approach of the anti-narcotic forces. Though an inadequate compensation package was designed for the poppy cultivators, the benefit hardly reached the farmers due to a variety of reasons—the predominant being the presence of corrupt local government officials. Various US officials, including the former US State Assistant Secretary for the Bureau of International Narcotics and Law Enforcement Affairs, Thomas Schweich, has on record said that opium production was protected by certain elements within the government as they hugely benefitted from it.[4] But in this coalition era, no one is willing to take a tough call in the power corridors of Kabul.

The Taliban did not waste any time in rendering succour to the agitated farmers. The farmers resorted to violence in order to protect their poppy fields from destruction. 'We cannot allow the government to take away from us the only means of income that we have,' said an agitated farmer. Even the unaffected poppy-growing farmers turned hostile to the Afghan government with this state-led poppy attack, anticipating that the sword of Damocles would eventually fall on them, at some stage. The state-sponsored attack on the poppy-growing farmers coupled with reported corruption in granting compensation generated tremendous political goodwill for the Taliban. They sparked low-level revolts, alienated the rural populace from the government and drove

---

[4]Schweich, Thomas, 'Is Afghanistan a Narco State?' *The New York Times*, 27 July 2008, https://www.nytimes.com/2008/07/27/magazine/27AFGHAN-t.html, accessed 18 June 2021.

them into Taliban hands. The Taliban presented themselves as protectors of the poppy, and cast the Afghan government and its international sponsors as infidels trying to kill the Afghan people by snatching away the primary means of livelihood. The US was confronted with a typical catch-22 situation. Opium-profits fuel insurgency, but so does destroying poppy crops of the farmers.

The increasing support of the poppy farmers for the Taliban could not have come at a more opportune time, as the Taliban were aiming to step up their resistance against the US invasion. This was another international blunder that fuelled the Taliban insurgency in the restive poppy belts of Afghanistan. In a way, the poppy farmers were mobilized for the Taliban, by the flawed poppy eradication strategy of the US and other western countries.

Tweaking the strategy

In late 2004, after nearly two years of outsourcing opium control to its British allies and police training to the Germans, the White House was suddenly confronted with troubling CIA reports emanating from Afghanistan, which suggested that the poppy money was fuelling a revival of the Taliban. The poppy eradication strategy was revised but without much success. The poppy cultivation area jumped to a record high of 193,000 hectares in 2007. Fuelled by the poppy proceeds, the Taliban were getting more lethal and were continually expanding their war chest. They started attacking US interests within Afghanistan at frequent intervals. The writ of the state of Afghanistan was openly challenged in the poppy-growing belt. This was disastrous from the counterinsurgency perspective, since it cemented the Taliban's political capital rather than bankrupting it. The US military think tank was once again compelled to revisit the strategy of their ongoing poppy eradication campaign.

Realizing that the current method of manual opium poppy eradication was a gross failure and counterproductive, a more centralized opium eradication programme, which negates corruption along with the possibility of attack on the ground forces, was explored. For the first time, the US think tank proposed the application of aerial herbicide on the standing poppy crop. Global Positioning System (GPS)-enabled technology was put to play for precise targeting of poppy fields. Poppy eradication under a centralized command would also help in better execution, monitoring and control. The process of land confiscation of errant farmers based on aerial reports could be further directed from Kabul. Aerial spraying of glyphosate, a commonly used weed killer, was seen as the only way to eradicate large-scale poppy cultivation in a complex country like Afghanistan. A wide range of merit was argued on behalf of the proposed method, which could spare the ground forces from any possibility of attack and build access to areas under Taliban control. This would further evade corruption, which stymied prior poppy eradication efforts in Afghanistan.

The US officials suggested that the Colombia model be emulated in Afghanistan, where the aerial herbicide application on coca crops has decreased narcotics production by 50 per cent, over a period of 10 years. Colombia is the only country in the world where drug plantations are targeted from the air. US Air Force pilots have been dodging treetops, mountain peaks and rebel gunfire for the past two decades while spraying herbicide on Colombian drug plantations. The US-backed aerial eradication programme aims to destroy coca leaves before they can be turned into powder cocaine. However, eradication of plantations never bankrupted insurgents anywhere, including the much-prescribed Columbia, nor is it sustainable without an on-ground solution.

The prospect of applying aerial herbicide was met with sharp criticism from both within Afghanistan as well as other western allies, who were sceptical of its benefits and afraid that it would further increase Taliban support among the farmers. Britain, which led anti-narcotics efforts in Afghanistan, firmly opposed the aerial eradication and argued that it would only worsen the insurgency. Even a few White House and Pentagon officials expressed their disagreement. Russia was the lone supporter of the aerial spray of glyphosate over the standing poppy crop. Moscow's tough stance on narcotics stems from its own rising internal consumption levels, which have steadily reached epidemic proportions. According to 2008 records, up to 21 per cent of the world's production of illicit opiates ended up in Russia, resulting in an estimated 30,000 deaths annually from heroin-induced overdoses.

The previous Hamid Karzai government in Afghanistan had been loud and vocal in its resistance. Karzai's advisors feared that aerial spraying would trigger a domestic backlash against Karzai, who was already politically weak, and deliver a propaganda bonanza to the Taliban. The political fallout could have been too high and gone against his overarching aims of winning the hearts and minds of Afghan farmers. Government officials traditionally have rejected aerial spraying, saying low-flying planes dispersing clouds of herbicide could destroy licit crops and arouse painful memories of Soviet-era carpet-bombing. Karzai's agriculture ministry said it opposes spraying because the chemicals could destroy legal subsistence crops, often cultivated alongside poppy. The public-health ministry warned of the threat that spraying poses to drinking water, 80 per cent of which comes from streams and open water sources.

Irrespective of all resistance, the US was prepared to test the waters. In 2004, US-contracted aircraft secretly sprayed harmless plastic granules over poppy fields in Afghanistan to gauge public reaction. The mysterious granules ignited a widespread outcry and protests from poor farmers, tribal chiefs and government officials up to President Karzai, who demanded to know if the spraying was part of a poppy-eradication programme. At the time, US officials, up to the level of Ambassador Zalmay Khalilzad, denied knowledge of the programme.

It is not known if the US applied the aerial spray on a large scale. However, in the later part of 2007, Karzai agreed to it in a desperate bid to deflate the soaring drug trade and the growing Taliban influence. Many experts still feel that spraying herbicide is the only way to curb poppy in the southern heartland of the Taliban. The size and diversity of the opiate economy have their own set of challenges, particularly that a successful intervention in one region doesn't mean success in the other regions.

Collapse of the alternative

After facing strong resistance from farmers to the process of direct eradication, a greater emphasis was put on exploring alternative livelihoods, including crop substitution. Development interventions by the North Atlantic Treaty Organization (NATO)-led International Security Assistance Force (ISAF) force, the Afghan government and the UN aimed to entice farmers away from cultivating the flower. The much-hyped crop substitution and the search for an alternative livelihood were pursued with great zeal and enthusiasm. Various international non-governmental organizations (INGOs) too jumped on the bandwagon and aligned their intervention with the newly set direction. Considerable investment was made in developing and further repairing irrigation infrastructure to enable the farmers for dual cropping. A whole range of cash crops, including cotton, was introduced for the first time in Afghanistan. Farmers were trained in modern techniques of farming to boost production. This was further complemented by a supply of high-quality agricultural inputs like seeds, fertilizers and pesticides. Besides these, big investment in skilling the landless farmers and unemployed youth was made to explore alternative livelihoods.

The government-backed national priority programme, along with those of the INGOs, set up revolving funds for people to access small and mid-sized loans for setting up micro businesses. The INGOs were leading the chart. However, these investments made little headway in solving the poppy conundrum. But there were pockets of success. The UK forces made a significant investment in this respect. The British government spent more than £290 million on a three-year programme of eradication, support for farmers and pursuit of drug barons and traffickers. This was further complemented by a surge in military presence in the restive poppy belt of Helmand.

Soon, the planners had something to cheer about. The UK prided itself on the fact that poppy cultivation in the province of Helmand—where it had run the military and development effort since 2006—had fallen dramatically since 2008, from an estimated 103,590 hectares to 75,105 hectares in 2012. The much-claimed success was largely due to large-scale investments ably complemented by huge concentration of military efforts in a single province. Such was the purported success of the Helmand effort that the Afghan Ministry of Counter Narcotics and the US government even thought of replicating the approach in eight other provinces, including Kandahar. The British military along with the Afghan ministry assumed that poppy cultivation had reached its saturation and things were only going to improve from here on. The UK military was not keen on continuing its aggressive role in Afghanistan, after David Cameron was sworn in as the British prime minister. Unlike his predecessor, Cameron was not an Afghanistan enthusiast, and had none of the passion that Tony Blair had for counternarcotics. The UK military was in a tearing hurry to give up the lead role in counternarcotics, despite the performance indicators being on its side. It wanted to exit at a high, probably because it had doubts about the sustainability of the results.

A number of farmers who switched to traditional crops such as cotton complained that the prices had fallen and that there was no market for the produce, either at home or abroad. The farmers had another gripe—the promise of high-quality seeds and fertilizers, to carry out developmental projects and promote alternative cropping, had not been kept. Afghanistan lacks agriculture-enablers like cold storage, warehouses and even a minimum support price (MSP) system to ensure remunerative prices of the farm produce. The cash crop failed to make money because the farmers could not afford to play the waiting game and sell their produce at a better price. They were in a hurry to sell their produce before they perished. Some produces had no takers. The local market did not have the demand to sustain the burgeoning skilled labour, and the urban growth engines like Kabul, Mazar, Kandahar, Herat, etc. were choked with an oversupply of labour, leaving no room for migration.

The bulk of loans accessed by the entrepreneurs turned into non-performing assets leading some of the largest banks to bust. The BRAC Bank, which was known for its impeccable profit-churning abilities, suffered the biggest loss in its Afghan adventure. Big-ticket investments like dairy and food-processing plants too failed to pick up, after showing an initial spark of success. Most of them collapsed. Experts suggest that sustained security is required for alternative livelihoods to work, and that remains elusive in Afghanistan. With an economy which was largely powered by dwindling international aid, the demands in the local economy were also falling. Robust demand remains imperative for the success of the alternative livelihoods and labour market. However, it would be unfair to conceal everything under the garb of growing insecurity and slowing demand, which has always been a strategy in Afghanistan to hide failure. Many alternative livelihood interventions were poorly designed and thus ineffective, rarely generating sound and sustainable incomes for poppy growing farmers. Even the bulk of choices made by the INGOs to promote alternative livelihoods was below average, to say the least.

Nothing in Afghanistan happens without collateral damage. The investment in crop substitution left a breed of trained farmers with better irrigation facilities and advanced knowledge of reducing input cost to maximize production. From the application of enhanced knowledge to new investments made in solar-powered tube wells, farmers in Afghanistan at large have used improved inputs and technology to subsequently increase opium production. The British military forces highlighted their model of poppy eradication as a grand success in Helmand and called for broader replication within Afghanistan. They were able to cut the net poppy sown area by 28 per cent in

2012, with a massive investment running over $500 million, along with the heavy presence of their military in almost every district's headquarters of Helmand. However, their model was untenable and highly unsustainable, and the UK started the process of exiting from Helmand after 2012, with a goal of completing the exit process by 2014.

The net sown area of poppy cultivation went up to 100,693 hectares in 2013 and further jumped to 103,240 hectares in 2014, giving up all the gains of 2012. The British military had prematurely assumed that poppy cultivation had reached a saturation point in 2012, in Helmand, if not the entire Afghanistan. The poppy farmers were once again under the influence of the Taliban, resulting in a continuous rise in poppy production. Local media reports strongly suggested that the Taliban manipulated the fall in net sown areas of poppy in 2012. They did it on purpose to facilitate the heavy investment made by the British military in the sector of agriculture in Helmand. They knew well in advance that these investments would eventually benefit them, once the British forces left Helmand. Any kind of conflict with the British forces in 2012 would have halted these critical investments.

By 2015, the Taliban had decisively seized the combat initiative, and opium seemed even more deeply embedded in its operations. In October 2015, the UN released a map showing that the Taliban had 'high' or 'extreme' control in more than half the country's rural districts. Within a month, the Taliban unleashed offensives countrywide, aimed at seizing and holding territory. Not surprisingly, the strongest attacks were witnessed in the poppy heartland of Helmand province, where half the country's opium crop was then grown. The next hotspot of the burgeoning conflict was Kandahar—another poppy belt of the war-torn country.

In 2016, exactly 15 years after Afghanistan was 'liberated', and in a significant reversal of the Obama administration's drawdown policies, Washington launched a mini-surge with the help of hundreds of new US troops into Helmand province to deny insurgents the 'economic prize' of the world's most productive poppy fields. Despite support from US airpower and 700 special-operations troops, in February and March 2016, the embattled Afghan government forces retreated from two more districts, leaving the Taliban largely in control of 10 of the province's 14 districts. After the fall of Helmand, there was no looking back and soon the Taliban attained its strongest position, with more than 50 per cent of Afghanistan under their control.

As more areas started falling under the control of the Taliban, the impact was seen in poppy production too. In 2017, opium cultivation in Afghanistan spiralled to a historic high with an estimated 3,28,000 hectares under poppy cultivation. The net sown area of poppy grew by 63 per cent compared to the figures of 2016 (201,000 hectares). In Helmand alone, cultivation increased by 63,700 hectares (79 per cent), accounting for about half of the total increase. The increase in the net sown area in Helmand once again exposed the flaw in the UK model. The 2017 harvest produced approximately 9,000 tonnes of heroin. It was valued at $6.6 billion, which accounted for almost 32 per cent of the country's GDP by most conservative estimate. The Taliban reportedly made $183 million by taxing the opiate production in their areas of control. The income would swell further, if the taxes on trafficking are added to it.

The steep rise in production created multiple challenges for the country, its neighbours and many other countries that are recipients of Afghan opiates. But it also provided lucrative incomes to the farmers and secured employment to the landless labourers in rural areas, where employment options are otherwise skewed. The most worrisome part was that it continued to strengthen the Taliban. The filled coffers allowed the Taliban to hire fresh recruits and buy arms and ammunition. This provided them the momentum to step up attacks and spread unrest in Afghanistan, resulting in new areas falling under the Taliban's control.

At the international level, people were realizing that the status quo couldn't be allowed to prevail as it could give teeth to the Taliban to capture Kabul by overthrowing the then incumbent government. Afghanistan was also witnessing another change in its poppy value chain. In the past, the opium latex would be dried and smuggled out of Afghanistan as a sticky paste to be refined elsewhere. Now, Afghan and western officials were estimating that more than half of Afghan opium was being processed either into morphine or heroin in low-investment processing laboratories within Afghanistan. This would make smuggling easy and further add to the coffers of the Taliban. Also, the spike in opium production came at a time when the US was struggling to contain its own opioid crisis at home. The White House declared it a national public health emergency in October 2017. More than two million Americans are addicted to opioids, and opioid overdoses have become the leading cause of death in the US, ahead of car crashes and even gun violence. The bulk of the heroin produced within Afghanistan would reach the US market pushing the prices down, making it even more accessible for Americans, thereby swelling the number of drug addicts.

With the looming danger and the war against poppy slipping, the US military think tank once again jumped into action in order to arrest the growing poppy cultivation and choke the supply of finance to the Taliban. The old and haggard poppy eradication strategy did not produce any results on the ground. Besides, there was a continuous rise in production along with the income of the Taliban. The failed campaign was calling for a fresh approach, and the US military think tank did oblige by going back to the drawing board in the quest for halting poppy production. Volleys of new approaches, including a few last-ditch efforts were announced. The most noteworthy was a bombing campaign targeting the heroin laboratories at the heart of the Taliban's $200 million-a-year opium trade. 'We're hitting the Taliban where it hurts, which is their finances,' claimed the Commander of Forces, General John Nicholson, in a press conference a day after the first wave of bombing.[5] The year-long air bombing was code-named 'Iron Tempest'. Launched in November 2017, the campaign witnessed 200 air strikes to drug laboratories spanning over a year. In the first week of November, the US military published an online video of nine such attacks hitting their targets with precision and killing eight Afghan civilians. The video demonstrated the lethal air power and precision bombing, using some of the most advanced military technology ever devised, including a B-52 strategic bomber, an F-22 Raptor stealth fighter and an M-142 tactical rocket launcher—US airpower at its best.

The air strikes on the opium laboratory were inspired by US air strikes in Syria, where aerial bombings targeting the ISIS's illegal oil industry had destroyed rigs, tanker trucks and other heavy machinery. The campaign in Syria was celebrated for its success, as it dramatically reduced the so-called Caliphate's revenues and made it very difficult to pay its fighters. The campaign did irreversible damage to the ISIS by cutting their chief source of finance. But, as is so often in

---

[5]Ferdinando, Lisa, 'U.S., Afghan Forces Target Taliban Drug Labs, Hit "Where it Hurts"', 20 November 2017, US Dept. of Defense.

the history of the conflict in Afghanistan, this campaign would not be as straightforward as the military planners had hoped.

By the end of 2018, almost after a year-long bombing, ground studies revealed that despite excellent intelligence, the multimillion-dollar campaign was having a negligible effect on the Taliban and the drug trafficking networks in Afghanistan. The high claim of air strikes' success made under the campaign was not matching the ground reality. The cost-benefit analysis of such a complex air campaign was also put under serious question. The so-called labs are the ordinary mud houses with minimal facilities and operate intermittently. Some were even operating inside caves. These dormant labs would store chemicals, equipment and heroin in smaller quantities. The finished products would be moved to hidden places due to the fear of attack. As the air strikes increased, the owners of drug cartels started moving the drug labs, with new facilities being commissioned in less than a week. At best the value of one lab can be put at sub-$15,000. The F-22, the most advanced stealth fighter in the world, was largely employed to hit the target. Each aircraft costs at least $35,000 an hour to fly. Assuming that the F-22 takes off from the US airbase in Bagram, it would take approximately three to four hours to hit the target and return to its air base. Before the plane takes off, a plethora of ground intelligence is gathered, which has its own cost and implications.

What is the loss to the Taliban's incurred? The then Air Force Secretary Heather Wilson was worried about the cost-benefit analysis more than anyone else. Experts also questioned the rationale of employing an F-22 for attacking the drug labs in a mud house. A few military veterans argued why heroin labs needed to be bombed when one could kill a Taliban? After a year-long bombing, the campaign was stopped in 2018. The much-hyped Iron Tempest too adds to the sordid tales of the US military failures in Afghanistan. It went down in history as a failed air strike campaign, both in its design and outcome, and proved to be a forlorn hope.

The net sown area of poppy reduced by almost 20 per cent in 2018, after registering an all-time high of 3,28,000 hectares in 2017. Consequently, the amount of opium produced also dropped by almost 29 per cent, from its peak in 2017. The sharp decline was due to lack of rain and snow during the 2017–18 season of poppy cultivation. The drought of 2018 exacerbated many of Afghanistan's challenges. The already impoverished farmers now witnessed crop failure due to drought and their living standards further slipped, potentially making opium cultivation an even more attractive option in the coming years. The US Government estimate of the 'Afghanistan Poppy Cultivation and Potential Opium Production' found that poppy cultivation decreased in 2019 compared to 2018, but potential pure opium production increased. Poppy cultivation in Afghanistan declined by 28 per cent, from 221,000 hectares in 2018 to 160,000 hectares in 2019. Conversely, potential pure opium production increased by 21 per cent, from 5,550 metric tonnes in 2018 to 6,700 metric tonnes in 2019. Low opium prices at planting time drove the decline in cultivation. The rise in potential pure production is a direct result of favourable weather and harvesting conditions. The fall in cultivation area did not change the overall narrative, with the Taliban making more money with a 21 per cent increase in opium production in 2019.

After more than a decade long, exorbitantly expensive US and international counternarcotics operation, poppy cultivation is not exhibiting any sign of significant reduction in Afghanistan. On the contrary, opium production is expanding at an alarming pace. It is further spiralling from its traditional origin of the highly volatile southern region, which remains under the fierce grip of Taliban insurgency, to the northern and even western regions of Afghanistan. According to the latest UNODC data, opium production has increased from 185 metric tonnes in 2001, a year that witnessed the toppling of the Taliban regime, to 5,500 metric tonnes in 2019, depicting an alarming thirty-fold rise.

The inept poppy eradication programme has inadvertently ceded the control of Afghanistan to the Taliban guerrillas. The US alone has employed a massive $10 billion on counternarcotics efforts in Afghanistan, since launching the campaign in October 2001, after the fall of the Taliban. It comes to almost $1.5 million per day, in addition to more than $2 trillion spent on the war in Afghanistan to defeat the Taliban. The atrocious rise in opium production, despite funnelling billions of dollar, calls into question the approach and effectiveness of the US counter-narcotics intervention in Afghanistan. This clearly shows that the poppy eradication mission has completely failed in Afghanistan. It can be considered as the single most ineffective programme in the history of American foreign policy for Afghanistan. The late Richard Holbrooke, the administration's coordinator of Afghanistan policy, by his own admission, said that the strategy was ineffective and wasteful.[6] This, in fact, has proven to be counterproductive, as the poppy farmers have turned towards the Taliban for succour. Launched with an aim to cut the finances of the Taliban, it has ended up filling their coffers and bolstering them like never before.

Poppy cultivation continues to feed power to the Taliban and fuels insurgency in Afghanistan. Poppy is weakening all

---

[6]Pain, Adam, 'Afghanistan's Opium Poppy Economy', Mei@75, 20 April 2012, https://www.mei.edu/publications/afghanistans-opium-poppy-economy, accessed 18 June 2021.

international efforts to weed out terrorism from Afghanistan and stabilize the war-torn nation. Poppy is boosting the finances of the Taliban and they appear to be now better funded than ever, and they are less reliant on traditional sources of funding from their neighbour and the Gulf. This has emboldened the Taliban and they seem to be more threating than ever before. Insecurity, opium production, terrorist attacks and territory controlled by the Taliban are now at a record high. Afghanistan is the 165th least corrupt nation out of 179 countries, according to the latest Corruption Perception Index (CPI) ranking released by the Transparency International in 2020. The Government of Afghanistan is unable to extend the most basic services to its people. Poppy is inextricably linked to all of the above. It has further jeopardized the state-building process and economic reconstruction initiatives of the US-led international efforts.

There is no solution to fix the problems of Afghanistan unless poppy production is arrested. The US is utterly short to solve the poppy mess that continues to poison Afghanistan. The US's failure in Afghanistan offers broader insights into the limits to its global power. The persistence of both opium cultivation and the Taliban insurgency suggest that the policies imposed on Afghanistan by Washington since 2001 have reached a dead end. In fact, the failure of the US strategy has planted the seeds, quite literally, for the Taliban's strong revival.

The illicit poppy economy inevitably determines the survival of a large segment of the population. The farmers and landless labourers in Afghanistan who grow or work on poppy are some of the world's poorest people. They indulge in an illicit form of livelihood out of desperation, and the US need to be understanding and empathetic towards their plight. Better opportunities should be afforded to opium growers to draw them away from their economic dependence on poppy. Even amid dauntingly complex policy problems, there are alternatives. Investing even a small portion of all that misspent military funding in the country's agriculture can produce viable economic options for the millions of farmers who depend on the opium crop for employment. Perhaps a more patient approach is required to eliminate poppy from both the mind as well as the fields of the farmers. The policy experts should press the extensive network of democratically elected Community Development Councils (CDCs)—village-level community structures—to arrest poppy cultivation in Afghanistan. This is doable through social mobilization and appropriate financial incentives. Rather than destroying standing crops and providing compensation later, it would have been prudent to provide incentives before, in order to arrest poppy cultivation.

Some western countries provide financial incentives to their farmers to influence certain farming decisions, for economic reasons. Why could Afghanistan not implement the same model for eradicating poppy? It could have been a good idea if the anti-narcotics fund was used to provide performance-based incentives to the CDCs in order to actively engage them in the poppy eradication drive. Perhaps it needs to be mentioned here that the private telecom companies are protecting their towers in the Taliban-infested areas by paying incentives to the CDCs. The usage of anti-narcotic funds in Afghanistan is another area of concern. The fund is largely employed for construction of community infrastructures like roads, bridges, etc. Without undermining the importance of infrastructure, one fails to understand how the same can eradicate poppy. The fund should have been specially used for its intended purpose.

The whole counternarcotics strategy needs to be revisited and revamped, in the interest of Afghanistan. The sooner it is done, the better. A common complaint from Afghan farmers is that traditional crops, grown legally, do not bring enough money. The new strategy should emphasize improving pre- and post-harvest agriculture infra, along with setting up a pan-Afghanistan MSP structure for ensuring secure and remunerative returns of farm produce. More realistic alternative livelihood opportunities should be explored and further steamrolled into the overall economic development and human capital development. Additionally, a national employment guarantee scheme (like the Mahatma Gandhi National Rural Employment Guarantee Act, India) should be launched for providing secure employment to the youth and landless labourers in Afghanistan. The daily wage rate could be kept higher, with an aim to dry the supply of labour to the poppy fields. The proposed scheme could be dovetailed with the sector of agriculture and allied sector. Overall, the above investments would create more jobs in the primary sector and make economic returns from agriculture more secure and lucrative. A large component of subsidy should be built into the MSP in order to make it lucrative for farmers to turn to alternative crop cultivation, such as wheat.

Afghanistan lacks a formal credit infrastructure in the rural areas, often compelling famers to remain under the clutches of drug lords and merchants charging exorbitant interest. This forces the farmer to perennially remain under debt and offer little leeway to break away from poppy. The new strategy should include a formal banking system to ignite a wide array of micro and small businesses at subsidized interest rates. The private banks failed, as they charged rates as high as 22 per cent per annum, making the business in a struggling country riskier.

A formal banking system would open up the key sectors and create more employment opportunities. This would further save the farmers from the highly exploitative moneylending nexus that operates under the control of poppy merchants. All the suggested investments, which would mount to just a fraction of the botched military aid, could create millions of jobs and improve the rural infrastructure, thus easing rural livelihoods.

Afghanistan's neighbours are either accomplices or victims of the opium trade. They need to be part of the solution too. Russia alone has a reported 3.5 million opium addicts. They should work in tandem to improve intelligence sharing and border security to seize cross-border smuggling. Concerted efforts should also be made in the consumer countries to curb drug addiction. Together, this would go a long way in arresting poppy production in Afghanistan.

The option of legalizing poppy cultivation to some extent under the watch of local government can also be explored. This will not only solve the illicit poppy production in Afghanistan but also lower the price of prescription drugs worldwide and make healthcare more affordable. A licencing system would further bring the state in a supportive relationship with the farmers. Such legalization was done in Turkey long ago. Australia, India, France, Spain and Turkey grow poppy but with better control and regulation. They currently dominate the global prescription medicine market. With a village governance structure, such as the CDCs in place, in every village, legalization and regulation of poppy in Afghanistan too may not be a distant reality.

The Senlis Council (or the International Council on Security and Development), in its report titled *Poppy for Medicine* has proposed a technical model for implementation of poppy licencing and the legal control of cultivation and production of Afghan morphine. But if Afghan poppy starts dominating the international market, it may hit the interest of the established international market players. Hence, one is not sure as to how much of this would be allowed in the present situation, where policy goals of Afghanistan are set and determined by the donor countries.

Of late, revenue from the poppy model has been extended to many other commodities within Afghanistan. Opium poppy is not the only source of funding for insurgency groups any more. The Taliban have started taxing minerals, marbles and even wood. The diversity of the Taliban's income portfolio will have serious implications. The growing revenue would only make them increasingly lethal and fuel instability and insurgency leading to more violence and bloodbaths. There doesn't seem to be any easy way to bankrupt the Taliban.

After fighting the longest war in its history, the US stands at the brink of defeat in Afghanistan. At this juncture, it looks like a small pink flower—the opium poppy—has stopped Washington's massive train of military juggernaut. The pink flower has brought the American military to their knees in Afghanistan with no solution in sight. As snow melts from the mountain slopes and poppy plants rise from the soil every spring, there will be a new batch of teenage recruits from impoverished villages ready to fight for the Taliban cause. And the unending cycle of violence would continue unabated. But does the US have the luxury of treating narcotics as a 'lesser evil' in Afghanistan? 'Without drugs, this war would have been long over,' Afghanistan President, Ghani, said recently.[7] 'The poppy is a very important driver of this war,' he further added.

---

[7] https://twitter.com/MujMash/status/924977955775893504, accessed 18 June 2021.

2

On-Again, Off-Again Peace Process

The US is smoking the peace pipe with the same Taliban that it had set out to eliminate. What made the US turn an apostle of peace? Will the on-again, off-again peace process, spanning over a decade, ever conclude? What is blocking peace from returning to Afghanistan?

Famous for his unpredictable policymaking style, Twitter-obsessed Trump, the then US president, had called off the peace talks with the Taliban after claiming that he was due to host the Taliban and the Afghan President at Camp David, the presidential retreat in Maryland, on 8 September 2019. He arrived at the decision after the Taliban claimed responsibility for a car bomb attack in the city of Kabul, a week before he was supposed to ink the deal. The attack killed 12 people, including one US soldier. This came after a deadly bomb strike in the province of Baghlan and Kunduz in the same week. Analysts were speculating some such development in the US camp after the abrupt cancellation of the planned US visit of President Ghani on 6 September 2019. However, little did anyone realize that the announcement could have far-reaching consequences.

While the world was trying to comprehend the abrupt cancellation of the peace process, President Trump surprised everyone once again. Though this time it was a pleasant surprise. During his maiden India visit, he stunned the international community, especially the Indian leadership, by announcing that he would sign a peace deal with the Taliban soon. There was little that New Delhi could do but play a great host and not raise the purported peace deal for fear of making the visiting president uncomfortable. As it is, the apprehension that President Trump might raise the Anti-Citizenship (Amendment) Act issue was looming large on the minds of the Indian leadership. Hence, it was in the interest of the Indian leadership to keep silent on the Afghan peace process. However, deep down, India was preparing for the upcoming storm in Afghanistan.

President Trump followed suit and a peace deal was inked between the Taliban and the US on 29 February 2020, at Doha, the capital of Qatar, to end the more than 18 years of conflict, and facilitate the return of the residual US forces from Afghanistan. The key patch-up terms included the release of over 5,000 hardcore Taliban militants against the 1,000 Afghan government officials lying in the custody of the Taliban. Another key condition remained the withdrawal of all US soldiers within 14 months from the conclusion of the agreement. Perhaps it needs to be mentioned here that about 14,000 US troops and approximately 17,000 troops from 39 NATO allies have been stationed in Afghanistan in a non-combatant role. Even though there was no explicit mention of the Taliban shunning violence under the peace pact, there was a tacit understanding that the Taliban would reduce violence in order to generate a favourable press around the peace deal.

'This is a hopeful moment, but it is only the beginning. Achieving lasting peace in Afghanistan will require patience and compromise among all parties,' said the then US Defence Secretary, Mark Esper, who met Afghan President, Ghani, in Kabul, where they announced a joint declaration parallel to the US-Taliban accord.[8] He sounded somewhat unsure, and so was the then US Secretary of State, Mike Pompeo. Addressing the historic moment, Pompeo said Washington would closely watch the Taliban's compliance to the agreement. He further called on the Taliban to keep their promise to cut ties with the al-Qaeda and keep fighting the militant Islamic State group. President Ghani, on his part, said that he hoped the Doha deal would pave the way towards lasting peace. 'We hope the US-Taliban peace [deal] will lead to a permanent ceasefire... The nation is looking forward to a full ceasefire,' he told a news conference in Kabul.[9] The Afghan government said it stood ready to negotiate and conclude a ceasefire with the Taliban, and affirmed its support to the phased withdrawal of the US and coalition forces, subject to the Taliban's fulfilment of their side of the commitments. President Ghani was happy to get direct control of the peace process for the first time, as until

---

[8]Baibhawi, Riya, 'Pentagon Chief Says "Road Ahead Will Not Be Easy" After US-Taliban Deal,' *Republic World*, 1 March 2020, https://www.republicworld.com/world-news/us-news/pentagon-chief-says-road-ahead-will-not-be-easy-after-us-taliban-dea.html, accessed 18 June 2021.

[9]Sediqi, Abdul Qadir and Alexander Cornwell, 'US, Taliban signs historic troop withdrawal deal in Doha,' *SundayGuardianLive*, 29 February 2020, https://www.sundayguardianlive.com/world/ustaliban-sign-historic-troop-withdrawal-deal-doha, accessed 2 July 2020.

then the White House was driving it all, with practically no say of the incumbent government in Kabul.

Some deal at last

The Afghan peace process, largely viewed as the brainchild of the White House, had been zealously pursued by the US for almost a decade. After decades of relentless military operations, it was becoming increasingly clear that the Taliban were far from vanquished. In fact, the Taliban were getting stronger with every passing day, and the war on terror clearly looked like a losing cause. The US launched four phases of its peace endeavour, since 2011. Even though separate in terms of approach and course, these phases were driven by a common goal of signing a peace deal with the Taliban and exit from Afghanistan, from what seems to be an un-winnable war. The previous three attempts of peace process had not yielded any result and the situation had spiralled from bad to worse in Afghanistan. However, a lot of hope was pinned on the fourth attempt, as for the first time, the Taliban seemed to engage directly with the top leadership of the US to cut a peace deal. Both parties were interested for their own reasons. And finally, a peace deal was worked out on 29 February 2020. It is worthwhile to know the brief history of the peace process with the Taliban to understand and analyse the recently inked peace deal in totality.

The first instalment of the Afghan peace talks was initiated with the Taliban in September 2014, much before the withdrawal of the US-led NATO forces from a combatant role in Afghanistan. A distinction was further made between the good (moderate) and the bad Taliban to kick-start the peace negotiation. The moderate Taliban refers to those who are ready to abjure violence and willing to join the mainstream political process. This was a marked departure from US policy of having no truck with all of Taliban, good or bad. For the first time, there was a formal recognition that the moderate Taliban could stabilize Afghanistan. An underlying principle was drawn—that the peace process would be led, controlled and owned by the Afghan government. The Government of Afghanistan even contemplated the concept of *Afwa* (forgiveness or political amnesty) for the moderate Taliban. The patch-up terms included the Taliban laying down their weapons on the terms of the Afghan government followed by an oath to abide by the Constitution. The Government of Afghanistan led the peace talks from the front, but away from the glare of 24x7 international media. However, the souring relationship between the then US president, Barack Obama, and the then Afghan president, Hamid Karzai, prevented the peace process from gaining full momentum.

During the last phase of the Karzai government, it was reported that President Obama was not even on speaking terms with President Karzai. The peace process eventually slowed down after showing an initial sign of promise and potential. This stemmed from the continuous tirade by President Karzai against the US, for not talking tough with Pakistan for fanning terrorism in Afghanistan. The people of Afghanistan subscribed to the aggression of President Karzai, as Pakistan was aiding and abetting the Taliban for spreading unrest in Afghanistan. The assassination of Rabbani, the chair of the Afghan high peace council, by suicide bombers in Kabul on 20 September 2011, dealt a devastating blow to the nascent peace process. The political fallout between Karzai and the Obama administration, coupled with the killing of the peace chair Rabbani by the Taliban gave a deathblow to the first leg of the peace process, after gathering some initial momentum. The process did not accomplish any results other than striking some resonance with the Taliban that a durable peace in Afghanistan is possible. In the peace process, there was a hidden realization for both the US as well as Afghanistan that a political solution is the only way out from the long-standing Afghan conflict. The war in Afghanistan against the Taliban and its proxies was un-winnable, and an escape through a peace deal was the best option for the US.

For the second time, in pursuit of peace, the US policy drivers in Afghanistan played a cardinal role in assembling the famous Quadrilateral Coordination Group, or QCG (comprising Afghanistan, Pakistan, the US and China) in 2015. This was done to bring the warring factions of the Taliban to the negotiating table, in order to stabilize the conflict-ridden country. Russia too joined the group at a later stage. The second phase of the peace process was also contingent on Islamabad to 'change its policies' towards militancy and regional peace, under the influence of the US. The China card was also brought to play by the US to impress upon Pakistan to use its influence over the Taliban in order to bring them to the peace table. Pakistan, under pressure from the US, made some half-hearted attempts in pushing forward the peace deliberations with the Taliban, mainly due to the fear of losing its strategic influence over Afghanistan. With the passage of time, it was amply evident that both Pakistan and its all-weather ally China were refraining from putting enough pressure on the Taliban to cut a peace deal with the Afghan government. The efforts lacked intent and was mainly done at a superficial level to gain favourable headlines in the international media.

A series of deliberations with the Taliban via the QCG hardly yielded any peace dividends. While a political settlement was the only solution to the Afghan conflict, the peace process struggled to clear the China-Pakistan axis. There was also no one voice from the Taliban, with the terrorist group riddled into various factions and warring leaders. The second phase of the peace process failed in bringing the top leadership of the various factions of the Taliban to the peace table. Things did not move beyond tacit negotiation and obscure deals between the Taliban and the independent members of the quadrilateral group. The Pakistan army refrained from employing full force for compelling the Taliban to negotiate with the Afghan government for a political settlement. This was largely due to the inherent conflict between the political and military establishments within Pakistan. The reluctance of the Taliban to surrender their position of strength at a time when the US was exhausted with the Afghan battle and desperate to somehow close the war also stopped them from surrendering to the peace process. Unlike the first leg of the peace process, a great degree of hope was pinned on the all-weather duo of Pakistan and China to assist the peace process by employing their strategic influence over the Taliban. Also, there was overdependence on Pakistan to deliver, knowing well that the army and the civilian government of Pakistan were not on the same page.

The second phase of the peace process exposed the differential approach of the quadrilateral group members with each of them reaching out to the Taliban independently rather than as part of a group. In a way, they launched a separate peace window without paying much attention to the common and binding goal of the Afghan peace process. In some sense, it was a freelance peace process initiated by the member countries rather than a unified and coordinated approach for peace in Afghanistan. The approach adopted by the member countries further exposed their inherent policy and strategic contradictions in search of the elusive peace deal in Afghanistan.

Frustrated with the peace process showing no sign of moving forward, coupled with an emboldened Taliban threatening to step up the turmoil in Afghanistan, President Trump took the reins of the dormant peace process directly at the White House. In the month of July 2018, he launched the third phase of the peace process, also the most potent phase, with a renewed vigour. The third phase began with the appointment of Khalilzad, an Afghan-origin US diplomat, who would directly negotiate with the Taliban. Washington clearly wanted to strike a peace deal with the Taliban and Khalilzad seemed to be the right person for the daunting task. He had served as a State Department policy planner during the Reagan administration. He spoke the major Afghan languages, Pashto and Dari, knew the key political players and was well-known in the elite circles in Kabul. He seemed to be aware of the problems and the challenges that lie ahead, much better than anyone in the White House administration. Armed with a clear brief, he aggressively went ahead with the Herculean task of exploring peace in Afghanistan.

The Pakistan angle

The actual source of the present-day crisis in Afghanistan boils down to Pakistan. Hence, Pakistan also has to be part of the solution. President Trump was not keen on subscribing to this hypothesis during his initial months at the White house. After some dilly-dallying, he realized and thus emphasized the centrality of Pakistan in solving the Afghan mess. This was a 180-degree turn from his long-standing position articulated through many rants in social media squarely blaming Pakistan for aiding and abetting terrorism in Afghanistan. He justified his turnaround by blaming the previous rulers of Pakistan. Trump said that a lot more could have been done in Afghanistan if it had the right leadership. His volte-face suggested that the Trump administration viewed its relationship with Pakistan largely through the prism of Afghanistan, even though the White House tried to pitch otherwise. After years of discord over Afghanistan, Pakistan too started cooperating with the US by influencing the Taliban to participate in the peace process, and thus helping the US in toying with the prospect of extricating from its longest war in Afghanistan. Pakistan did this to get into the good books of the US to escape its worst financial crisis. The fresh approach adopted by President Trump provided the real impetus to the third phase of the peace process. For the first time, it appeared that the US was inching towards a conclusive peace deal in Afghanistan.

But, the acerbic tweet of President Trump on 8 September 2019 whereby he called off the peace negotiations with the Taliban,[10] put an abrupt and screeching halt to the third phase of the peace talks, that the US was so heavily invested in. If the previous version of Khalilzad is to be believed, nothing was standing in the way of peace in Afghanistan. The tumultuous peace process led by its chief architect Khalilzad was almost on its penultimate phase. Both sides had almost agreed on a 'draft framework' for a peace agreement. While keeping the finer print of the draft peace deal under wraps, the US Special Representative for Afghanistan Reconciliation, Khalilzad,

---

[10]Shams, Shamil and Masood Saifullah, 'Why did President Donald Trump call off Taliban talks?' DW, 8 September 2019, https://www.dw.com/en/why-did-president-donald-trump-call-off-taliban-talks/a-50344189, accessed 18 June 2021.

announced on the popular TOLO TV that the US had 'in principle' agreed to withdraw over 5,000 troops from Afghanistan in exchange of guarantees by the Taliban to not allow the war-torn country to be used as a launch pad for transnational terror attacks and further fight the growing menace of ISIS within Afghanistan. Breaking their personal pledges to the al-Qaeda and not allowing them to grow within Afghanistan was another precondition set for the Taliban. President Trump was also warming up to the peace draft. 'We're going down to 8,600 [troops] and then we'll make a determination from there as to what happens,' Trump told Fox News.[11]

If Khalilzad's account was to be believed, nothing was standing in the way of peace in Afghanistan. His view was not in isolation. All those who mattered—starting with the Afghan civil society, which welcomed the Taliban's participation in the talks, down to the governments in Pakistan and Iran—seemed to be on board. The Afghan government wanted to see the fine print of the draft peace deal before conclusively voicing its opinion on the same. Pakistan on its part facilitated the travel of Mullah Abdul Ghani Baradar to Qatar by lifting the ban on his travel. Mullah Baradar co-founded the Taliban with the slain one-eyed supreme leader Mullah Omar, and often seen as perennial number two in the ranks of the Taliban. He was reported to be a votary of peace, as he was of the understanding that the Taliban could make a good bargain from their position of strength. He remains the most acceptable face and a bridge between the moderate and the dogmatic Taliban leaders, within the Taliban. His participation was imperative

---

[11]ANI, 'US plans to maintain 8,600 troops in Afghanistan after peace deal: Trump,' *Business Standard*, 30 August 2019, https://www.business-standard. com/article/news-ani/us-plans-to-maintain-8-600-troops-in-afghanistan-after-peace-deal-trump-119083000089_1.html, accessed 21 June 2021.

for the peace process to gain any serious traction.

Afghanistan did not extend the same privilege to jailed Anas Haqqani, son of the founder of the dreaded Haqqani network—a Taliban affiliate. His name was proposed by the Taliban as part of the 14-member delegation to negotiate the peace process. Kabul did not oblige as it sensed a strategic ploy to get him out of jail. In his absence, another representative from the Haqqani group was made part of the delegation.

Even though the third instalment of the peace process was halted because of President Trump's tweet, some seasoned diplomats from both the US as well as Afghanistan immediately aired the opinion that the peace process could no longer be delayed. The Taliban lost no time in increasing the level of violence in Afghanistan. And soon the reality dawned on President Trump that perhaps reaching out to the Taliban was the only way forward to exit from the war-torn nation.

In the fourth instalment of peace offering, he once again relied on his blue-eyed peace envoy Khalilzad to repair the damage and pick up the threads of the process. Unlike last time, he directed Khalilzad to conduct the dialogue with the Taliban behind closed doors, away from the glare of the international media. While for the Taliban, the ongoing peace deal was one of the options in Afghanistan, for the US, it was their only option to exit Afghanistan. President Trump was left with no option, as the defeat of the US forces was looming large. Khalilzad soon stormed into action and picked up the thread with the Taliban from where he had left it in Doha. As the nuts and bolts of the peace deal had already been hammered out, it did not take much time to conclude the fourth phase of the peace deal, which was announced on 29 February 2020.

The new agreement was confronted with several hurdles.

The nascent peace deal faced its first stumbling block on the prisoner swap. President Ghani was not warming up to the idea right from the beginning of the deal. Less than 24 hours after signing the peace deal, he questioned several elements of the deal, including the timeline for releasing the Taliban militants and the conditions surrounding the talks between the Taliban and his government. As per the condition of the agreement, the Government of Afghanistan had to release 5,000 Taliban prisoners before 10 March 2020 to kick-start the intra-Afghan political dialogue with the Taliban. 'Freeing Taliban prisoners is not [under] the authority of US but the authority of the Afghan government,' Ghani told reporters in Kabul on 1 March 2020.[12] 'There has been no commitment for the release of 5,000 prisoners,' he further added and mentioned that the prisoner swap could be discussed during talks with the Taliban, but could not be a precondition.

This jolted the US policymakers as well as the Taliban, and the prospect of the deal falling flat, once again, was real. However, with US brute diplomacy coupled with an aid cut made President Ghani sign a presidential decree for the release of 1,500 Taliban prisoners after more than a week of dilly-dallying. The Afghan authorities started releasing Taliban prisoners in a phased manner clearing the roadblock for the direct negotiation of the Afghan government with the Taliban. The Afghan grand assembly of elders, the *Loya Jirga*, approved the release of 400 hardcore militants accused of serious crimes, in the second week of August 2020. Ghani earlier had said that the decision to free the 400 Taliban prisoners with serious charges, was outside his authority. However, analysts were of

---

[12] 'Afghan conflict: President Ashraf Ghani rejects Taliban prisoner release,' BBC News, 1 March 2020, https://www.bbc.com/news/world-asia-51695370, accessed 18 June 2021.

the opinion that the engagement of *Loya Jirga* was an attempt to develop a broad-based consensus on the release of these 400 most dreaded militants, in case the peace deal went sour and the released militants picked up the gun again. In a way, this was to safeguard his political stake. The *Loya Jirga* said in a resolution that the decision to free the 400 militants was made in order to 'remove an obstacle, allow the start of the peace process and end of bloodshed.'[13] It coincided with the US announcing that its troop level in the country would drop below 5,000 by November.

After the approval of the *Loya Jirga*, a majority of the 400 militants were released. The Taliban were determined not to have any talks with the Afghan government until all them were freed. While the government has released more than 5,000 Taliban militants so far, the Taliban are yet to proportionately release the government officials under their custody. This is perhaps preventing the Afghan government from releasing the remaining hardcore Taliban militants. The delay in releasing the government officials questions the sincerity of the Taliban to follow suit.

The Taliban representatives and the US have remained tight-lipped over the various sticking points, which have the potential to scupper the peace process much before reaching its goal. The success of the peace deal is contingent on the subsequent 'intra-Afghan dialogue', especially with the elected government of Afghanistan. The Taliban, in the past, had overtly rejected any direct engagement with the elected Afghan

---

[13]'Afghan assembly approves release of 400 "hard-core" Taliban prisoners,' *The Times of India*, 9 August 2020, https://timesofindia.indiatimes.com/world/south-asia/afghan-assembly-approves-release-of-400-hard-core-taliban-prisoners/articleshow/77443549.cms, accessed 16 June 2021.

government and termed it as a 'puppet regime of the US'.[14] The international media was critical of the policy stance adopted by the Taliban and further questioned the leeway provided to the Taliban amid peace talks.

Seeking broad acceptance

In the midst of mounting criticism over ignoring the elected government of Kabul, the drivers of the peace process made a few representatives from the Afghan government participate in the third phase of the peace talks in Doha, which was held from 7–8 July 2019, albeit in their personal capacity. This was to circumvent the Taliban's rejection of any direct talks with the Afghan government. The talks intended to break the ice for direct negotiation on Afghanistan's future after the much anticipated exit of US forces. It was also to portray the right optics in order to make the peace process seem more broad-based and inclusive. This assuaged the growing concerns of the US media on the future of the peace talks in the backdrop of the continual rejection of the Taliban to engage with the elected Government of Afghanistan.

Representatives from media, civil society and even political parties were invited to the same meeting to blur the participation of government representatives. This round of talks grabbed the headlines for different reasons though. Social media mistakenly included the baby's name who accompanied her mother on a list of conference participants. Maybe it was befitting, as of all the participants, his future stakes remain

---

[14]Reuters Staff, 'Afghan government has concerns about U.S.-Taliban peace deal', Reuters, 4 September 2019, https://www.reuters.com/article/us-afghanistan-taliban/afghan-government-has-concerns-about-u-s-taliban-peace-deal-idUSKCN1VP16K, accessed 15 June 2021.

of prime importance. News of another round of carnage killing children came as the delegates deliberated peace in the sprawling Sheraton resort in Doha. This was the irony of the peace process. You have to sit with the same people and search for peace who are hell-bent on killing anyone and everyone in order to prove their upper hand in this theatre of war.

Under the peace deal, the Taliban would directly speak to the Government of Afghanistan, as a part of the intra-Afghan dialogue to hammer out the real deal. Why did the Taliban after refusing to accept the Afghan government as a legitimate and credible party agree to speak to the Government of Afghanistan directly? Actually, the Taliban wanted the US to announce the blue print for withdrawing the remaining 14,000 troops from the soil of Afghanistan. They knew that the Kabul government would be very weak once the US, especially the US airpower, is out of the equation. With their grand objective achieved under the peace deal, the Taliban softened their stand and agreed to open negotiations with the Afghan government, popularly referred to as track II negotiation.

The media believes that as the talks begin with the elected government, the Taliban will make a demand for representatives from other political parties and civil society to minimize the influence of the top leadership of the elected government. This will also enable them to align with their long-standing position of not recognizing the incumbent government and speaking to a broader group. While being a part of the peace deal, some Taliban leaders continue to question the legitimacy of the incumbent Ghani government. And even after the release of the bulk of Taliban prisoners, they are not showing any real intent or urgency to talk to the elected Afghan government. The proposed talks are being deferred on some pretext or the other. This makes analysts question if the Taliban are serious about recognizing the position of the Afghan government.

The Taliban's resistance to any direct business with the government was consistent with their long-stated policy. However, it also stems from the fact that any association with the Afghan government would affect the morale of the fighters in the actual battlefield. There was also a lurking fear that the radical lot of the Taliban fighters might revolt and challenge the diktats of the top leadership, thereby exposing the flaw in the chain of command. The chances of low-level revolts against the leadership could have made the Taliban look fractured, thereby seriously eroding their ability to make the most out of the peace table.

While the intra-Afghan dialogue is in the offing, the Taliban continue to employ violence as a means of boosting their power. The US soldiers are spared from the ambit of their attacks, especially after signing the Doha deal. The Taliban are resorting to attacks in order to gain leverage in the intra-Afghan peace talks, so that they can benefit the most. Fourteen rockets crashed in different parts of Kabul city, including the heavily fortified presidential compound, while the nation was celebrating its 101st Independence Day. There is a new twist in the Taliban strategy now. They refuse to claim responsibility for most of the attacks engineered in Afghanistan. And the US comes to their rescue after every attack giving them a clean chit.

The attack on the Kabul hospital maternity ward, killing 35 people, including mothers and newborn babies, is one such instance. While all local intelligence was pointing towards a typical trademark Taliban attack, the US special envoy blamed the Daesh or the Islamic State militants behind the same. Hours after Khalilzad's tweet, Kabul openly rejected the US assessment that the Daesh militants were behind the attack; it claimed to possess evidence implicating the Taliban and the Haqqani network. The recent attack on peace negotiator and ex-Member of Parliament, Fawzia Koofi, tasked with carrying forward the peace discussion with the Taliban, is another case in this regard. Local intelligence officials blamed the Taliban. The Taliban, sticking to their new strategy, denied their role. The US put the blame on the enemies of the peace process and refrained from naming the Taliban directly. The Taliban have the military momentum going with them, and will not accept any ceasefire, despite repeated calls from the US and its Afghan counterpart to shun violence amid the peace process. The recent spate of attacks underscores a grim reality in Afghanistan: the government's pleas to spare civilians means little, as the combatants seek leverage by continuing attacks that endanger the lives of civilians. The Taliban are further invigorated with the release of the prisoners. This is in gross violation of the established standard operating procedures in any peace process. Terror and talks do not go together.

However, the Taliban write their own rulebook and rarely follow any other. They are in no mood to stop the mayhem and wait for the peace process to conclude. The media along with the civil society of Afghanistan is highly critical of the dual approach adopted by the Taliban. The spate of attacks stems from the fact that the Taliban are not willing to surrender the position of their strength. It will not be a surprise if the Taliban raise the level of attack as the embattled country inches closer to the elusive peace deal. This is anticipated in light of their growing greed to get the most from the peace process in a position of strength.

For the time being, the US is ignoring the lethal attacks led by the Taliban in Afghanistan. But it is not possible for them to turn a blind eye to the growing attacks and casualties in Afghanistan for a longer duration. The US media has been getting critical of the peace process and seriously questioning the strategic leeway provided to the Taliban amid the peace talks. Some are even mocking the strategy adopted by the US for rapprochement with the Taliban. Earlier, the US wanted to fight and talk, simultaneously. Now, the Taliban seem to be adopting the same strategy. The Taliban are aping the US military strategy in Afghanistan.

Post-withdrawal fears

Some voices in the Afghan government and many among the ordinary citizens fear that the Taliban would simply wait for the US military departure and proceed to overthrow the Afghan government with brutal force. It is quite a potent possibility, given the way the Taliban have reorganized themselves into a lethal force, with swelling numbers of fighters and extension from their traditional stronghold in the south to the northern region of Afghanistan. The Taliban of 2020 are very different from the Taliban of 2001. Today, they are well equipped with a lethal range of sophisticated weapons for causing mass damages. Their coffers have swelled to an all-time high and the fighters seem to be ready to go for the final kill. There are genuine fears that, without the US's support, especially air power, the Afghan government will be as powerless as the government of Dr Najibullah—whom the Afghan Mujahideen replaced in 1992. Experts have started drawing a parallel between the premature withdrawal of the Soviet forces in 1988 to the exit of the US forces under the peace deal. Can the Afghan government keep itself in power if the US military decides to leave? The Taliban look more organized, motivated and lethal than before to take over Kabul, subduing their opponents. The Taliban would be in an even stronger position and will not see the need to engage with the US anymore and keep working on their larger desire of capturing and ruling Afghanistan. If the US exits prematurely, Afghanistan may turn into another Iraq where large parts of the Iraqi army collapsed in the face of the rising Islamic State group.

The complete US withdrawal may also create a serious vacuum and Afghanistan may turn out to be nobody's concern in the international community—a repeat of the post-Soviet withdrawal scene. This time round, its location is right next to the rising superpower China, and its all-weather ally Pakistan, eyeing the vast mineral resources and more strategic grip over Afghanistan makes it furthermore complicated. India too remains a contestant in the economic and strategic race driven by the larger objective of keeping the China and Pakistan duo in abeyance. And Iran too is vying for more space and influence in Afghanistan. It is posturing more aggressively than ever for regional supremacy. This means that outsiders continue to remain seriously interested in Afghanistan's stability.

More importantly, there is a very real threat of the rise of the Islamic State (ISIS), or Daesh, in Afghanistan, which has already expanded its sphere of influence in the country. From a few wolf attacks, they have emerged as a serious threat to Afghanistan, after the Taliban. The Afghan Taliban and ISIS are sharply divided over ideology and tactics, with the former mainly targeting government interests and international security forces. The Taliban are still the larger, more penetrated, imposing and lethal force at play. At this stage, it will not be hyperbole to suggest that the ISIS and the Taliban appear to be competing for the title of the 'most feared terrorist' in

Afghanistan. ISIS could take advantage of the security vacuum that an American withdrawal might create; it may reorganize quickly and deploy its underemployed leadership and cadres from Iraq and Syria to Afghanistan. The world can ignore this threat only at its own peril. This was evident when the West, albeit involuntarily, allowed the ISIS to gain root in Iraq and Syria and witnessed the fatal consequences of the same. Any fecund ground created in Afghanistan with the premature withdrawal of the US forces will only make the ISIS thrive and turn into a more lethal force in Afghanistan. And if successful, the ripples would be felt in Iraq and Syria too. The Taliban may try to control them, but the civilian populace would ultimately face the major brunt of it.

The ongoing peace negotiation is cryptic about the thorny issue of the political arrangement in a post-US exit scenario. The eventual power-sharing idea floated by the chief negotiator was set aside by the Taliban as something to be discussed only after the complete withdrawal of the US forces from Afghanistan. It would come up in the much-anticipated political dialogue with the Afghan government. The Taliban have remained officially vague and tight-lipped about what kind of government they envision. This would be the most arduous task, though it might come up only after the Taliban and Afghan officials agree to work out a new political structure to rule Afghanistan in future. Islamabad, a key player in the negotiation, overtly supports that the Taliban need to be given a share of political power in Kabul, and further term it as a key to bring peace in the neighbouring Afghanistan. A few pragmatic US generals with Afghan credentials support this argument with an extended analogy that such an arrangement would make the peace process enduring and provide long-term stability. Pakistan's interest stems from its long-standing

Afghan blueprint of fixing ISI sympathizers in the new political order of Kabul, so that they enjoy and retain their strategic influence in Afghanistan.

The intra-Afghan political settlement in all probability may throw up the formation of a unity government that has representation from the incumbent government as well as the Taliban. The US would further employ its influence to accommodate a few civil society representatives to make the unity government look more inclusive, representing broader Afghan society. Any such government in Kabul had to be further ratified by the *Loya Jirga*, for the unity government to be legitimate. The problem will unfold once the unity government comes to play. Leaders like Karzai and a few others have tremendous influence in the *Loya Jirga* and can single-handedly sway and influence their decision. The support would come only when these leaders find their immediate interests and followers are adequately accommodated in the unity government. If there's the slightest of disagreement, the *Loya Jirga* might not approve the arrangement.

Some insights to how the Taliban view power and exercise governance can be found in a constitution that the group drafted while it ruled Afghanistan. It remains the only known official document depicting the Taliban's political vision. It is conservative and extreme, to say the least, and will not be acceptable to any contemporary democratic society. It is marred by inherent contradictions on issues such as women's education, protection of minorities and justice. It has flashes of occasional brilliance too. There lies the catch. The devil lies in the details. What is amply clear is that the Taliban are not fighting the war to assume power through the ballot box, which they have shunned long ago. They will never give up arms and allow the Afghan people to choose or reject them in an election. Nor will they dilute their radical doctrine and philosophy primarily based on a crude interpretation of Islam.

Also, the Taliban don't want to be part of the ruling coalition in Kabul, given their long-cherished ambitions and penchant for ruling the country. Those who know the Taliban leadership from inside are doubtful that it would be willing to share power within a political arrangement, which it has long since banished. The Taliban have abrogated the Constitution of Afghanistan, and it will not be prudent to think that they would abide by the same Constitution in a post-peace process scenario. President Ghani and his government have clearly stated that the Taliban need to have unflinching commitment to the Constitution and not the emirates that Taliban openly advocate. Will these two streams of conflicting political ideology and diametrically opposite views coexist in a ruling conclave in the largely anticipated political set-up, post-US exit from Afghanistan, remains unanswered. Looking into the past history of the Taliban, there are serious doubts that they would be willing to govern within a system that the Taliban's hardliners are grossly uncomfortable with. Consensus building on critical issues amid two contrasting ideologies and views would be the ultimate victim. We witnessed a precursor to that effect, even without the formation of the envisaged political arrangement between the elected government and the Taliban.

In a video statement after the Doha talks, Taliban spokesperson Sher Mohammad Abbas Stanekzai claimed that the Afghan army would be dissolved after the conclusion of the peace deal. The Afghan government strongly protested, prompting Stanekzai to clarify that what he, in fact, meant was that large-scale reforms would be brought in all government institutions and bodies, including the army. This tiff was symptomatic of a bigger trust deficit between the Taliban and the Afghan government. This is only the trailer of what is to follow. There is also a fringe view that the Taliban's more moderate new guard might be willing to stand up to the hardliners and be part of the ruling dispensation post the US exit from Afghanistan. There is a possibility of a split among the Taliban on the issue of power sharing. And if so, this will once again put the much-anticipated peace deal under a great deal of uncertainty.

There are various factions within the Taliban that have started to believe that they can soon achieve their end-goals and thus will not shun violence under any circumstances. The Taliban of today is not the Taliban of yesteryears under the supreme leadership of Mullah Muhammad Omar, the group's founding father, who enjoyed ultimate authority and decision-making power. Even his announcement at the mosque became a diktat for the rank and file of the Taliban with no room for laxity and disobedience. The modern-day Taliban are riddled with factions and groups not necessarily owing their allegiance to the incumbent Mawlawi Hibatullah Akhundzada. Some factions operate under the broader vision and umbrella of the Taliban, but they are driven by their own set of interests and political aspiration.

The Haqqani network, largely viewed as an affiliate of the Taliban, is one such faction. They are also referred to as the blue-eyed boy of the ISI for their additional curiosity in targeting the Indian interest, especially the Indian embassy in Afghanistan. The Haqqani network is part of the peace process, but there is no guarantee that they would subscribe to the outcome of the peace deal. Besides these, all the factions are eyeing the big cake of the post-US exit political set-up in Kabul. Should they find themselves marginalized and not adequately accommodated in the new power structure, the crack would open up, as opposed to the unified face the Taliban have presented so far. Some factions may walk out of the peace deal and will not hesitate to wage their own battle, in case of the slightest disagreement and slide of their personal interest.

Threat to women

The crude and blatant abuse of women's rights during the Taliban's rule is another pressing issue in the peace negotiation. The scar of abuse and torture of women during the Taliban rule still remains fresh and refuses to fade away even after close to two decades. The US think tank did make a few women representatives participate in the Doha peace talks with the Taliban to assuage the growing concern of women.[15] However, women leaders within Afghanistan doubt that this interaction has served any purpose beyond rhetoric and photo op. The inclusion of women is not just about ensuring their passive participation at the peace table. It also means bringing their voices, perspectives and aspirations in the ongoing negotiations and ensuring that there are appropriate safeguards to protect their interest.

Stanekzai, according to *The New York Times*, said the Taliban were 'committed to all rights given to women by Islam ... such as trade, ownership, inheritance, education, work and the choice of partner, security and education, and a good life.'[16] He also said that the Taliban did not recognize Afghanistan's current Constitution, calling it a copy of western constitutions,

---

[15]Saifullah, Masood, 'How successful were the Afghan peace talks in Qatar?' *The Wire*, 10 July 2019, https://thewire.in/south-asia/afghan-peace-talks-qatar, accessed 2 July 2021.

[16]https://www.facebook.com/tayyabSaqibSafi123/posts/1265545550261277, accessed 18 June 2021.

and assured that the Taliban 'did not seek to monopolize power inside Afghanistan.'[17] There lies the real problem. The Afghan Constitution recognizes women's rights in all spheres and guarantees their freedom. However, the repressive Taliban draw women's rights from their crude interpretation of Sharia law, as was evident during their rule in Afghanistan. Women suffered immensely due to the archaic decree passed by the Taliban to control their lives. Hence, there are genuine fears regarding women and their rights, and these fears cannot be set aside.

The Taliban treat women as second-class citizens and subservient to men. During their rule from 1996–2001, women were banned from schools and work, faced public torture and execution, and endured severe restrictions on their movements. A large section of women will be seriously uncomfortable if the Taliban were to decide the contour and scope of their rights. It would be a recipe for more turmoil in the lives of women, if the past sufferings were any standards to go by. Women leaders are of the opinion that some of the basic issues that should be addressed in the intra-Afghan dialogue are education for girls, equality of rights, opportunities for women, etc. Experts, however, think that women's issues would be simply put off or just blurred, in any eventual peace deal to avoid internal resistance from the Taliban's influential and dogmatic military commanders. This remains a huge obstacle to the peace process, as the Taliban have always maintained a rigid and inflexible stance towards women's liberation and empowerment.

There are serious concerns about how much the US can arm-twist the Taliban to safeguard women's rights under the

---

[17]Ibid.

peace deal, if at all. There are lurking fears that the US may trade away women's rights in order to give a real chance to the impending peace deal with the Taliban to fructify. This has left Afghan women fearing abandonment after years of considerable gains in every arena of public life. Women's rights activists and women parliamentarians fear that their hard-won rights and status in Afghan society post the fall of the Taliban would be washed away if the Taliban become part of any new power structure, as a part of the peace deal. To ensure that the Taliban do not change their stance, they demand that more women should get representation in the High Peace Council, the apex official body created by the Government of Afghanistan to carry out negotiations with the Taliban and other militant groups. They also insist that no agreement at any level will be acceptable to them unless Afghan women are made a party of all negotiations. A reputed female journalist from Afghanistan puts it in perspective, 'I do not want such a peace which brings stability but puts me in chains.'[18]

The Government of Afghanistan has included women in the peace council to spearhead the peace talks with the Taliban. However, accommodating the growing concern of women in the peace deal will not be easy, if the established standards and position of the Taliban on women's rights are anything to go by. The US is already reeling under serious pressure from the Taliban and does not enjoy an edge over them. Neither is the Taliban expected to soften their stance.

The ongoing peace process was the cardinal strategy for the Pentagon, but for the Taliban, it was merely one of the options at their disposal. The failure of the peace process

---

[18]Khan, Behroz and Faisal Shakeel, 'Which way the Afghan peace process is headed?' *Herald*, 16 April 2019, https://herald.dawn.com/news/1398847/which-way-the-afghan-peace-process-is-headed, accessed 2 July 2021.

would not cost them anything. While everyone advocates peace dialogue to be the only option, it is imperative for both parties to be equally invested in the same for a meaningful and durable solution. The Taliban control both war and the peace process at this stage. They are in a position of strength. The onus of steering the peace process was completely left at the behest of the US. At this critical juncture, the peace process is heavily tilted towards the Taliban, which is not an ideal scenario for striking a win-win deal for the US to end the longest and the most complex war in US military history. There is a saying that peace cannot be kept by force; shared understanding and mutual cooperation can only achieve it. So far, the Taliban have proved to be a tough negotiator and have made significant gains in the peace process.

The regional game

An Afghan political settlement will not be durable unless regional powers and Afghanistan's immediate neighbours— Pakistan and Iran—support and subsequently endorse it. Russia and China too are included in this strategic list. However, every country is trying to muscle the peace process in a way that it suits its larger geostrategic interest and political design. The Afghan peace process is facing a series of hurdles in passing through the multiple and often competing strategic design of its neighbours. Rather than being complementary to the Afghan peace process, these countries are focusing on keeping their strategic interest and relevance growing, even at the cost of impeding the peace process.

Pakistan Prime Minister, Imran Khan, would leave no stone unturned to make the newly elected US President, Biden, understand the indispensability of Pakistan in the intra-Afghan dialogue. The former US President, Trump, has already awarded the 'good Samaritan' certificate to Imran Khan, as he wanted to ride the influence of Pakistan over the Taliban to conclude the peace deal. For its part, Pakistan has been instrumental in making the talks happen and has received some accolades for its efforts to facilitate these crucial negotiations from none other than President Trump. Pakistan did not turn as the peace angel without a reason either. The US swiftly engaged Saudi Arabia and the UAE, Pakistan's close friends in the Arab world, to create a three-pronged pressure on Pakistan to bring the Taliban to the peace table.

Pakistan too expected that its strong support to the desired peace process will finally yield some dividends in terms of release of blocked funds from the Pentagon and mediation of the White House in the Kashmir dispute. In the past, the Trump administration has suspended security and other assistance to Pakistan, arguing that Islamabad in return has only given 'lies and deceit'.[19] The US on its part made some positive gestures in terms of releasing the first tranche of blocked funds from the Pentagon and offering mediation for solving the Kashmir conflict between the two arch-rivals. To keep Pakistan in good humour, the Pentagon even put Tehrik-e Taliban Pakistan (TTP) and the Balochistan Liberation Army under the specially designated global terrorist list.

Trump pursued Pakistan to pressurize the Taliban to sign a peace deal with the Government of Afghanistan and give the US a window to exit from the Afghan mess. He further influenced Pakistan, especially the powerful army, to persuade

---

[19]Daiz, Daniella, 'Trump's first 2018 tweet: Pakistan has "given us nothing but lies & deceit,"' CNN Politics, https://edition.cnn.com/2018/01/01/politics/donald-trump-2018-pakistan/index.html, accessed 18 June 2021.

the Taliban to announce a temporary ceasefire. He anticipated that the conclusion of the peace talks would give the much-needed fillip to his image in the recently concluded presidential election in the US. Even a face-saver Taliban ceasefire would have given a temporary reprieve to Trump from the Afghan disarray. It would further embolden his image as a dealmaker and generate electoral dividends in the recently concluded presidential election. However, all his efforts turned out to be futile as he lost the presidential race to Biden. The international community is keenly watching if President Biden would give his approval to the peace deal concluded with the Taliban by his predecessor.

It looks unlikely though that President Biden will stick to the deadline of US withdrawal from Afghanistan under the peace deal, though he has not ruled it out. This may jeopardize the peace deal. The suspended US security assistance to Pakistan will be leveraged by President Biden to lure Pakistan into some arm-twisting of the Taliban for a better version of the peace deal. As a strategic compromise, the US is expected to soften its stand towards dismantling externally focused terrorist groups like the Lashkar-e-Taiba and the Jaish-e-Mohammem in Pakistan without explicitly mentioning it in their future policy briefs. It may further allow Pakistan to tackle the externally focused terrorist network with the vicious cycle—arrest, free and re-arrest—so that the right optics are maintained in the international discourse.

However, it is very unlikely that the 'Naya Pakistan' would go against the established military doctrine of old Pakistan and surrender all the levers to play against the US in case their topsy-turvy ties turn sour. Pakistan has supported the Taliban since the mid-1990s. The support goes beyond providing safe sanctuaries. It has enabled Pakistan to keep its rival India from exercising greater influence in Afghanistan. This relationship has given Islamabad more leverage than any other country over Afghanistan. It is not expected to surrender its trump card so easily.

For the time being, Pakistan would wait and watch the fate and future of the intra-Afghan political dialogue without pressing the Taliban to compromise. Should that process falter, Pakistan would continue with its strategic dividend yielding age-old policy of deceit and duplicity in Afghanistan. This is more of a strategic compulsion for it to stay potent and relevant in the resolution of Afghanistan, as and when the opportunity arises. Under no circumstances would Pakistan like to lose its grip and influence over the Taliban and make them sign the peace with the Government of Afghanistan, sans proper accommodation of its long-term strategic interest. Pakistan views the Taliban as a strategic asset, which can be diverted against its arch-rival India and further checkmate the US in Afghanistan. The Taliban are also expected to help Pakistan settle its long-standing boundary dispute (Durand Line) with the Afghanistan government to its advantage. Hence, even if Biden arm-twists Pakistan to deal with the Taliban firmly, the Pakistan army would not subscribe to any such Pentagon aspirations.

In such a scenario, the new-found bonhomie between the US and Pakistan around Afghanistan would dissipate soon and return to rancorous exchange of allegations and counter-allegations just like before. However, the optics and gestures of the White House suggest that President Biden has not given up on the prospect of a full employment of Pakistan to tame the Taliban in Afghanistan. Biden's dependency on Pakistan is not confined to providing momentum to the stalled peace process. Land-locked Afghanistan can be accessed only through Pakistan, Iran or Russian allies Tajikistan, Uzbekistan and Turkmenistan. Since the US is on increasingly bad terms with Iran and Russia, they are stuck with Pakistan to maintain an active military logistic supply lines in Afghanistan. The presence of a minimum US military deterrent is a must for checking an overt aggression of the Taliban to run over Kabul. Hence, the US has to keep Pakistan in good spirits for both scenarios.

At a time when Pakistan is going through its worst economic meltdown, it will not be easy for it to refuse subscription to the US design in Afghanistan completely, in lieu of quick and easy green bucks. This will also give Pakistan its best chance to escape from the threat of the Financial Action Task Force (FATF) putting it in the black list and further add to its persistently deteriorating image of a terror-friendly state. The country is also looking for rebalancing its regional geostrategic position. Hence, the extension of the deceit and duplicity game by Pakistan would be largely in play. Some believe that while overtly they will make half-hearted attempts to show that they are with the US, covertly they will continue to aid Taliban and fan unrest in Afghanistan. More than the peace process, Pakistan would aspire to build its strategic clout in the new political order and arrangement that the conclusion of the peace process may throw up in Kabul.

Pakistan would, however, play its cards carefully without conceding any ground to India, which is elbowed out of the peace process completely. India would see the stalled peace process as an opportunity to get into the thick of things to make itself a potent player in the greatly contested 'peace game' in Afghanistan. India will try to gain in the whole process, as it has failed to stay relevant in the Afghan peace process so far. All the half-hearted attempts like sending two retired diplomats to the Moscow round of peace talks as observer to gain a grip in the peace process has not worked in its favour.[20] This, however, was a marked departure from the publicly articulated diplomatic stance of the Indian government of having no truck with the Taliban. The 'non-official' participation triggered widespread speculation that India was reversing its policy on the Taliban. India defended the charges with a bizarre argument that the delegation attended in their personal capacity and it should be seen as a 'non-official' delegation to Moscow. While this was done at the behest of the incumbent Government in Kabul, the diplomatic outreach made a further mockery of its slipping status in Afghanistan. It was done as a last-ditch attempt to get a seat in the peace negotiation to safeguard and promote India's interest.

India's rigid stance towards the Taliban is solely responsible for its isolation from the Afghanistan peace table. When the world was exploring ways and means to engage with the Taliban for political settlement in Afghanistan, India even failed to recognize the distinction between good and bad Taliban. India assumed that the big investment it made for the public good would make them an indispensable player in any high table for fixing Afghanistan. This may sound as a fair expectation for the top leadership of India but is diplomatically unrealistic. It rather smacks of diplomatic arrogance. The second flaw in India's Afghan policy stems from its underlying assumption that deep investment in civilian goodwill and diplomatic penetration are interconnected. It may be true for other

---

[20]Haider, Suhasini, 'In a first, India to send two former diplomats to talks that include Taliban representatives,' *The Hindu*, 8 November 2018, https://www.thehindu.com/news/national/taliban-talks-in-moscow-india-to-attend-at-non-official-level/article25445933.ece, accessed 18 June 2021.

countries, but it does not stand pragmatic for Afghanistan at least. Despite its extensive and leading developmental role, India continues to remain a peripheral player in the Afghan peace process.

After 2012, it was getting clear that Afghanistan could not be fixed without engaging with the Taliban. Most of the western countries, including the US revised their stance and made fresh overtures to the Taliban. India stuck to its guns and failed to smell the tea. With India slipping, a lot of hopes were pinned on President Ghani to make it win a seat in the peace negotiation. But the Taliban's refusal to engage with the elected government made the case worse for India. After investing close to $3 billion and generating tremendous civilian goodwill, India failed to make the cut and faces diplomatic marginalization in Afghanistan. On this ground alone, Pakistan's establishment considers it as a major achievement. However, Pakistan's sole intention would be to fix the pro-ISI radical Taliban into any political arrangement for the future in Afghanistan. This would give them the leeway to promote and further advance the agenda of Pakistan, and by extension China. It will keep India at a safe distance from any influence in Afghanistan, even after the new political order assumes power, in a post-US exit scenario.

China so far has kept its cards close to its chest and let Pakistan muscle into the peace process. They know that they are fully in control of the Afghan peace process by extension. China's interest is largely confined to the rich mineral resources, rather than any serious strategic aspiration. China aspires to monopolize the mineral resources thereby riding the strategic influence of Pakistan over the Taliban. Afghanistan is also an integral part of their grandiose 'Belt and Road Initiative (BRI).'

China needs Afghan peace no less than others. The success of its multibillion-dollar China-Pakistan Economic Corridor (CPEC), a vast transport and infrastructure project and key part of the BRI is not possible without peace in the region. Beijing is concerned that if the situation in Afghanistan deteriorates after the US withdrawal, it could endanger the CPEC. They further have a grand plan for a CPEC-type investment in Afghanistan too, should peace return to the war-torn nation. Besides economic gains, this proposed investment would offer China greater strategic depth in Central Asia. The latter aligns well with the grand ambition of the economist President Ghani to make big ticket infra spending in Afghanistan and create jobs for the largely unemployed youth population. President Ghani has made repeated calls for Chinese investment in Afghanistan. With the rising trade war with the US, China is in constant search of newer markets. And Afghanistan fits the bill. Any Taliban-laced political arrangement in Afghanistan would suit their economic agenda with the proxy power of ISI in full display. Prolonged insecurity would water down China's economic plans. China is expected to support Pakistan to step up diplomatic efforts to drive the Afghanistan peace process in order to safeguard its interests in the region after the US withdraws its troops from the war-ravaged country. Interestingly, under the influence of Pakistan, the Taliban have also called for China to play a bigger role in the peace process in Afghanistan.

Russia's engagement in the peace process boils down to the not-so-immediate fear of a spillover of terrorism to its backyard—Central Asia. But more than that, Moscow is uncomfortable with the US military presence in the region. In a way, it is the return of the same pre US-Soviet Cold War, with Afghanistan being the epicentre. Russia also has to counter the flooding of drugs originating from Afghanistan and swelling millennial addicts at an alarming rate. Russia has further an abiding interest owing to its regional proximity. It has hosted talks with Taliban delegates and members ofAfghanistan's high peace council, as Moscow seeks a role as peace broker between Islamist rebels and the US-backed government in Kabul. Russian peace overtures are more of a freelance attempt than a coordinated approach in sync with the US outreach. The US, on its part, has constantly pitched the Afghanistan peace process as a futuristic spot for bilateral cooperation.

It is in shared interest for both the US and Russia to collaborate and fix a durable political settlement in Afghanistan. Russia is heavily tilted towards the Taliban in the peace process. It was alleged that Moscow supplied arms to the Taliban in 2018 in its bid to expand their influence over the Taliban. The US was miffed with the alleged development and called it grossly irresponsible. Russia's peace overtures can be graded at best as suboptimal, if not a spoiler, with the spotlight being on the US. The collapse of US-Taliban relations after nine rounds of Doha peace talks provided an opening for Russia to reassert its diplomatic authority and expand its bandwidth in search for peace. This was a major concern for the US after it has done all the spade work on the ground. The chemistry between President Putin and President Ghani is far from cordial. President Putin overruled Kabul's strong objection and invited a Taliban delegation to Moscow in November 2018 for peace talks. This was followed by a few other intra-Afghan dialogues well attended by the Taliban as well as the opposition camp of President Ghani. The Afghan foreign ministry has time and again criticized the Kremlin-backed peace negotiation stating that it has been largely unhelpful to the central Afghan peace process spearheaded by the White House. As the relations between Kabul and Moscow have deteriorated over the recent years, Putin is slowly investing in the Taliban and the opposition political camp as a hedge for staying relevant in Afghanistan. This has polarized the political class and made the Ghani government appear even weaker. Putin's recurrent invitation to former President Karzai to participate in the Kremlin-backed peace negotiation and giving him ample place in the State-controlled media to vent out against the US is seen as another investment by Russia to expand its stake in Afghanistan. With the White House exploring ways to kick-start the intra-Afghan dialogue, Washington will watch Moscow with a great deal of suspicion. Moscow has the ability to put a spanner in the intra-Afghan political dialogue should it be sidelined in Afghanistan.

Iran has a direct stake in Afghanistan. Tehran faces a threat with the presence of the US forces. Additionally, Iran has to counter the drug trafficking and overflow of refugees from Afghanistan. Iran also nurses the desire to supply oil and gas to India and Afghanistan with an arrangement like Turkmenistan, Afghanistan, Pakistan and India (TAPI) gas pipeline. For that to happen, they need to have considerable clout and influence in Afghanistan. Being a Shiite country, it is guided by an additional interest of ensuring that the minority Hazara Shiites have a distinctive political and social status in Afghanistan. It would be unfair to expect Iran to be of any help to the US in stabilizing Afghanistan, given the country is reeling under harsh sanctions imposed by Trump. However, the Afghan government is more than welcoming about the growing role of Iran in solving the Afghan deadlock. With growing isolation and the economy in a deep mess, Iran's role and influence will always be suboptimal. Iran has been supportive to the Taliban with arms and ammunition and their targeting of US interests in Afghanistan. There will not be any change in their policy and they would continue to bolster the Taliban in their bid to damage the US military in Afghanistan without coming to the forefront. Iran covertly or overtly would continue to direct the peace process in a way that the outcome suits its larger design and interest in Afghanistan.

Afghanistan's neighbours are not going to make it easy for the US to conclude the peace deal with the Taliban. There are so many questions that don't have easy or direct answers as of now. This amplifies just how fraught and complex the current peace and reconciliation process has been. And even after the first cut of the peace deal signed on 29 February 2020, there are still massive challenges that lie ahead.

The US is left with very limited bandwidth in terms of strategic options in Afghanistan. Surging the military boots in Afghanistan is not an option anymore as it has been proven counterproductive. This would embolden Taliban further and increase US casualties, as has been proven in the last 19 years. The 'body-bag syndrome' (Americans seeing many dead American soldiers in body bags on TV arriving from Afghanistan) would severely damage the image of President Biden and help democrats gain traction with American taxpayers. The status quo in Afghanistan also does not align with Biden's frequently articulated desire to pull back from Afghanistan with a better deal with the Taliban.

While Biden too is desperate to leave Afghanistan, like his predecessor, his advisors have made it clear to him that a sudden and complete withdrawal—particularly in the absence of a better deal between the Afghan government and the Taliban—will be most dangerous. It may turn Afghanistan once again into a hotbed of terrorism. The peace process has been paused for the time being with both the Afghan government and the Taliban blaming each other for the stalled intra-Afghan political dialogue. The Afghan government is putting the blame on the Taliban for reneging on their commitment to release government officials as a part of the prisoner swap deal. 'The Government of Afghanistan is committed to complete this (prisoner swap) process, but the reason this process is not completed is the Taliban's failure to free government prisoners,' said President Ashraf Ghani's spokesman, Sediq Sediqqi.[21] But the Taliban's Qatar-based office's spokesman, Suhail Shaheen, said that the Afghan government made excuses to postpone the negotiations. At this juncture, both the Afghan government and the Taliban are killing each other amid intermittent dose of peace dialogue, and security spiralling from bad to worse. Civilian casualty remains at a historic high. As of now, both the Taliban and the military forces of Afghanistan are killing each other while intermittently talking peace.

The Taliban know that it is a Saigon moment for the US forces. The writing is on the wall. The US is not winning this war anytime soon. The imminent peace deal is the only face-saver to exit from Afghanistan after a 19-year-long war. It is imperative for the President to find a political cover to exit from Afghanistan. The US was desperate to end an un-winnable war in the region where they over committed themselves.

Exactly when one thought that the Afghan peace process is on its way to a resolution, it once again went off track. Now it seems we still have miles to go before stability and calm can be achieved. It is not clear if the Afghan government-Taliban talks

---

[21]Shalizi, Hamid and Abdul Qadir Sediqi, 'Afghanistan frees nearly 200 Taliban prisoners to push peace talks,' Reuters, 16 September 2020, https://www.reuters.com/article/afghanistan-taliban-prisoners-int-idUSKBN25T13R, accessed 18 June 2021.

have hit a permanent deadlock at this juncture. The Taliban have escalated the attacks. It is not going to be easy months for Afghanistan. The stalled peace process is not the end of the game in Afghanistan; the real game has just begun.

Everyone agrees that the US President, Biden, is more politically mature than his predecessor. But will his maturity revive the intra-Afghan political dialogue in Afghanistan? It will be interesting to watch if he can pull a rabbit out of the hat to resolve the mess and mayhem in Afghanistan. For the time being, it appears there are no easy pathways to peace.

3

The Flailing and the Failing State

After the fall of the Taliban regime, building the state of Afghanistan was the most pronounced priority of the West. Even after pouring in billions, the state of Afghanistan is grappling with poor capacity, rising corruption and dwindling legitimacy, and is ill-prepared to render succour to the citizens. The prolonged status quo is only ceding more ground to the Taliban.

The US-led War on Terror (WoT) project did not end with the collapse of the Taliban regime, but rather, it was transformed into a grandiose state-building intervention in Afghanistan. Along with the effort to irreversibly degrade the capabilities of the Taliban and the al-Qaeda, the US along with its western allies endeavoured to reinstate the lost political stability of Afghanistan, build a functioning state and launch a long-term economic recovery process.

By 2001, it was evident that Afghanistan was a failed state, with weak and fragmented state institutions struggling to provide either effective public services or even the basic security to its citizens. The economy had severely contracted due to more than two decades of war. The World Bank in 2002, estimated the total cost over the period of conflict, measured in terms of lost growth along with the cost of humanitarian assistance as well as military expenditure, to be a massive $240 billion.[22] More than two-thirds of the population was either internally displaced or took refuge outside Afghanistan, especially in Iran and Pakistan.

A war economy had emerged, which transformed the socio-economic dynamic of the country and made post-2001 recovery and state building a daunting task. It is crucial to note that some of the causes of state fragility have their roots in Afghanistan's modern history. These include prolonged political isolation, unsustainable fiscal basis of successive regimes, subsistence-based economy, landlocked nature of the country and its complex social mosaic. The state's fragility was further exacerbated by a chequered history of internal armed conflicts and the rivalry of great powers for domination of the region resulting in multiple invasions. While the key dimensions of state fragility varied over time, in the last two decades following the Soviet invasion in 1979, the vulnerability deepened. State and non-state violence and repression became dominant, and the state's capacity to perform deteriorated.

The different forms of political structures in the late twentieth century (constitutional monarchy, republic, communism and Islamic theocracy) failed to provide lasting stability and render succour to its citizens. It also failed to bind

---

[22]World Bank, 'Two Decades of Conflict Cost $240 Billion: Now Afghanistan Will Need $27.5 Billion to Recover,' World Bank Group, Press Release, 30 March 2004.

the citizens under the fabric of a nation as such. Afghan society is a complex conglomeration of ethnic, linguistic, religious and tribal lineages, more closely united at the local level than under the banner of a homogeneous Afghan identity at the national level. The fractured social capital can be attributed to the legacy of civil wars and external proxy interferences over the past three decades. The citizens were more organized under the region, rather than the State of Afghanistan. The trust and loyalty of the citizens rest on the ethnic regional leaders more than the national government, at any given time.

After the fall of the Taliban, the task of the US and NATO forces were clearly cut out. The immediate tasks in 2002 were to stabilize the country and build a legitimate and functioning state, along with a viable and sustainable economy. The building of the state's executive, legislative and judiciary pillars was pursued with great zeal and enthusiasm, although the progress has been largely uneven. State-building endeavours adopted by the international community to 'fix' Afghanistan from 2002 onwards had become a major preoccupation of international aid agencies too, with colossal resources allocated to the task at hand. The new government, empowered with financial aid and technical assistance from the international community, carried out a plethora of reforms in the key areas of the public financial management system and vital state institutions (e.g., finance, health, education, police, army and judiciary) along with security and governance, including decentralization of power through creation of local governments. The delivery of public services was also revamped with an aim to cater to a greater section of the Afghan populace. This was critical as the bulk of the citizens were devoid of public services in the past. And public services could have brought the citizens under the fold of a nation, under the new government in Kabul.

Crumbling apparatus

However, these international efforts failed to bring the desired stability and meaningful changes to the life of its citizens, struggling with more than three decades of war and devastation. For ordinary Afghanistan, how much has life changed after the fall of the Taliban? Afghanistan's HDI value for 2019 was 0.511—which put the country in the extremely low human development category—positioning it at 169 out of 189 countries and territories.[23] The State of Afghanistan is deeply entrenched in corruption, ranking as the fifteenth most corrupt nation out of 179 countries, according to the 2020 Corruption Perceptions Index reported by the Transparency International. Even though there has been a marked improvement compared to the ranking of 2019, it is far from acceptable. Corruption remains an integral part of daily life of the citizens, which undermines the trust over the Afghan government, across all levels. People need to pay a bribe or rely on *wasata* (connection to government officials) for accessing basic government services. All efforts towards improving governance have been derailed by pervasive corruption in governing systems. Widespread corruption has further eroded the legitimacy of the public institutions, making the government weaker.

The World Justice Project (WJP) places Afghanistan's rule of law at 122, out of 128 countries, depicting a pitiable law and order, and justice sector, in the 2020 edition of the report.[24]

---

[23]'The Next Frontier: Human Development and the Anthropocene,' Human Development Report 2020, http://hdr.undp.org/sites/all/themes/hdr_theme/country-notes/AFG.pdf, accessed 14 June 2021.

[24]'Afghanistan ranked 122 out of 128 countries on rule of law, rising three positions,' https://worldjusticeproject.org/sites/default/files/documents/Afghanistan%20-%202020%20WJP%20Rule%20of%20Law%20Index%20

Perhaps it needs to be mentioned here that the WJP 'Rule of Law Index' measures countries' rule of law performance across eight factors: constraint on government powers, absence of corruption, open government, fundamental rights, orders and security, regulatory enforcement, civil justice and criminal justice.

There is not much to cheer about the economy either. Afghanistan faces daunting economic problems, including very slow growth, high unemployment, weak private investment and anaemic government revenues. The process of economic recovery has been tardily slow. The broader economy of Afghanistan has performed far below the popular expectation and continues to rely heavily on foreign aid. The revenue proceeds are barely enough to support the operation budget of the government, let alone the development budget, which remains integral to address the crying infrastructure and critical needs. The overall macroeconomics in Afghanistan since 2001 can be divided into two distinct phases: pre- and post-2014 security transition, when international troops handed over security responsibilities to the Afghan National Security Forces (ANSF). The pre-transition phase was marked by a sustained period of higher economic growth with share of revenue peaking at 11.6 per cent of GDP in 2011–12 (higher than Pakistan's corresponding ratio and Iran's non-oil revenue to GDP ratio). While Afghanistan's economy was on an upward trend, between 2002 and 2011, the upswing slowed down thereafter.

After the ascension of the unity government in 2014, the economic growth has declined and touched a historic low (post the fall of the Taliban) of one per cent in 2015. With the

Country%20Press%20Release.pdf, accessed 14 June 2021.

withdrawal of most international troops and the steady decline in aid (both security and civilian aid) since 2012, the economy witnessed an enormous shock to demand, from which it is still struggling to recover. The share of revenue to GDP slipped to 8.5 per cent of GDP in 2014, depicting an alarming state of the economy.

As with any country, Afghanistan's central government revenue remains an important fiscal indicator and determinant of macroeconomic stability. Afghanistan's revenue picture throws a mixed picture. Since the fiscal crisis around the 2014 presidential election, Afghanistan's total revenue has recovered and has further grown considerably. In 2018, the total revenue was almost 90 per cent higher than in 2014 in nominal Afghan currency (Afghanis), and rose to 13.4 per cent of GDP, from its nadir of 8.5 per cent in 2014. However, there was a 9 per cent depreciation of the Afghani against the US dollar between the first half of 2018 and first half of 2019, because of artificially inflated customs receipts (including both customs duties and other taxes collected by customs departments at the border). This is because the same receipts valued in US dollar yield a higher amount denominated in Afghanis than in the first half of 2019. Additionally, there was a one-time Afghanis (local currency) 8.9 billion transfer of administrative profits from the Central Bank to the budget in the first half of 2019. These Central Bank profits also stem almost entirely from the depreciation of the Afghani currency, which appears to have generated gains from foreign exchange transactions and asset valuation.

Taking the currency depreciation into account, the underlying growth of revenue to GDP, in real terms, seems negligible. The revenue growth has continued in the first half of 2019, with total revenue up by 15.1 per cent from the same period in 2018. This looks noteworthy, especially considering the surfeit of negative forces weighing on collections, primarily being the weak economy and political instability coupled with the terror unleashed by the Taliban. The budget execution rate has been steadily improving, since 2014. Another optimistic note in Afghanistan's otherwise bleak economy is that by the end of 2019, the Afghan government had cash reserves of more than $1 billion with the Central Bank (Da Afghanistan Bank), up from Afghanis 74 billion at the end of 2018. This accumulated cash cushion contrasts sharply with the situation in June 2014. As the fiscal crisis unfolded that year, cash reserves fell to as low as Afghanis three billion, reaching a point where the government could no longer manage its daily cash flow and pay its bills. There is no question that the government is in a better situation now than it was immediately before the crisis, five years ago (2014). However, most of the apparent improvement—at least in 2018 and 2019 on the revenue front—can be attributed to the weakening of the Afghan currency against the US dollar, a development that offers no sustainable path to long-term revenue growth.

In short, a half-decade of economic progress, since 2014, was lost because of the economic shock triggered by the draw down of US and international troops from 2011 to 2014, the lingering effect of the 2014 fiscal crisis, the political uncertainty that plagued Afghanistan's previous National Unity Government during much of its tenure followed by clouds hovering over the US-led peace talks and the unprecedented spike in the Taliban and ISIS-led attacks.

The World Bank in its flagship annual economic publication *Afghanistan Development Update 2020* calculated

Afghanistan's GDP growth rate at 3.9 per cent in 2019.[25] This was fuelled by strong agriculture growth following recovery from drought. The GDP in Afghanistan is projected to decline sharply as a result of the COVID-19 pandemic, and rising security and political challenges. The Asian Development Bank in its *Asian Development Outlook 2020*, forecasted Afghan GDP to contract by an alarming 5 per cent in 2020.[26] This is disturbing for a country where over half of the population is poor and living off less than a dollar a day.

Afghanistan has to create a viable economy in order to transition to a sustainable financial base, as the current economy is heavily reliant on foreign aid. More than 75 per cent of the public expenditure budget of Afghanistan comes in the form of foreign aid through a variety of ways. The country could barely generate 2.5 billion out of the 11 billion public expenditure budget, through its modest revenue base.[27] There is a series of 'off-budget support' by several international donors which keeps the development process going. The current state of economic affairs is untenable with the dwindling foreign aid amid the US in a hurry to exit Afghanistan. The emergence of other global hotspots like Syria, Yemen, Iraq, Somalia, etc., are also vying for foreign aid and attention. An imminent flight of resources is on the anvil. This makes it impossible for the Afghan government to maintain the budget status quo in its current form and

---

[25]'Afghanistan GDP', countryeconomy, https://countryeconomy.com/gdp/afghani stan#:~:text=Afghanistan%3A%20GDP%20increases%203.9%25,of%201.2%25%20 published%20in%202018, accessed 18 June 2021.

[26]'Afghanistan's GDP to Contract in 2020 Due to COVID-19; Small Recovery Projected for 2021', Asian Development Bank, News Release, 15 September 2020, https://www.adb.org/news/afghanistans-gdp-contract-2020-due-covid-19-small-recovery-projected-2021, accessed 2 July 2021.

[27]Mashal, Mujib, 'Afghanistan needs billions in aid even after a peace deal, World Bank says', *The New York Times*, 5 December 2019.

scale. No matter how much government revenue improves, the country will continue to rely on international assistance to support its budget. A recent World Bank and International Monetary Fund joint report suggests that the country will continue to rely heavily on foreign aid, and not achieve fiscal sustainability—defined as occurring when domestic revenues cover operating expenditures—until 2030.[28] The sudden halt or abrupt cut in aid would precipitate a fiscal crisis, which would choke the government and lead to further weakening of the state. Any budgetary constraint would also fail to support the sustained flow of its critical services and create jobs from its own sources. The public services are already running at a deficit level and any cut would significantly stress Afghan citizens, who are already frustrated with the government in Kabul. The development of the country hammered by more than three decades of war and destruction is not even taken into the equation. With the severe reduction of international aid on the cards, an imminent economic collapse too seems to be on the anvil.

Unemployment is particularly problematic in Afghanistan because of the country's 'youth bulge', roughly 63 per cent of Afghans are young and more than one-third of them are unemployed, as of 2018. Lack of employment is disillusioning the youth from the State. And the Taliban have resolved to fish in the troubled water. They have shore up fresh recruits with salaries more than twice as high as those offered by the Afghan National Army (ANA). Young Afghans have a huge untapped potential and can unleash a large pool of human capital, which if used productively can not only lead to faster growth and prosperity, but also stem the supply line

---

[28]Staff of International Monetary Fund and International Development Association, Joint World Bank/IMF debt sustainability report, November 2011.

of terrorists for the Taliban. A higher number of Afghans in employment can make the country more equitable and stable. The informal economy is huge, but is dominated by the opium industry that has fuelled and further reinforced corruption and insurgency. And the State has been grappling to reduce the growth of opium cultivation, since declaring a war on opium after the fall of the Taliban.

Fixing the economy

The State of Afghanistan has no option other than fixing its struggling economy, if it aims to survive and provide a better model of inclusive growth and transform the lives of the Afghans. Sustaining a robust revenue growth in the coming years will require economic expansion, buoyancy of the existing tax system (meaning whether revenue growth will keep up with or better yet exceed the growth of the economy) and broadening the tax base, which is currently very narrow. With regard to base broadening, one question that counts is when and how can the Afghan government implement its ambitious but long-delayed plan for a value-added tax (VAT). The longer-term benefits of VAT in providing strong positive incentives for base broadening and avoiding cascading taxation of multiple transactions along the value chain are unquestionable. Moreover, VAT allows zero-rating of exports so they are not at a competitive disadvantage vis-à-vis the other World Trade Organization-compliant countries.

However, the critical policy draft has been lingering in various ministries for quite some time. The cardinal challenge, however, is to improve the business climate and investor confidence for a nation that has been gifted with abundant mineral deposits, which can be explored to build a modern and prosperous country. The spur in the growth of the private sector would create the much-needed jobs for the youth. However, this appears more academic than anything given the contemporary climate of political uncertainty and imminent threat of the Taliban taking over Kabul, that exists today.

Economic growth, in the first instance, hinges on real progress towards a durable peace and at least a modicum of political stability including an accepted outcome of the recently concluded presidential election. Tax system buoyancy, in turn, will be critical if the Afghan economy starts growing again—so that government revenues at least maintain or rise as a share of GDP by growing at a faster rate than the economy as a whole.

The government has taken some strides in luring the private sector, but the deteriorating security has largely crippled investor confidence. A rare bright spot in Afghanistan's otherwise bleak fiscal and economic landscape has been its steady increase in the ease of doing business. Afghanistan climbed 16 positions in the rankings from 2018, advancing from 183rd in 2018 to 167th in the 2019, as per a report in ease of doing business published by the World Bank.[29] The World Bank credits Afghanistan's unprecedented advancement in the rankings to a record number of business reforms in the past year, which made it easier to start a business, access credit, pay taxes, resolve insolvency and protect minority investors. It showed remarkable improvement in at least four of the 10 indicators measured: Starting a Business (47th), Protecting Minority Investors (26th), Resolving Insolvency (74th) and

---

[29]'Doing Business Report: Afghanistan is a Top Improver with Record Reforms to Improve Business Climate', Press Release, The World Bank, 31 October 2018, https://www.worldbank.org/en/news/press-release/2018/10/31/afghanistan-is-a-top-improver-with-record-reforms-to-improve-business-climate, accessed 15 June 2021.

Getting Credit (99th).[30] Afghanistan's impressive rise in the Doing Business rankings manifests the Afghan government's firm commitment to improve the legal and regulatory business environment, as well as bolster institutions to increase private-sector engagement in the country. However, the improvement in the ranking has not translated into new foreign direct investment (FDI) in the country. Foreign direct investment has remained volatile so far. The FDI inflow steadily increased between 2002 and 2005, but declined sharply thereafter. Afghanistan is a gold mine of natural resources, with estimates ranging from 1 to 3 trillion dollar in value, yet very few private companies have invested in this resource potential. The country needs foreign investment to explore vast amounts of oil and mineral reserves to ramp up the revenue and service its citizens plagued by endemic deficit of public services. With poor infrastructure, weak public institutions/legal system, Afghanistan is a high-risk country for investment.

The lack of access to cost-effective electricity, corruption and growing insecurity have continuously constrained the development of the private sector. Despite these challenges, the country offered an opportunity for investment with a high return because of an immense gap that existed in the market. The growth of the telecom sector in Afghanistan is an eye-opener. In 2020, a well-organized public-private partnership has delivered communications services to 75 per cent of the country, connecting people from the most isolated areas to the rest of the country and to the world. It has further created the much-required jobs in big numbers across all levels.

---

[30]Majidyar, Ahmad W., 'Afghanistan Declared a Top Improver in 2019 Doing Business Ranking,' *The Diplomat*, 7 November 2018, https://thediplomat.com/2018/11/afghanistan-declared-a-top-improver-in-2019-doing-business-ranking/, accessed 15 June 2021.

Improving the business environment is essential for Afghanistan to stimulate domestic investment and create jobs. Despite reforms initiated by the government, Afghanistan still faces critical barriers to doing business. Due to the deteriorating security situation, the private sector is unable to grow at the pace it needs to in order to boost employment for the youth, when the State records of providing employment has been pathetic. Some of the Chinese and Indian companies winning bids for exploring minerals in Afghanistan are unable to start production to scale due to targeted attacks by the Taliban. Where resources have been employed, however, local conflicts and rivalry over the control of such resources have stalled production. Recently, a CEO of a telecom company on condition of anonymity confided to the author that his company had the resources and expertise to trial and execute 5G telecom services in Afghanistan. But, he will not endeavour to do the same as the Taliban in volatile provinces routinely blows up the towers of the company. And furthermore, his company is very apprehensive of a Taliban takeover of Kabul. Deteriorating security has increased the cost of investment, making business highly risky and unsustainable. It has also hampered private-sector development and further increased the vulnerability of the country. The sharp fall in private investment and almost zero pipeline of foreign investment are a testimony to the same. This puts the whole plan of attaining financial sustainability of the State by bolstering the private sector into jeopardy.

With the bulk of the socio-economic indicators still placing Afghanistan among the world's poorest countries, and conflict still a fact of daily life, the state-building attempts continue to grapple with unprecedented challenges like poor capacity of state institutions, resource constraint, deteriorating security crippling the State to a grinding halt and endemic corruption along with a slipping democracy. The poor performance of the successive government coupled with lack of accountability is making the State of Afghanistan largely unpopular to its citizens and inadvertently gravitating them towards an alternative (read Taliban in some cases).

Despite some progress in building state institutions and thereby expanding public services, Afghanistan remains fragile and highly susceptible to shocks. The successive Afghan governments suffered from a deficit of legitimacy. Growing insecurity coupled with almost two decades of war has severely undermined different sources of political legitimacy in Afghanistan. Presence of pervasive corruption has further dented the legitimacy of the State. Legitimacy generates social and political trust as well as public acceptance of the State and goes a long way in attracting reciprocated rights and responsibilities of citizens, thereby lending stability. If these are not present, the possibility of State systems being able to act effectively becomes very difficult. The path to legitimacy was always going to be a daunting task, in light of the new sociopolitical order and change, post 9/11.

Two distinct tasks as a part of state building were—how to build legitimacy and, given the lack of it, how to manage it. Deepening democracy through fair and transparent elections and helping the elected government to deliver a broad range of public services to its citizens were chosen as a preferred mode of building legitimacy by the successive governments in Afghanistan.

A belief in the building of State legitimacy through elections was something that international donors, the *Loya Jirga* represented by Afghan elites and citizens, by and large, subscribed to. This was a major effort in building

State legitimacy, post 2004. However, it was not going to be a cakewalk. Due to the role of political parties in armed conflict (since 1978), people lost confidence and trust in these parties, perceiving them as a major driver of factionalism and patronage with self-serving objectives. The first presidential elections in 2004 (with 70 per cent turnout including 40 per cent female) and the parliamentary elections in 2005 (with 50 per cent turnout) were a stupendous success in the direction of building legitimacy of the State. Such a massive turnout of voters was seen as the desired mechanism in building political legitimacy.

The country was up for building a modern form of legitimacy through elections. People welcomed the idea of a transfer of power through ballots, not bullets. With a few registered complaints about irregularities and fraud, those who did not win accepted the results. A Joint Electoral Management Body, which included the Independent Election Commission of Afghanistan and the UN Assistance Mission for Afghanistan (UNAMA), administered and oversaw the electoral process during the transition period. The role of the UN as an impartial actor helped build the trust of different local actors at a time when society was highly polarized on ethnic lines. Elections, by and large, changed the concept of power and authority in the country. However, while the first presidential and parliamentary elections were a major success, the subsequent elections did not achieve the intended outcomes. The electoral process soon lost its legitimacy because of growing cases of fraud and sharply declining voter numbers.

Irregularities and fraud damaged the electoral process more than the threat that the Taliban insurgency posed. The government, however, failed to derive learning insights from its failure and deliver on its promise to undertake necessary political and institutional reforms. The established political system increased the incentive to commit electoral fraud and further initiated a culture of refusing to accept the outcome of elections, especially by the losing candidates and their followers. Voters were not properly registered. By 2010, the number of voter cards exceeded the 12.5 million eligible voters, considerably. Moreover, the way elections were designed was very costly and depended on foreign aid. The 2004 elections' estimated cost (excluding International Security Assistance Force and NGOs' contributions) was $200 million for over 8 million votes. The 2009 presidential elections went to the second round because of widespread allegations of fraud.

In the first round, according to the Independent Election Commission of Afghanistan, incumbent Karzai secured 49.67 per cent of the votes.[31] But Abdullah Abdullah, who secured 30 per cent of the votes, refused to run in the second round because Karzai did not accept his demands for reforming the Independent Election Commission of Afghanistan, including replacing the head of the commission.[32] While Karzai was declared the winner, Abdullah refused to accept the outcome. This process severely undermined public trust in the Afghan government and thereby went on to become a set precedent in the beleaguered country. The second round of the 2014 presidential elections further exposed the weakness of the electoral system. Despite threats by the Taliban to kill or cut off fingers of those who would vote, voter turnout was high at 58 per cent in the first round. The Taliban, for instance, cut off

---

[31]'Afghanistan Review', ReliefWeb, 21 October 2009, https://reliefweb.int/report/afghanistan/afghanistan-review-21-oct-2009, accessed 15 June 2021.

[32]Boone, Jon, 'Afghanistan Election Challenger Abdullah Abdullah Pulls Out of Runoff', *The Guardian*, 1 November 2009, https://www.theguardian.com/world/2009/nov/01/afghan-election-karzai-abdullah, accessed 14 June 2019.

the fingers of 11 men in East Afghanistan because they voted in the first round of elections.[33]

As none of the candidates secured over 50 per cent of the votes, the election between Abdullah Abdullah and Ashraf Ghani went to the second round, in which they respectively secured 44.9 per cent and 31.5 per cent of the votes. However, the allegation of fraud in the second round severely undermined the legitimacy of the upcoming government in which Ghani, according to the Afghanistan Election Commission (which announced the result after the two candidates reached an agreement), secured 55.2 per cent of the votes and Abdullah 44.7 per cent.[34] Abdullah threatened to announce a parallel government under his leadership. The Electoral Integrity Project of Harvard University categorized Afghanistan's election of 2014 as the third worst elections worldwide, after Bahrain and Syria.[35]

After pressure from Afghanistan's major development partners threatening to freeze their aid to Afghanistan and mediation by US Secretary of State John Kerry, Ghani and Abdullah agreed to form a power-sharing system referred to as a National Unity Government (NUG), with Ghani as President and Abdullah as Chief Executive. This arrangement helped to mitigate the risk of conflict. But this type of arrangement in the absence of the necessary political reforms in the governance

---

[33]Bizhan, Nematullah, 'Building Legitimacy and State Capacity in Protracted Fragility: The Case of Afghanistan,' https://www.theigc.org/wp-content/uploads/2018/04/afghanistan-report-v3.pdf, accessed 15 June 2021.

[34]Reuters staff, 'Commission releases disputed 2014 Afghan election results,' Reuters, 14 February 2016, https://www.reuters.com/article/us-afghanistan-election-idUSKCN0VX1O8, accessed 2 July 2021.

[35]'Afghanistan, Syria and Bahrain the worst elections of 2014,' Harvard Kennedy School, 17 February 2015, https://www.hks.harvard.edu/announcements/afghanistan-syria-and-bahrain-worst-elections-2014, accessed 15 June 2021.

practices made the new government ineffective. The initial years froze all decision-making abilities of the state institutions due to a tug of war between the rival camps within the NUG. It led to an almost policy paralysis in the first few years of the NUG.

The saga of the controversial election did not end with the NUG. Allaying fears, President Ghani's government went ahead and conducted the fourth presidential election on 28 September 2019. Along with the past election, this election too revealed the challenges of immature democratic politics. The prime contender seeking to unseat the incumbent is Abdullah Abdullah, President Ghani's ostensible partner in the NUG. Abdullah lost to Karzai in 2009 and Ghani in 2014 and accused each of wide-scale fraud. In both cases, some US cajoling was required to prevent the slide from a political fight to a militant one.

After expressing some initial reservations, the international community was largely supportive of Afghanistan's decision to hold elections. Roland Kobia, the European Union's special envoy to Afghanistan, recently said that elections 'become more necessary by the hour'[36] after the collapse of the US-Taliban peace negotiations. Although the US expressed concern about political violence during the vote, it hasn't questioned the timing of the elections. The latest presidential election in Afghanistan, on 28 September 2019, witnessed a grim turnout of only 26 per cent, the lowest since 2001. It has dismally fallen from a record voting of 70 per cent in the 2004 presidential election. The democratic observers are questioning the constantly falling voter percentage of the presidential and parliamentary election.

[36]Reuters, 'Elections in Afghanistan becoming more necessary by the hour, says EU special envoy,' Thomson Reuters Foundation, 8 September 2019, https://news.trust.org/item/20190908111229-9ywra, accessed 18 June 2021.

Apart from the serious question about whether such a miserable turnout can grant sufficient legitimacy to the forthcoming president elect, it reminds Afghans of a crucial fact that they direly need to rethink the democratic process in the country. The low turnout was not by coincidence and neither due to the threat issued by the Taliban. In the past too, the voters have thronged to polling booths in big numbers despite severe threats issued by the Taliban. The low turnout is largely attributable to many grievances that have built up over a long period of time, at least since the contentious 2014 presidential election. By and large, the performance of the NUG in the past five years has yielded endemic corruption, increasing unemployment, an alarming rise in poverty, persistent insecurity, undermined rule of law and, most importantly, increasing death and destruction, all of which in turn have caused distrust in the government and democratic institutions.[37] In light of these struggles, democracy and freedom have become only a second priority for the Afghan populace. It is difficult to ask the people to commit themselves fully for democracy when they think that democracy is incapable of giving them food to eat, providing them with jobs, providing security or of placing a definitive end to the terrible scourge of corruption that, in the eyes of the entire country, is eating away at the institutions of [the country] with each passing day.[38]

The problem of Afghanistan's tryst with democracy does not end with the low turnout of voters alone. The primary result of Afghanistan's controversial elections has been

---

[37]Rahyab, Jumakhan, 'Is democracy dying in Afghanistan?' *The Diplomat*, 11 October 2019, https://thediplomat.com/2019/10/is-democracy-dying-in-afghanistan/, accessed 2 July 2021.
[38]ibid.

announced in the third week of December 2019, after three months of counting amid allegations of fraud and rigging. Overlooking petitions to scrap over 3,00,000 controversial votes, state election authorities tallied all ballots and reported that Ghani was the frontrunner with more than 50 per cent of the 1.8 million votes. The results followed many complaints flooding the complaints commission, which launched a major classification of all filed grievances. An aggregate of 16,500 complaints had been filed to challenge the primary outcome of the presidential election. Chief Executive Abdullah, who had almost 39 per cent vote, was challenging the result claiming his rival Ghani had manipulated the polls and stuffed thousands of ballots including one-third of his tallied votes.[39]

The number of election frauds and irregularity-related complaints have multiplied by over three times, since the first presidential election in 2004. This comes amid harsh criticism that the complaints tribunal doesn't have the capacity to deal with such a magnitude of complaints to the satisfaction of the warring candidates. The reputation and integrity of the election commission are shoddier and more disputed than in 2004. It was a no brainer to assume that Abdullah's team will accept an opponent's controversial win without giving it a fight. And in lines of popular anticipation, the country witnessed another term of unity government, with Uncle Sam coming to the rescue at the last hour. However, the legitimacy of the new government is more stained and eroded than ever. And there is a continuous slip of democracy after giving up all the gains, post-2004. The trust in the government in Kabul is more eroded than ever, a situation which would only bolster

---

[39]Presidential race; Investigation into election fraud nears end,' *The Frontier Post*, https://thefrontierpost.com/presidential-race-investigation-into-election-fraud-nears-end/, accessed 5 July 2021.

the already threatening Taliban. This scenario benefitted the Taliban, offering them more leverage at the ongoing peace negotiation.

Afghanistan is in the throes of giving up the modest development gains post-9/11, as the Taliban gain recognition and appear stronger both on paper and on the ground. Afghan democracy is at serious risk, if necessary measures are not taken to save it. The Taliban and other fundamentalist groups threaten Afghanistan's fragile democracy and the weak government, on the one hand; on the other, a corrupt and dysfunctional government weakens the democratic institutions and undermines the rule of law. The behaviour of the leadership of the Afghan government since 2014 has largely pushed democracy to the brink as they made practically no efforts to strengthen democracy. The bickering between political and government leaders in Kabul is also having a negative impact on the smooth running of the government.

While most Afghans see peace with the Taliban as critical, many are also determined to protect and build upon the governing principles and processes their country embraced after 2001. With all the difficulties that the Afghan people are grappling with, and with all the challenges the country is facing, there is still no alternative to democracy in Afghanistan. While remembering that it is not easy to rescue democracy and put it back on the right track, one ought to remember that it is possible and achievable. For that, an all-out engagement effort is needed on different fronts. At this juncture, the Independent Election Commission and Independent Complaints Commission can play a significant role to put an end to scepticism about the democratic process. And direct election in whatever form keeps reminding the country's fractious strongmen, who historically grabbed at power through violent conflict, that their imperfect democracy is still the best bet in town. Despite the shortcomings of the system, all stakeholders towards building political legitimacy still view elections as one of the desired mechanisms to form government and further lend legitimacy.

Another preferred route towards building legitimacy was enabling the government in Kabul to expand the reach of key public services in Afghanistan. It has been universally accepted that effective public service has a fundamental influence on the quality of lives and often adjudged as a significant determinant of poverty. The challenge is not only to prioritize public service to best reflect the local demand, but also develop mechanisms and processes that empower the poor and marginalized section of the society to actively participate in the process of decision-making around public services and further benefit from it. The history of Afghanistan depicts a scarce example of the state providing public services to its citizens. And even if some regimes have provided them, they were grossly inadequate when compared to the complex and varied need of the people in this war-torn nation. The continued gross deficit of public services has widened the gap between the citizens and their rulers and pushed the citizens away from the State. The prolonged status quo has further disillusioned the citizens from the state and made them gravitate towards the local/regional power structures. Armed with a strong mandate and considerable resources, the new government in Kabul, after the fall of the Taliban, was in an excellent position to expand the public services and render succour to the people exasperated with more than two decades of war and destruction.

There was an emerging need to build accountable public services delivery, whereby the citizens are empowered to hold the service providers accountable. It was anticipated that effective delivery of public services would go a long way in connecting citizens with the Kabul-based government, in a setting where people are mobilized more around ethnicity and regions. Such a development would further aid the state-building process. The rudimentary state institutions, and by extension the Government of Afghanistan, would have further gained sustained legitimacy, providing critical need-based services to the masses and assuage their plight. However, the new government was struggling with multiple challenges to step up the public services. In addition to poor capacity of key state institutions, there was a set of inherited structural, procedural and contextual policy issues to deal with. To address the challenges, the international community reformed the public sector and helped to build the Afghan government capacity in a way that strengthens Afghan public sectors, builds credible systems and values, and is ultimately accountable to the Afghan people. They adopted a three-pronged strategy to build the capacities of the public sector.

The first strategy was to buy capacity from outside the public sector and country by hiring national and foreign consultants, and by outsourcing some of the government's core functions. The second entailed donors to bypass the Afghan state and national mechanisms to deliver public services directly through the private sector under the oversight of the relevant line department. The third focused on building the capacity of the various government departments through reforms, training and new hiring. The results were largely mixed. The provision of public services since 2002 has significantly expanded. Access to public health facility within a one-hour walk has increased from 9 per cent in 2002 to 57 per cent in 2012. The total number of enrolled school students increased from one million, despite girls being banned from school under the

Taliban rule, to nine million in 2013. Nearly two out of three households have an improved water source. A vast network of metallic roads has been constructed throughout Afghanistan. There has been a significant rise in access to electricity, especially in the urban areas. The scale and outreach of public services increased considerably and benefitted a large number of citizens for the first time in Afghanistan. Despite a plethora of challenges on multiple fronts, the ability of the state institutions to deliver on the popular expectation of the citizens was noteworthy. Afghanistan was steering on the path of recovery at a reasonable pace. This was lending legitimacy to the Government of Afghanistan and aiding stability.

But even this was short-lived. The progress on the front of delivering public services was throttled by growing insecurity. From early 2013 onwards, the Taliban started to capture various parts of Afghanistan, as soon as the US exit started. According to the UN's latest data, 50 of Afghanistan's 370 districts remain under the control of the Taliban.

There is a considerable number of districts where the Taliban enjoy a dominating influence, if not a direct control. Beside these, the Kabul government is constantly losing geographical influence—its armed forces are abandoning rural outposts to protect provincial and district capitals and road connections between major cities are getting obstructed. The status quo has not only impeded the extension of public services after the exit of US forces, but also squeezed the existing range and outreach of public services. The slash in public services has affected the citizens, who are already grappling with poor livelihoods, recurrently affected by drought and insecurity. The employment rate remains at the lowest in 2019, since the reconstruction process started in 2002. Cut in public services on top of poor income has only aggravated the plight of the people leading to an erosion of the public trust in their government. This, in turn, is denting the new-found legitimacy and reversing the gains made by the State of Afghanistan in the pre-transition phase.

The problem of public services goes even beyond the Taliban. The sustainability of the existing range and scale of public services delivered by the government is under a cloud. In the current scenario, the bulk of the cost in providing the existing level and range of public services are borne by international donors, through on or off financial support. According to a conservative estimate half of the financial support comes via various bilateral and multilateral donors. With the international funding on the slide, Afghanistan's public sector has started facing the heat. The receding appetite of the newly elected President Biden foretells a drastic reduction of state funding to Afghanistan, in the coming years. Absence of international resources would paralyse the state institutions and compel them further to cut a severe chunk of public services, which are already constrained due to a resource crunch. Any further cuts in public services would seriously affect the lives of the people and may lead to public revolt. Such a situation would be catastrophic for the new government in Kabul.

There has also been concern over the quality of public services provided by the government. Most of the basic services, especially education does not meet the regional standards. Public health services too fall far short of the World Health Organization's prescribed standards. There is lack of proper systems and community oversight mechanism for feedback on the quality of public services. Even if there are some, they are largely defunct and dysfunctional. Some pilot exercise by INGOs in Afghanistan has demonstrated that the active engagement of citizens in the oversight of public services can not only lead to better quality and outreach of public services, but also arrest leakage of public resources.

The delivery of the health services was subcontracted to INGOs. The quality of health services provided by the INGOs is better than that of the public health department. While this approach helped in improving public service delivery, both in terms of quality and outreach, it increased the cost of services, which the government may struggle to support in the future due to the dearth of financial resources. The bulk of aid that came in through parallel mechanisms outside the state system helped to improve the performance and outreach of the public sector. However, this type of service delivery increased project costs because of multilevel subcontracting arrangements. It also diverted financial resources and political attention from building permanent state institutions. Any resource crunch at the state level will endanger the continuity of these arrangements. The government has expressed its willingness to take these services under its direct command, given the private service providers are being viewed as competitors and the government has expressed serious reservations about bypassing them. The top ministers, including the incumbent President has been very critical of preferring INGO subcontracting to the state, as they feel it erodes the influence and authority of the State.

In addition to these issues, the structure of the state itself as well as the neglect of local state institutions are the two major challenges for service delivery vis-à-vis state building. In particular, the state structure and lack of clarity within different departments and amongst staff presented an obstacle for effective service delivery. Excessive centralization of public administration, beyond what the Afghanistan constitution envisages, and a blurred institutional role, adversely affected the delivery of public services. The roles of the ministries in Kabul, the line of ministry directorates in the provinces and districts, and the elected provincial councils, are not clearly defined. Further, each ministry relentlessly fought a turf battle against another over their respective authority and jurisdiction. The infamous tussle between the Independent Directorate of Local Governance (IDLG, equivalent to the ministry of local government in other countries) and the Ministry of Rural Reconstruction and Development (MRRD) is well-documented in Afghanistan.

While government departments exist in Kabul as well as the provinces and districts, the subnational departments at the provincial and district levels do not effectively participate in and contribute to planning and budgeting associated with public services. The participation of subnational governments in the planning and budget is at best academic in nature. The ministries and line departments in Kabul perform or coordinate most of the state functions with excessive centralization of power. The fragmentation of state institutions and the flimsy institutional link between Kabul and the provinces might have further encouraged the government to excessively centralize governance processes to extend the reach of the central government and curb the power of strong local actors. Donors also found a centralized administration more convenient to work with. While this approach seemed plausible at the beginning, it has undermined the ability to effectively identify and finance local priorities, build local capacity and enhance local participation in the long run. The provincial departments are dependent on Kabul for many of their day-to-day operations and budget. These deficiencies have inadvertently led to waste and poor delivery of public services. It remains a daunting task to maintain the right balance between centralization and decentralization in Afghanistan, a situation that has also been observed in other conflicts and fragile contexts. A notable example was re-centralization of the revenue collection process. In 2002 and 2003, regional commanders and strongmen controlled provincial revenue and customs. The government in Kabul recentralized revenue collection and allocation through a consensus-building process, organizing a meeting in Kabul to discuss the centralization of revenue with the commanders and strongmen, and issuing a decree after an agreement of sorts was reached with them.

While the concerns regarding decentralization in Afghanistan—that it may lead to corruption and empower local strongmen in some cases—seem valid, some of the programmes in which people fully participated and were managed in a decentralized manner were more effective. The National Solidarity Programme is a major success in the history of development in the country. By allowing people to participate in the design, implementation and monitoring of their local projects, this programme mitigated the risk of corruption and waste. It also helped in building the capacity of local communities and establishing an extensive network of communities that practised power in a democratic manner. But instead of learning from this highly successful programme, the Government of Afghanistan in communion with the World Bank designed an overcomplicated Citizen Charter programme as a successor to the National Solidarity Programme. The new programme aimed to guarantee certain key services at the village level. However, it stopped the flow of budget to the locally elected village bodies (community development councils) and centralized the resources in the hands of the key line ministries.

The IDLG has been making polices for separation of powers and functions between federal, provincial and district authorities. However, none seems to have taken roots at the ground level. The policy has been mostly confined to papers. The confusion prevails still today. This process has had adverse implications for service delivery, project implementation, monitoring and downward accountability.

Most academics and analysts of the conflict agree that the project of building a viable and effective democratic State in Afghanistan has failed. The state institutions have failed to deliver on popular expectation of the people and inevitably created a vacuum, a by-product of which is growing disillusionment with the incumbent government at Kabul. There is a mounting dissatisfaction among Afghans that the successive governments in Kabul have failed to bring any meaningful improvement in both security as well as the living conditions of the people. And any further cut in aid will slash public services, thus further aggravating the process of citizens' disenchantment with the State of Afghanistan. This will make way for the Taliban to gain more ground. This would significantly erode legitimacy of the incumbent government in Kabul. This was certainly not the outcome the US along with its western allies was expecting after pouring in billions of dollars. It is very convenient to bury every failure under the garb of deteriorating security in Afghanistan. The deteriorating security did have an impact on the state building. Intensifying cross-border insurgency and terrorist activities create insecurity, obstruct development and provide space for illicit activities that weaken the rule of law and thereby the State.

The graph of state building was on an upward trend between 2002 and 2005, the upswing slowed down thereafter. The US and its allies' attention in particular slipped from

Afghanistan, after they invaded Iraq in 2003. The Taliban insurgents, with support from Pakistan, were able to reorganize and increase their attacks. In response to the deteriorating security situation, the US eventually increased the number of troops and its development and military aid to Afghanistan. Additional aid and troops helped to stabilize the situation to some extent, but the plan to withdraw from Afghanistan by 2014 created a sense of uncertainty. This situation along with a sharp decline in the flow of aid to Afghanistan and a disputed presidential election in 2014, referred to as a triple transition, increased the level of threats and reversed many of the gains. The Taliban only got stronger with every passing year. But the dangerously slipping security was not the sole reason behind the failure of the state building.

The process of state building in Afghanistan since 2001 has been complicated by a diverse set of problems, including the unintended consequences of early political decisions, the choice of institutional forms, dysfunctional policymaking and the slide towards increased centralization of power. The existing system and structures of governance at the subnational level are still not coherent, effective or functional in a way that is capable of meeting the current expectations of the Afghan populace. The government at this level is composed of a range of entities whose roles, responsibilities and interrelationship along with accountability mechanisms are not yet fully defined in law and whose competencies and resources are inadequate for addressing local needs and aspirations. These problems have had a corrosive effect on the state-building enterprise, leaving an ambiguous legacy as Afghanistan proceeds towards one of the most challenging phases of its modern history. However, the biggest waste was the capacity building of state institutions followed by impractical policymaking.

Given that the state suffered from an acute deficit of capacity, it was crucial to devise ways to add new and higher capacity in the overall bid to build the state capacity. The international aid agencies hired multiple subject matter and policy experts, mostly foreign consultants from outside the public sector and country, and de facto outsourced some of the government's core policymaking role. The UN agencies too jumped with their share of expertise to contribute to the state capacity building agenda and further aid policymaking. Besides these, the US and its western allies empowered their provincial reconstruction team, an assisting unit of their ground military, to aid the state-building agenda. From 2002 to 2014, on an average, donors spent between $250 million and $1 billion annually on technical assistance projects, recruiting highly paid national and international staff. A large portion of technical assistance programmes was off-budget.

A large number of state-building experts wearing the military robe entered the state building. The INGOs too were not to be left behind in the state-building game and employed their resources and expertise at full scale. With all foreign players jumping onto the state-building bandwagon, it soon catapulted to a situation whereby foreign consultants and UN agencies overcrowded the federal ministries and captured the policymaking domain completely. The provincial administrations too met with the same fate with the Provincial Reconstruction Team completely dominating their affairs due to the sheer power of their financial resources. This sidelined the Afghan bureaucracy, further depriving local intelligence from the domain of policymaking. The top bureaucracy of the Afghan public sector became the cheerleader for their foreign counterpart, posted as advisors in relevant ministries. With the Afghan bureaucracy restricted to a clapping club, the foreign consultants got an open licence to drive the policy in a way they felt appropriate, rather than context-specific merit. The policymaking domain was completely hijacked by several foreign experts from different agencies, including the UN and PRT via various federal ministries. These experts hardly had their feet on the ground and attached minimal importance to learning from their Afghan counterparts. Their inputs were largely driven by what worked in other locales rather than what would work in Afghanistan. Broad-based consultation before policymaking was grossly lacking. Hence, realistic policymaking was the ultimate fatality. The policymaking was driven by the foreign agenda, rather than an Afghan agenda. This phase witnessed a series of faulty policymaking in every ministry, barring a few, thus deteriorating the development process, both in terms of quality and outreach. This continued till the exit of US forces, i.e., until the end of 2014.

Too many cooks

The overcrowding of foreign experts did not just damage the prospect of realistic policymaking, it also seriously affected capacity building. The US and its international players focused on building the capacity of the various government departments through reforms, training and new hiring. Due to excessive concentration of resources and efforts around capacity building, there was a glut in the supply line. The supply surpassed the demand. In a province, on a daily basis, there would be a training conducted by some or the other agency with little or no coordination. The food supply was best in its class for the participants. A few agencies would further sweeten the deal by attaching a component of seating fee, making it all the more lucrative for the Afghan bureaucracy to attend the capacity-building activities.

The generosity was not limited to training only. The key bureaucrats would be perennially on an international exposure visit to countries as unrelated as South Korea and Honduras. The training on gender was in the oversupply territory, with each INGO competing with the other in bolstering its gender credentials. How much of it was useful still remains a big question. Once a director of the department of women's affairs in the province of Baghlan said, 'If I ask for $1,500 to run the generator for conducting computer classes for women participants for six months, I will not get it. But if ask for $5,000 to send two members of my staff on a gender exposure visit to Indonesia, I will get more than one donor.' The glut in availability of capacity-building training peeved the ministries no end. As such there was a deficit of key staff in the line ministry, across all levels. 2009 onwards, an official position was commissioned by the State of Afghanistan in each province to coordinate the capacity-building activities at the provincial level. But that was perhaps too late, if not too little. Without a proper decision-making framework, it was completely left at the whims and fancies of the said officer. The march of flood in capacity building continued even after the position was institutionalized in the provincial administration. However, the coordination improved to some extent. The INGO had its way in getting the training schedule approved from the concerned officer. In some cases, the concerned officer was sent on an international exposure visit.

A provincial director once confided to the author on condition of anonymity that he had to depute his entire staff to training alone, throughout the year, if he had to entertain all the training invitations. But there was a smarter director too in the race. Once the director of the Ministry of Agriculture,

Irrigation and Livestock of a northern province confided to the author that he had to recruit a clerical-level staff just to entertain the training invitations of all the stakeholders. Further, the duly trained line department officials would often switch their jobs to lucrative INGOs at the first opportunity knocking on their door, pushing the institutional capacity of the respective department to almost ground zero again.

These capacity-building players hardly assessed the ill effect of the glut and particularly if their training-cum-capacity building had any desired impact on the relevant line ministry/department. With a few exceptions, none of these capacity-building interventions were tied to a long-term institutional development plan of state institutions. In 2014, a study sponsored by the Agency Coordinating Body for Afghan Relief found that even though 'one quarter of all aid to Afghanistan has been allocated to technical assistance which is intended to build government capacity, much of this assistance has been wasteful, donor-driven, and of limited impact.'[40] Everyone was in a race to burn the budget. The international donors too were suffering from the same syndrome. The UN agencies were leading the chart. As there was a travel restriction for international donors and even the UN agencies, there was no critical questioning around the impact of the capacity building. Most of the provincial line ministries would be provided with computers with rare arrangement for an in-house trainer to transition them to full use of computers. In some cases, the supply of computers was often provided without adequate arrangements for electricity. One recalls, how with a proper approach and follow up,

---

[40]Bizhan, Nematullah, *Building Legitimacy and State Capacity in Protracted Fragility: The Case of Afghanistan*, Commission on State Fragility, Growth and Development, 2018.

the official communication in the province of Bamian was switched to online completely in 2014.

The story of mindless capacity building does not end here. Another circus was taking place at the civil service front, which remains rigid and outdated till today. A considerable amount of resources and focus was allocated to revamp the civil services in Afghanistan after the fall of the Taliban. The first step in this regard was the restructuring and commissioning of the Independent Administrative Reform and Civil Service Commission (IARCSC). A new benchmark of civil service was formed and a comprehensive recruitment drive was initiated to recruit civil servants as per the newly designed eligibility criteria, purely based on meritocracy. It was a massive recruitment drive by any stretch of the imagination. It was difficult to discard much of the old civil servants. The old civil servants posted at the district level were getting a much lower salary than the newer ones, thus resulting in friction and simmering tension between the old and the new cohort of civil servants. In every ministry, there was a combination of old and new civil servants with two different range of salaries, which only increased tension and consequently hampered effective functioning.

However, a gross blunder was committed in the arena of capacity building. There is a famous Afghan capacity-building model for public officials: spend in some training around project management, general management skills along with basic governance, and top it up with English and computer courses. The UN would super top it up with an international exposure visit. The capacity-building design for the newly recruited civil servant, including the district governor (equivalent to the district magistrate in India) was no different. In training modules spanning over two to three weeks, the Afghan civil service commission would train the newly recruited civil servants and send them for field posting, when their counterparts in India or Pakistan would be trained for almost a year before any field posting. And the task at hand for the Afghan civil servants is more complex and varied compared to their peers in the neighbouring countries. This would make the civil servants mostly unprepared, lacking the depth to tackle governance challenges on a daily basis.

Good governance remains a significant determinant of poverty. It further has a fundamental influence on the quality of life. And for a country where corruption is endemic and pervasive in the system, extending good governance remains an arduous task. An international aid agency initiated a long-term capacity-building process to build the capacities of Afghan civil servants, especially the district governors in 76 districts across four provinces of Afghanistan. The idea was to run a pilot and showcase the impact and influence of the Afghan civil service commission to replicate the model for all civil servants across 350 plus districts in Afghanistan. It was by far the most comprehensive capacity-building programme designed for civil servants after carefully studying the course curriculum offered for newly recruited civil servants in India, Pakistan and Bangladesh. The contemporary governance challenges along with the local context was also built in the design. The model gained traction within a year and started showing impact.

One of the components of the capacity-building design was to expose the district governors to all elements of good governance. This was needed as they were just briefed sketchily on the broader aspects of good governance without unpacking the greater details. Once in a training session on pro-poor governance in Baghlan, a district governor shouted at another, 'We don't have even $300 budget per month to spend on the poor, and you have been preaching pro-poor governance. This training is a useless exercise for us.' Soon the other participants in the workshop joined the camp and voiced the same set of concerns. One asked the district governor to map the most popular services for which citizens thronged to their offices on a daily basis. Everyone voted for Tazkira (national identity card), which the Afghans need for availing any services and entitlements from the government. With a secret and independent voting, it came to notice that an Afghan has to pay a visit to the district governor's office for 3.8 times (rounded to four times) to receive the said service.

And, the cost incurred by a poor Afghan for visiting the district government office four times was calculated at $98. It was also honestly confessed by the district governors that the rich find a way to get the said service within two visits only. The district governors were challenged to find out how fast they could provide the said service by reforming their systems. This time the number of visits came down to 1.8 visits (rounded to two visits). This meant that they could provide the same service within two visits if they reform their internal system. And the cost to avail the service for poor Afghans would come down to $36 from $98. The participants were stunned. Few participants shared that before this training, they thought that doling out resources to the poor is pro-poor governance. As they didn't have resources at their disposal, they felt that it was not possible for them to facilitate pro-poor governance in their respective districts. The exercise excited the participants to the extent that they volunteered to undertake a similar exercise for all the services provided under the ambit of the district governor's office, in order to expedite the process of public service delivery and save critical resources of the poor people. Later, an independent evaluation report commissioned by Altai Consulting in May 2014 found that poor Afghans are receiving public services much faster from district offices than before, in the project districts.

The district governors were encouraged to switch to social media, so that they could have a dialogue with the broader Afghan citizens on governance affairs. Afghanistan has relatively good internet connectivity and the younger generation is quite social media savvy. Soon, the office timings were decided on the basis of public voting on Facebook. Complaints started pouring in from social media, making the district official seriously guarded against corruption. There were many positive results. However, it failed to change the course curriculum of the Afghan civil services, as the relevant ministry was keen on regulating the capacity-building mode more than learning from it. A bilateral donor agency came to its rescue to expand the model within Afghanistan. There was a component of over $1 million for innovation. They were keen to use the money to stir a competition among the district governors to come out with an innovative public service methodology/approaches for providing faster services or even exploring a new range of public services. In the course of various capacity-building events, it was amazing to see the extent of new ideas that the district governors had to come up with to deliver public services.

The relevant ministry was more excited to use the money for introducing training on accountability as was envisaged under the new subnational governance policy. The concerned donor representative wanted to remain in the good books of the relevant ministry and hence did not challenge it strongly. Ultimately, the INGO was asked to return the money to the donor. There are endless stories of such misadventures. A considerable number of the ministers in the Kabul government are rookies and first-timers. And they do not have the technical bandwidth to make an independent choice, based on the merit of the proposal. The advisors deputed in most of the ministries are not experienced in technical matters and mostly err over the professional choices they make in the interest of Afghanistan. Pragmatic policymaking has been the ultimate fatality.

There are occasional bright spots too in the midst of this gloom. A few ministries and departments that remained under the greater influence of donors have improved significantly. The finance ministry is a notable example in this light. The budget-making and execution capacity of the finance ministry has improved remarkably with time. However, unrestricted aid to Afghanistan has done more damage to state capacity building than any good.

The civil services continue to remain weak and further choked by the deterioration of security. The district governor remains the first target of the Taliban, when they want to send a stern message to the present-day government in Kabul. The media has lost count of civil servants killed by the Taliban in recent years. One trained a considerable number of such martyred officers personally. It is a pity to witness these civil servants sitting like a lame duck at the district offices to become the next target of the Taliban attack. The morale of the district governors is lying at a historic low with most of them contemplating the takeover of their districts by the Taliban, any time soon. At a time, when the Kabul government has influence and control over only 50 per cent of the districts, one wonders how the battered State of Afghanistan is going to revamp the civil services and, more importantly, connect with the citizens. The Taliban have appointed their district governor in several districts that remain under their direct control. With no official representation of Kabul in such districts, the Afghans are switching to the Taliban en masse. This will make the government's fight for legitimacy even more complicated, as not only will they have to defeat the Taliban but also win back the citizens under the fold of the government. At this juncture, it looks simply improbable. If the Afghan government has to find its feet and fix governance, it has to revamp the civil services at least in whatever geography that remains under its control.

The supply of excessive money has done more harm to state building than any good in this war-ravaged nation. Aid to Afghanistan could have been more useful had it been phased out over a longer period than dumped in a rush. Further, most of the aid should have been linked with performance and predetermined growth criteria. It should have followed the laid path of aid leading to investment, investment leading to growth and growth leading to poverty reduction. This was how the US's Marshall Plan had provided financial aid to West Europe after the Second World War. Such a path adopted in some of the African locales ridden with conflict has also yielded better results. But in Afghanistan, unlike the Marshall Plan, foreign money is mainly converted into expenses and no significant amount is invested in the economy, leaving a negative impact on the country and making it even more dependent on foreign aid. Foreign currency in aid inflows appreciate Afghan currency, making domestic goods less price competitive in the export market, and prevents exporters from competing. It also kills domestic demand for Afghan goods, as they become more expensive. This causes businesses to close and people to lose their jobs, resulting in increasing poverty and unemployment.

The supply of excessive green backs has had other ramifications too. Unrestricted aid has bred corruption. Much of the corruption in Afghanistan stems from an inflow of aid money, giving the country one of the worst reputations in the world—British Prime Minister David Cameron once called the country 'fantastically corrupt'.[41] The state head of every donor country has warned Afghanistan to curb corruption or lose the money. Yet, aid is flowing unrestricted sans any strict monitoring, and mostly ends up in the pockets of politicians, corrupt officials, warlords, power brokers, and even to the Taliban in a system that seriously lacks downward accountability. As Peter Bauer, the famed development economist, has rightly said, foreign aid is 'an excellent method for transferring money from poor people in rich countries to rich people in poor countries.'[42] Corruption is especially prevalent in construction, security, logistics and procurement, where most of the aid money is diverted.

The rich and the powerful people, with the tacit backing of the state, have floated a wide range of companies that procure lucrative contracts from the State of Afghanistan and even the aid agencies. And a significant chunk of that money inadvertently reaches the Taliban, after corrupting the bureaucracy and politicians on its way. Special Inspector General for Afghanistan Reconstruction (SIGAR) has time and again found out non-existent schools, clinics and roads in its report for which money has been claimed.[43] It does not end here. There are ghost teachers, health workers and even army

---

[41]'David Cameron calls Nigeria and Afghanistan "fantastically corrupt"', BBC News, 10 May 2016, https://www.bbc.com/news/uk-politics-36260193, accessed 15 June 2021.

[42]'A voice for the Poor', *The Economist*, 4 May 2002, https://www.economist.com/finance-and-economics/2002/05/02/a-voice-for-the-poor, accessed 15 June 2021.

[43]'US wasted billions on cars, buildings in Afghanistan: Report', *The Economic Times*, 1 March 2021, https://economictimes.indiatimes.com/news/international/world-news/us-wasted-billions-on-cars-buildings-in-afghanistan-report/articleshow/81270963.cms?from=mdr, accessed 2 July 2021.

personnel. Multiple reports from SIGAR have questioned the pervasive corruption in key sectors and warned of severe ramifications. However, people in power know well that these are nothing more than blank threats.

America's longest war continues and so does the West-sponsored state-building efforts in Afghanistan, with almost no sign of any tangible progress. After 18 years of major security, development and humanitarian assistance, the international community has failed to achieve a politically stable and economically viable Afghanistan. Despite a trillion dollars in aid, state institutions remain fragile and unable to provide good governance, deliver basic services to the majority of the population or guarantee human security at the least. Public resentment against the government due to lack of services, accountability and legitimacy is increasing and so is their disenchantment with the State of Afghanistan. The State of Afghanistan knows the problem, but has run out of solutions to steer the country out of this mess. The western allies, including their ringleader, the US, find them in the same boat; they do not appear any less confused than their Afghan counterparts.

Like the war in Iraq, the war in Afghanistan is a conflict that has evolved over time to encompass various different strategic objectives. Back to the wall, what was once viewed as a grand project to transform Afghanistan into a thriving, developed liberal democracy is now largely restricted to a narrower mission to combat terrorist threats and augment the capacity of the ANSF to counter the Taliban, by the US. For the time being, the state-building agenda is on the back-burner. Will this make any difference to the state building in Afghanistan? Not really; at least the recent past suggests so.

4

The March of the US Follies

As the US is all set to exit Afghanistan under the guise of an ambiguous peace deal with the Taliban, the question remains: has the US achieved anything tangible after losing more than 2,400 soldiers and funding the most expensive war on terror in the history of the human race?

By refusing to hand over bin Laden in the aftermath of 9/11, the Taliban prepared for a long and protracted war. The US military, with its all-weather ally UK, began a bombing campaign against the al-Qaeda and the Taliban, launching 'Operation Enduring Freedom' on 7 October 2001. The war's initial phase mainly involved air strikes on al-Qaeda and Taliban hideouts ably assisted by a partnership of the Northern Alliance and anti-Taliban forces within Afghanistan. The first contingent of conventional ground forces arrived 12 days later. The Taliban regime disintegrated rapidly after its defeat at Mazar-e-Sharif on 9 November 2001, at the hands of forces owing their allegiance to Abdul Rashid Dostum, an ethnic Uzbek warlord. Within a week, the Taliban strongholds started to crack with the loss of Taloqan (11/11), Bamiyan (11/11), Herat (11/12), Kabul (11/13) and Jalalabad (11/14).[44] By the third week of December 2001, the Taliban were driven away from Kandahar, their last stronghold and political-cum-spiritual capital. On 14 November 2001, the UN passed the Resolution 1378, calling for a 'central role' for the UN in establishing a transitional administration and inviting member states to send peacekeeping forces to promote stability and aid delivery in Afghanistan.

Osama bin Laden was tracked to the mountains of Tora Bora, south-east of Kabul, with a small contingent of al-Qaeda fighters. A fierce fight followed for a few weeks (3 December onwards) resulting in over 100 deaths and the eventual escape of bin Laden on 16 December 2001 to Pakistan. Twenty of his followers were arrested on 15 December 2001, before his escape to Pakistan on horseback. Despite credible intelligence of his presence, the US forces did not lead the assault from the front, rather allowed a rookie Afghan contingent led by Hazrat Ali, Haji Zaman and Haji Zahir to do the job for them. Some critics still question the move of US forces for not leading the assault. And what would have been the fate of the Afghan war, had the US captured bin Laden in the second week of December 2001 itself?

After the fall of the Taliban, Hamid Karzai was sworn in as interim president of the Afghan transitional government on 7 December 2001. His selection came after an emergency *Loya*

---

[44]CRF Timeline, 'The U.S. War in Afghanistan,' https://www.cfr.org/timeline/us-war-afghanistan, accessed 15 June 2021.

Jirga, a grand council of Afghan elders, convened in Kabul, and was attended by 1,550 delegates, including women from 34 provinces. Karzai, a powerful leader from the Popalzai tribe of the resourceful Durrani Pashtun, returned to Afghanistan after the 9/11 attacks to organize Pashtun resistance against the Taliban. His elevation was also bolstered by the failure of the Northern Alliance, dominated by the ethnic Tajiks, to come up with a consensus candidate for the top job. However, the Northern Alliance was successful in vesting power to Parliament to veto senior officials and further impeach a president in case of any wrongdoing. The selection of Karzai provided the much-needed political stability in Afghanistan beset with civil strife and misrule of the Taliban. As a follow up to the Bonn (Germany) Conference convened in December 2001, the international community pledged resources to rebuild and reconstruct the war-ravaged country after decades of war and destruction.

Approximately after one and a half years of relentless attack against the Taliban and al-Qaeda targets, the US declared an end to the 'major combat' in Afghanistan on 1 May 2003. The then Defence Secretary, Donald Rumsfeld, made an announcement to this effect, in a small ceremony held at Kabul. The announcement coincided with President Bush's 'mission accomplished' declaration of an end of fighting in Iraq. In a cheerful mood, the then US Central Command Chief Gen. Tommy Franks and then Afghan President Karzai concluded that Afghanistan needed to move from a combat phase to a prolonged stabilization and reconstruction phase.

The US achieved its first objective of dislodging the al-Qaeda and the Taliban out of Afghanistan and installing a representative government in Kabul. However, the US military thought that it was not sufficient. There was an emerging need to irreversibly degrade the capabilities of the Taliban to strike and control Afghanistan, again. Hence, the Predator UAV (long-endurance, medium-altitude unmanned aircraft system), armed with drone missiles, was employed in large numbers to target hardcore militants hiding in inhospitable mountainous terrains and the safe sanctuaries of the porous Afghanistan-Pakistan border. The US military kept hitting the Taliban hideouts by employing drones on both sides of the border, with an unfailing regularity.

In a historic development, the NATO assumed control of International Security Assistance Force (ISAF) in Afghanistan on 11 August 2003. Originally mandated to secure Kabul and the surrounding outskirts, NATO expanded both its role and strength aggressively, culminating in 65,000 troops in 2006, a thirteen-fold increase from the initial 5,000 troops in August 2003. Afghanistan started moving on the path of development and political consolidation too. In a historic national voting on 9 October 2004, Karzai emerged as the first democratically elected president of Afghanistan. He defeated his nearest rival, Younis Qanooni, a key Northern Alliance member, by a landslide margin. The election was also viewed as a democratic and political victory of Afghanistan. This was the second great achievement of the US after driving away the Taliban from the fragile nation.

The Afghan mission of the US was moving like a dream script and had all the makings of a perfect military manual of stabilizing any conflict-prone country. The first crack in the American dream appeared when bin Laden released a videotaped message three weeks after the historic election in Afghanistan and days after the election of Bush as the US president, for the second term. In a largely televised message, bin Laden taunted the US and took responsibility for 9/11 for the first time. 'We want to restore freedom to our nation, just as you lay waste to our nation,' bin Laden said.[45] The White House allayed all fears first by terming the video as fake and further that it was nothing more than a blank threat devoid of any real substance on the ground. The US military leadership assumed that the backbone of the Taliban and the al-Qaeda had been broken beyond repair. And a regrouping of the Taliban and the al-Qaeda remained next to impossible.

By 2005, the US started preparing for the next phase of consolidation in Afghanistan. Karzai and Bush issued a joint declaration that pronounced both countries as strategic partners.[46] The joint declaration gave unprecedented access to US forces to Afghan military facilities, and power to directly execute attacks against terrorists and violent extremism, with no accountability to the Afghan government. The agreement further called for Washington to 'help organize, train, equip and sustain Afghan security forces as Afghanistan develops the capacity to undertake responsibility,'[47] and to continue to rebuild the country's economy and political democracy. This perhaps meant that the US was not for a long haul combat role in Afghanistan. It also signalled a planned switch of role for the US in Afghanistan. Along with a hardcore combat role, the US was contemplating to build the rudimentary Afghan army, perhaps an indication that the US military was keen to play the role of a mentor than being in the frontline of the battle, in the longer run. The joint declaration remained largely silent on two major contentious issues: the status of US forces in Afghanistan and the limits on their military outreach.

---

[45]CRF Timeline, 'The U.S. War in Afghanistan,' https://www.cfr.org/timeline/us-war-afghanistan, accessed 15 June 2021.
[46]Ibid.
[47]Ibid.

In his private meeting with the US President, President Karzai expressed his desire for more control over US forces in his country and for the return of Afghan detainees from US custody. President Bush conveniently ignored both the requests made by his Afghan counterpart.

The script goes wrong

A few things were changing fast and beyond the US radar and wide network of intelligence. The Taliban were regrouping quickly by employing the poppy money. And the terrorist sanctuaries were popping up in the tribal-dominated and lawless Waziristan. The ISI wing of the Pakistan army began mentoring such camps by providing arms and training. In the latter half of 2005, the US's consolidation effort was quickly hit by the emergence of sporadic insurgency, with the Taliban, the Haqqani network, foreign fighters and disgruntled local tribes seeking to overthrow the new Afghan government. The Taliban, which had been pushed out of Afghanistan, began to plan attacks in Afghanistan from their sanctuaries located in Pakistan. Al-Qaeda was lending more than a supportive hand to the Taliban to plan attacks mostly in Kabul and the heartland of the Taliban—southern Afghanistan. The tacit but burgeoning nexus between the Taliban, the ISI and the al-Qaeda had to show up in the whole of Afghanistan. Violence increased across the country during the summer months, with intense fighting erupting in the south in July 2006. The number of suicide attacks quintupled from 27 in 2005 to 139 in 2006. The remotely detonated bomb attacks more than doubled to 1,677. The US was divided in fathoming the reasons behind the sudden spike in the terrorist attacks. Some White House officials blamed the fledgling and corrupt governance behind the growing attack, while the Afghan-stationed US military commanders squarely blamed the ISI for aiding and abetting unrest in Afghanistan. The Taliban were getting traction, especially in southern Afghanistan.

The White House officials blamed the inability of the Karzai government to render succour to the people, making them turn towards the Taliban. There was no consensus within the US leadership to deal with Pakistan either. The opinion was sharply divided between the military leadership and the top White House officials. While the bulk of the military commanders advocated handling Pakistan with an iron hand, the White House pursued with the policy of cajoling Islamabad to act tough against the growing sanctuaries and attacks emanating from such sanctuaries located within Pakistan. The US was stuck with Pakistan for another reason too. The logistic supply line of the US and NATO forces stationed in Afghanistan often termed as the lifeline, used to pass through Pakistan. The possibility of routing it through Tajikistan and Turkmenistan, largely seen as the backyard of Russia, was grim. Russia would not warm up to any such US aspiration. Hence, the US was stuck with Pakistan for practical reasons too.

The White House kept urging Islamabad to talk tough with the Taliban by providing more aid and diplomacy. Pakistan on its part was enjoying the growing attention and the flow of money, with no real intention to curb the growing menace of the Taliban. However, the barrage of the US persuasion effort earned them the licence to increase the drone attack and target Taliban leaders in the unruly Afghan-Pak border. This was met with some initial success in killing Taliban fighters, and some of their leaders too. But the situation was turning highly volatile in Afghanistan. There was no respite from the

Taliban-led attacks in the war-torn country. The signs of early US success were dissipating fast. The US was on the verge of facing its biggest and most arduous military challenge since their arrival in October 2001. Slowly, things started spiralling out of control. The casualty and death of the US military were mounting, putting the White House under intense pressure and media scrutiny back home.

The US was losing in another battle too. Despite funnelling billions of dollars to eradicate poppy, it was only increasing. In 2007, Afghanistan cultivated 193,000 hectares of opium poppies, an increase of 17 per cent over the previous year. As a result, in 2007, Afghanistan produced an extraordinary 8,200 tonnes of opium (34 per cent more than in 2006), becoming practically the exclusive supplier of the world's deadliest drug (93 per cent of the global opiates market). Poppy funds Taliban terrorism and continuing to grow it would make the Taliban even more lethal and dangerous in their design and attack. A multipronged poppy eradication strategy was on play to cut the finances of the Taliban, post the appointment of interim President Karzai, immediately after the fall of the Taliban. The bumper opium production in 2007 was a grim testimony that the US poppy eradication strategy was not working. It was not only aiding the Taliban, but also corrupting the Afghan bureaucracy, thereby turning the rural populace towards the Taliban.

The US strategy needed an overhaul in light of the deteriorating security, in order to make it more pragmatic and impactful. The US election in 2008 witnessed a new president and a change of guard from the Republican to Democrats at the White House. A fresh call on Afghanistan was awaited and President Obama did oblige after a while. He announced a military surge in Afghanistan. President Obama reaffirmed his poll commitment and sent a fresh contingent of another 17,000

US marines to Afghanistan. This was on top of the already stationed 37,000 US military commanders in Afghanistan. The additional reinforcement was aimed to focus on countering a resurgent Taliban and stemming the flow of foreign fighters over the porous Afghanistan-Pakistan border. He further reiterated that Afghanistan remains the most important US front against the terrorists, and no timeline for withdrawal of US military can be committed, unlike Iraq. The Pentagon further narrowed down the military objectives of Afghanistan to limited goals of preventing and limiting terrorist safe havens, terming the original goal too broad.

The newly elected US President did not stop here. He unveiled a new strategy for Afghanistan on 27 March 2009. The new Afghan strategy linked success in Afghanistan to a stable Pakistan, for the first time. Besides hitting the Taliban, the core strategy revolved around disrupting, dismantling and defeating the al-Qaeda and its safe havens in Pakistan and further choking their movement to Afghanistan (from Pakistan). For the first time, the strategy also linked the flow of aid to Pakistan against the preset framework to measure their progress in fighting the al-Qaeda and the Taliban. An additional 4,000 US troops were committed for Afghanistan to train the Afghan army and police forces. President Karzai welcomed the strategy in Kabul and expressed hope that the new strategy would bring success to Afghanistan. President Karzai was getting frustrated with the leadership of Pakistan for fomenting trouble in Afghanistan. He was getting vocal about the fact that the US needed to check Pakistan for fanning unrest in Afghanistan. However, he too hoped that the new US strategy would compel Pakistan to act tough against the Taliban.

Washington has for years blamed Pakistan for providing a safe haven to the insurgency, making it impossible to defeat the Taliban in Afghanistan. In an attempt to coax Pakistan to support America's Afghan war, the Obama administration ramped up military and economic aid, up to $3 billion a year, but Pakistan saw it as against its interests to fight the Taliban and ties soured in no time. The summer of 2009 witnessed a major offensive from both sides. The US marines launched major battles against the Taliban particularly in southern Afghanistan. The Taliban on their part gave it a tough fight. Besides the guerilla attack, the Taliban started a protracted war against the US and Afghan forces in their stronghold, in selected southern districts. The US forces were drawn into a long and conventional military battle. They retained control of a few and ceded control of the rest in the process of a long-drawn war. But for the first time, a few districts started falling under the control of the Taliban. In Kandahar, a bulk of the districts had fallen to the Taliban. The government officials would rarely venture into districts like Spin Boldak, Panjwayi and a few others. The province of Helmand too witnessed a fierce battle particularly in the districts of Sangin, Marjah, Sahedabad, etc. The surge in US forces was the reason behind these multiple battles at one go. Rather than clamping the terrorist attacks, the surge proved to be counterproductive. By August 2009, the US forces went up to 68,000 in Afghanistan. The new counterinsurgency of the US was put under acid test. The year 2009 was the most daunting one for the American-led war, since the fall of the Taliban government in late 2001. The US military fatality was counted at 310, over a two-fold increase from 153 in 2008.

The Taliban too suffered serious damage in their rank and file. However, there was no dearth of fresh recruits and supply line to fight the US forces with sanctuaries thriving inside Pakistan. The poppy money too played its role in making the

Taliban turn into a lethal and mean force, once again. The civilians bore the brunt of the fierce battle between the US and the Taliban with a reported 2,412 civilians killed by the war in 2009, a jump of 14 per cent over the number that lost their lives in 2008. 2010 was no different, with mounting attacks and lives being lost at both ends. However, more and more areas started falling under the Taliban influence and control. By the end of 2010, it was luminously clear that Obama's Afghan strategy was not working like his predecessor Bush's. The new strategy was neither changing the behaviour of Pakistan nor was it being instrumental in bringing down the Taliban-led attacks within Afghanistan. On the contrary, the ability of the Taliban to wage a battle and protracted war against the US forces was on the rise. The fatality on all sides surpassed the 2009 figures by an alarming gap. The cacophony between the US and Pakistan was no more confined to the peripheries of the White House anymore, but in full public glare.

The Afghan President with a fresh public mandate for the second term started squarely blaming Pakistan for fanning terrorism in Afghanistan. The top leadership of Afghanistan resorted to acerbic charges against their counterparts in Islamabad. As the patience of President Karzai was exhausting, the rancorous exchange between the top leadership of both sides was also on the rise. One fact was getting increasingly clear by 2010 that unless Pakistan was checked, the Taliban-led terrorism could not be controlled in Afghanistan. The US and NATO allies were for the first time exposed to the grim possibility of not winning the war in Afghanistan and getting their heels dug for a long haul.

The NATO leadership was smart enough to heed the early warning emanating from Kabul. At the Lisbon NATO Summit of 2010 (19–20 November), the member countries signed a declaration agreeing to hand over full responsibility for security in Afghanistan to Afghan forces by the end of 2014. The transition process in this effect was set to begin from July 2011, onwards. The local security forces would take over the security control in relatively stable provinces and cities. Many in the West and in Afghanistan, including members of the Afghan parliament were concerned about the ability of national forces to take control over from international forces. The Afghan media was very critical of the move and few even went to the extent of terming it as 'NATO surrender to the Taliban'. A significant proportion of Afghan law makers said, 'If the US and NATO forces with modern training and weapons are unable to control the Taliban, how is it expected from the beleaguered Afghan army to manage them? Will it not give more leeway to the Taliban to get further organized and lethal in their design and attack?' The NATO was unfazed by their mounting criticism and decided to go ahead with their plan.

The hydra-headed monster

The US war in Afghanistan marked its tenth-year celebration on 7 October 2011, with about a hundred thousand US troops deployed in Afghanistan for counterinsurgency operations. By then, the US forces were stretched and fighting the Taliban almost all over Afghanistan. The US had already deployed $444 billion in the Afghan war and suffered 1,800-troop casualties. Amid a resurgent Taliban, the US military goals were far from achieved and the terrorist sanctuary continued to operate in Pakistan. The writ of the central government in Kabul was openly contested in many areas; and in many other areas, it didn't even have a nominal presence. The military gains of the US were very limited even from the generous standard of the Afghan president. But his patience with Pakistan too died on the vine, after the fatal attack of the Afghan government's peace chair Burhanuddin Rabbani, by a suicide bomber at his office-cum-home. In no uncertain terms, he blamed the attack on the Pakistan-based Haqqani network, often referred to as the blue-eyed boy of the ISI.

More than a decade of relentless military operations made it clear that the Taliban were far from vanquished. President Obama's much-talked-about 'military surge' policy has delivered very little to rejoice about, both militarily and politically. Much to the dismay of the Pentagon, it has proven to be totally counterproductive. Despite the surge, the Taliban have been able to converge and effectively besiege strategic locations, with unfailing regularity. This has further emboldened the Taliban. In fact, as per the US intelligence reports, they had grown stronger and more organized, after the troop surge. Not only have they consolidated their position in their southern provinces' stronghold, but also wormed out their way into the once peaceful northern provinces like Kunduz and Baghlan. The Taliban were massing in the outskirts of Kabul and slowly turning the city into a hotbed of terrorism. Sensing that their military campaign would in no way reach their end goal, the White House wanted to smoke the peace pipe with the Taliban. Talks about a long-term political solution for building a durable peace with the Taliban started gaining momentum all of a sudden. A brainchild of the US military think tank, 'the peace process' was zealously pursued by the US and objectively linked with the transit of their army, from Afghanistan. The US further managed to get an international backing for the peace process from their western allies. This was a marked departure from the US policy standpoint, from having no truck with the Taliban to singing peace carol with the Taliban.

The US strategy in Afghanistan was changing again. If President Bush's strategy to make a lot of noise, declare victory and return home has failed, so has President Obama's policy of surge, sign blank cheque for Pakistan, declare victory and run. In a desperate bid to stabilize Afghanistan, President Obama turned to peace talks as a lender of last resort. It was prudent given the fact that the military option instead of providing a solution backfired. The US-based scholars and analysts in Washington who have been following the conflict for years warned President Obama that he was making a fatal error by trusting the very same insurgent group that once housed Osama bin Laden. But President Obama had no better option than engaging with the Taliban, as chasing them over a decade did not yield any dividends. He covered up the strategic shift in the US policy by coining the term 'Good Taliban and Bad Taliban.'[48] He further emphasized that there should be no harm in engaging with the moderate Taliban.

What turned the US and its western allies to apostles of peace overnight warrants some deep probing though. There are a number of strategic compulsions tied to this much-hyped peace process. The US and its western allies have been getting increasingly tired of the war and do not see it reaching anywhere near the end goal. The writing was clear on the wall. They are on the brink of a sad realization that it is beyond their capacity to drive away the Taliban, let alone irreversibly degrading their capabilities. To make a dignified exit, on the pretext of launching a peace process, was probably the best option for the US. International critics, however, saw this as an effort to buy peace from the Taliban rather than

---

[48]'Strategies for Negotiating With "Good" Taliban,' npr, 15 October 2009, https://www.npr.org/templates/story/story.php?storyId=113816617, accessed 15 June 2021.

build peace in Afghanistan. The Taliban on its part made some significant gains after the initiation of the peace talks—the most important being the recognition of their central position in the peace process. The fact that they have finally forced the Americans to have direct negotiations with them is an acceptance of their geostrategic advantage within Afghanistan.

The Afghan president was apprehensive about the US's sudden change of heart towards the Taliban. He was apprehensive that any direct access of the Pentagon to the Taliban would render him toothless. To allay the fear of the top leadership in Kabul, the White House insisted that any political-cum-peace settlement with the Taliban should be Afghan-led and controlled. In March 2012, the Taliban struck a deal to open an office in Qatar, a move towards the peace talks that the US viewed as a crucial part of a political settlement to ensure a stable Afghanistan. President Karzai, believing the office would confer legitimacy on the insurgent group and serve as a diplomatic outpost, did not subscribe to the US approach. President Obama made a series of failed attempts to rope in Pakistan to use its influence over the Taliban in order to advance the peace process in Afghanistan.

The Government of Afghanistan started to reach out to the Taliban on its own. This made the ISI nervous to the core. Pakistan was deeply averse to any direct connection between the Taliban and the elected government in Kabul. This would have made the ISI lose its strategic relevance and become redundant. The ISI soon started arresting the Taliban leaders settled inside Pakistan. This was a move to thwart the direct connect between the Taliban and the Afghan government and further lodge their strong protest against any freelance peace dealing. After finding out that the US was serious about the peace process, Islamabad too subscribed to the peace tunes after recalibrating their strategy. They pinned their hope to plant Pakistan sympathizers and radical Taliban leaders in a post-peace process political arrangement in Kabul to get uninterrupted strategic access and leeway.

In early 2012, a large number of media reports emanating from both Kabul and Washington suggested a tacit deal between the US and the Taliban for fixing peace in Afghanistan. The US vehemently denied any such negotiation with the Taliban sans Kabul's agreement. The first crack in the US theory was observed when the Taliban suspended the preliminary talks in May 2012, accusing Washington of reneging on the promise to take meaningful steps towards an agreed prisoner swap. The unilateral announcement on the part of the Taliban put a spanner on the peace process. The US was determined to move ahead with their departure plan. The US defence secretary made it clear that they aimed to conclude the combat role by mid-2013 and make a switch towards the security assistance role. This phase also witnessed US military excesses in civilian areas peeving President Karzai to the hilt. There were government reports of multiple air strikes gone awry and killing civilians. There were many cases of US military killing innocent civilians providing fodder to the Taliban for fanning anti-US sentiments.

The public image of the elected government was also eroding, being a collaborator of the Afghan war. President Karzai demanded that the foreign troops be withdrawn from civilian areas and that they should be made accountable for their actions. The White House subscribed to none of the demands. This created a void between Kabul and Washington, which continued to grow with time. The US military was confronted with manifold problems. They were suffering mounting casualties at the hands of the Taliban. The people of Afghanistan were agitating against the US military excesses.

And the Taliban were only getting stronger with every passing day. By then, almost 25 per cent of Afghanistan had fallen to the Taliban. And above all, their last ray of hope, the peace process was fading faster than its flourish.

The Afghan forces started taking the lead in providing nationwide security as NATO handed over control of districts, 2012 onwards. The US-led coalition goal was confined to military training and coaching, along with the special counterterrorism operation. The strategy was questioned by critics and supported by few. The cardinal arguments were the Afghan military's preparedness to face the Taliban and the performance metrics based on which the US resorted to the idea of localizing counterinsurgency. And if that was the end goal, shouldn't the US have made the move of training the Afghan military much in advance? Above all, if the US army, with all its military might and new-age machines, is unable to counter the resurgent Taliban, how can the same be expected from the rookie Afghan army confronted with the plethora of challenges like lack of number, training, mechanization and equipment, and the infiltration of Taliban supporters within the army? It was further confronted by attrition due to a combination of desertion and casualty. Just one day after NATO lowered its flag in Kabul (28 December 2014), marking the official end of the 13-year war in Afghanistan, the Taliban seized upon the occasion to declare victory, announcing the 'defeat' of the US-NATO joint mission. NATO allies gradually faded away as the long war began to stretch, leaving the US to determine the end of the conflict on its own.

In May 2014, President Obama made his decision of withdrawing most of the US forces from Afghanistan by the end of 2014. He further reiterated that the combat mission of the US forces would completely end by December 2014 sans demand-driven air strikes. With the US security mandate expiring in December 2014, it was imperative for the US to negotiate a bilateral security agreement with the Karzai government in order to maintain a military presence inside Afghanistan. President Karzai was not keen on signing the deal in 'as it is' form and wanted certain changes, especially making the US forces accountable for their action inside Afghanistan. Bombing in civilian areas was another bone of contention between the two states. However, he was not in any position to reject it either. All his requests for amendments fell on deaf ears at the Pentagon, and the critical security deal with the US remained unsigned till the last day of his office. The status quo created a serious rift between Washington and Kabul. The bilateral relationship hit a historic low. It was reported that President Karzai was not even on speaking terms with President Obama towards the end of his presidential stint.

Karzai's frustration was not restricted to the awry air strikes killing civilians alone. He was equally peeved with the long handle given to the US military forces, with no accountability, in Afghanistan. He was ranting against the US in full glare of the international media. President Karzai's public outburst against the US leadership also stemmed from the inability of the White House to check Islamabad from aiding and abetting the Taliban-led terrorism. He was not forgiving against Pakistan too, and openly challenged Pakistan for fomenting trouble in Afghanistan.[49] His intelligence chief even went to the extent of sharing the GPS coordinate of the terrorist camps sponsored by the ISI along with the point-wise

---

[49]PTI, 'Hamid Karzai slams Pak, defends India's role in Afghanistan,' *Business Standard*, 20 August 2016, https://www.business-standard.com/article/international/hamid-karzai-slams-pak-defends-india-s-role-in-afghanistan-116082000719_1.html, accessed 18 June 2021.

locales of the banned Taliban outfit in Pakistan. Pakistan was in no hurry to act and conveniently brushed aside the charges. Islamabad termed the accusation as a figment of imagination of the Afghan leadership devoid of any tangible evidence, a standard response provided by Islamabad to circumvent any terrorism-sponsoring charges by its neighbouring countries.

The US military arrived in Afghanistan with their sophisticated weapons to weed out the Taliban from Afghanistan and irreversibly damage their abilities. This was the whole point of the war and it was not accomplished. The insurgency in Afghanistan was more widespread and bolder than at any time, since the war began. The US decided to quit just when all the things that they promised were most badly needed but were nowhere to be seen. Life in Afghanistan was in many ways contrary to what the US had promised. In a way, the US withdrawal was an admittance of its failure. In his speech ending the combat mission in Afghanistan, President Obama said, 'the longest war in American history is coming to a responsible conclusion.'[50] In view of the undeniably worsening situation there, the phrase sounded so inconsistent to the laid US goal. Obama further admitted that the al-Qaeda still had a presence in Afghanistan, implying that the original reason for the invasion remained intact. The reduced goals of 'reversing' or 'blunting' the Taliban's momentum was not even mentioned in his speech. A peace deal was the only vague hope. A much better deal could have been crafted back in 2002, when many senior Taliban figures offered to support Karzai's government, but they were rejected, hunted, arrested and killed. The US, and many others, ultimately determined that fighting was the only option.

---

[50]https://obamawhitehouse.archives.gov/the-press-office/2014/12/28/statement-president-end-combat-mission-afghanistan, accessed 14 June 2021.

The US departure from the combat role in 2014 portrayed a sordid tale. In 2014, Afghan civilian casualties topped at 10,000, a 22 per cent increase compared to the previous year, continuing the grim trend.[51] According to the UN, 3,699 people were killed and 6,849 injured by the end of 2014.[52] The Afghan security forces suffered more than twice as many losses the previous year than US forces suffered during the entire war, with some 5,400 soldiers and policemen killed in 2014 alone. Even in the capital of Kabul, the ceremony ending NATO's mission had to be held in a secret location because the likelihood of a Taliban attack was very imminent. Despite the end of US and NATO combat operations in Afghanistan, the war was not over. It was now in its deadliest phase since the Taliban were bombed out of power 13 years ago. Ashraf Ghani, former finance minister of the Karzai government, was sworn in as the new President of Afghanistan on 29 September 2014, under a unity government. In Afghanistan, this patch-up arrangement was brought into play to escape the electoral deadlock and the consequent unrest that almost threatened a civil war. Immediately, after taking charge, Ghani signed the vital, long delayed security deal that allowed nearly 10,000 US troops to remain in Afghanistan beyond the final withdrawal of US and international forces by the end of 2014. Both the countries breathed a sigh of relief with the signing of the security deal put on the back-burner by the outgoing President Hamid Karzai.

The new political set-up in Kabul was showing some early sign of rapprochement with the Taliban, to drive the peace process. President Ghani was gravitating more towards the

---

[51]'Afghanistan civilian casualties up 22% in 2014, UN says', BBC News, 18 February 2025, https://www.bbc.com/news/world-asia-31515140, accessed 15 June 2021.
[52]Ibid.

all-weather duo of Pakistan and China. Afghanistan started relying on the political goodwill of China to influence Pakistan into cooperating in the peace process. By visiting China in his first leg of foreign tour, the president made his intention loud and clear. Ghani's approach of making Pakistan a key party to the peace process was sounding cynical but stood politically pragmatic. Ghani's outreach towards Pakistan was vastly different from his predecessor's approach. Islamabad had played a significant part in its own way in Ghani's victory in the presidential election and also viewed the present government in Kabul far more sympathetically than his predecessor.

As a result, the relationship between Afghanistan and Pakistan significantly improved in the first year of the Ghani government. This included a visit of the Premier Nawaz Sharif and Army head Raheel Sharif to Kabul. President Ghani worked hard to improve relations between the two neighbours. To address Pakistani suspicions, he toned down Afghanistan's traditional alliance with India and stepped up unprecedented security cooperation with Islamabad, despite facing a volley of domestic opposition. To allay fears of Afghanistan's growing proximity with India, President Ghani even sidetracked the issue of ongoing security cooperation with India. This created a renewed hope both in Afghanistan as well as the international community that Pakistan would amend its ways and assist Afghanistan in striking a political settlement with the Taliban.

In his twilight phase at the White House, President Obama's search for peace continued with no tangible headway though. In pursuit of peace, the US policy driver in Afghanistan later played their part in assembling the QCG (comprising Afghanistan, Pakistan, the US and China), to bring various warring factions of the Taliban on the negotiating table to stabilize the conflict-ridden country. However, a series of deliberations with the Taliban, via the QCG, did not yield anything to cheer about. The composition of QCG was also questionable with the absence of Russia and Iran, two of the most important players, enjoying access and influence on strategic matters in Afghanistan. Initially, there was a growing sense of optimism among the Afghans about China's role in the QCG. It was expected that China would set up the peace talks with Taliban through its strategic grip over Pakistan, but the red dragon was keen on protecting the strategic interest of its all-weather ally Pakistan than Afghanistan. The QCC group though kept the process of discussion going with the Taliban. Pakistan was found making a half-hearted attempt at cutting out a peace deal with the Taliban. The Pakistan army was keen to pursue with its time-tested strategy of deceit and duplicity in Afghanistan.

There was growing frustration among the top US leadership for their inability to make Pakistan toe the line. The US leadership was now very open and vocal about their criticism for Pakistan. The top leadership of the US too blamed Pakistan for harbouring the Taliban and further sponsoring terror attacks inside Afghanistan. They were questioning the performance metrics of Pakistan against the US taxpayer's money flowing for enlisting security cooperation. Pakistan on its part was not keen to neutralize the influence of the Taliban. But they had to act to curb their growing image of a terror-friendly state. They chased the cousin of the Taliban, the Pakistan-focused TTP, which caused serious damage inside Pakistan. This served the dual purpose for Islamabad—making the right optics that Pakistan is not soft against terrorists and quelling the TTP in the bud before it becomes a bigger problem for Pakistan. The act of the Pakistan military assuaged some nerves in the White House. But the top US leadership was not fully convinced that Pakistan was doing enough to stabilize Afghanistan. And for the first time the idea of strict performance-based payment was floated by the Pentagon. The idea itself put Pakistan on the back foot, as for the first time the US was cornering Pakistan to act against payment made to its mammoth military establishment. And the fear of losing out on billions of US dollars at the time when the economy was slipping sent jitters to both Rawalpindi and Islamabad. The abundant optimism of the outgoing President Obama over Pakistan to cooperate with the US, ended on a sour note.

The year 2016, witnessed an unprecedented surge in Taliban strikes, posing a serious threat to the internal security and stability of the country. The attack of the Taliban spiralled from its traditional bastion of southern provinces, bordering with the fragile terrorist sanctuaries of Waziristan, to the once relatively stable northern provinces. The Taliban were attacking the federal capital of Kabul at their free will. And the military and civil casualties escalated at an alarming rate. The Taliban appeared more threatening than ever. About 5,500 army and policemen were killed in the fight against the Taliban in the first eight month of 2016.[53] Civilian casualty stood at 3,498 by the end of 2016. The officials at the Ministry of Defence (MoD) reported ongoing counter-insurgency operations in 20 provinces, estimating the total number of districts facing grave security threats nationwide to range between 60 and 100. Afghanistan was going through the worst.

But there was no taker in the White House in 2016, as the country was completely occupied with electing the successor of the outgoing President Obama. The burning

---

[53]'Afghanistan Nato: "30 civilians killed" during Taliban fighting,' BBC News, 3 November 2016, https://www.bbc.com/news/world-asia-37857733, accessed 2 July 2021.

issue of Afghanistan was kept on the back-burner, allowing the Taliban to grow more dangerous in their design and execution. Policymaking on Afghanistan was frozen in the US. The longest and the priciest war in Afghanistan failed to make much of the election narrative of the cacophonous presidential campaign in the US. A war that drained the US exchequer by $600 billion and witnessed the death of 2,247 US military personnel (by the third quarter of 2016), along with 20,000 more wounded. Contrary to public opinion, Trump was elected as the new US president.

The costly and bloody war in Afghanistan failed to strike resonance with the US electorate, but it remained a critical priority for the newly elected US president. President Trump had inherited the toughest foreign policy challenge in the Afghan status quo, confronted with a surfeit of distinct challenges that required exigent attention. President Obama's eight years at the helm of US affairs solved very little in Afghanistan. It rather exacerbated the crisis. The pull out of US troops from Afghanistan has only led to an emboldened Taliban looking more threatening than ever to reverse the few gains made over the past 15 years. For the newly elected president, there was little to rejoice and more to ponder about resolving the Afghan deadlock. Any political and strategic complacency would have turned Afghanistan into a hotbed for the Taliban and ISIS offshoots.

President Trump had not spoken much about Afghanistan in the past. But the analysis of his comments clearly depicted a lack of coherent understanding of the Afghan challenge. His public statements have been consistently erratic on whether the US should maintain a long-term military presence in Afghanistan or not. For the US, the war in Afghanistan remains a strategic conundrum, bleeding it financially with no sign of a closure. The financial liability of the US due to the Afghan war was only increasing with passing years. Perhaps the previous US regime erred in assessing the potency of the Taliban in a post-US military exit scenario. Besides these, the US think tank pinned abundant optimism on the ongoing peace process. They harped on the peace process via the QCG as an alternative to the war against terror, with the long stretched military campaign showing no sign of progress towards their end goal in Afghanistan. The cardinal question boiled down to the new Trump administration's desired length and intensity of commitment in Afghanistan.

Given Trump's recurrent thrust on 'America first', it was difficult to believe that he would step up the accelerator and announce any big bang military surge in Afghanistan, like his predecessor Obama. 'I would stay in Afghanistan,' Trump said in a pre-election interview with Fox News. 'I hate doing it. I hate doing it so much.'[54] And in line with his election promise, Trump continued with a residual US military presence in Afghanistan. He assumed that the strategy would serve as an effective check on any overt aggression of the Taliban, as well as the ISI of Pakistan. However, Trump advocated that US troops should abandon state-building objectives and focus on combating more imminent security threats in Afghanistan. He has clearly refrained from playing a comprehensive role, beyond the peripheries of military support in Afghanistan.

Eventually, Trump was confronted with the bigger questions about the US's long-term plans for Afghanistan and its tumultuous relationship with Pakistan, an unstable partner with

---

[54]'Will free jailed Pakistan doctor who helped track Osama bin Laden: Donald Trump,' *DNA*, https://www.dnaindia.com/world/report-will-free-jailed-pakistan-doctor-who-helped-track-osama-bin-laden-donald-trump-2207500, accessed 2 July 2021.

clearly documented evidence of fanning unrest in Afghanistan. The conflict in Afghanistan was convoluted to say the least. The incumbent leadership of Afghanistan had apprised President Trump about the continual presence of the Taliban's cross-border havens in Pakistan, operating under the aegis of the ISI. The key Afghan officials have long been demanding to eliminate the terrorist sanctuaries located in Pakistan. President Trump was well aware of Pakistan's policy of deceit and duplicity in Afghanistan. But he was also privy to the fact that the key to stabilize Afghanistan lies in Pakistan. He had to be politically pragmatic in dealing with Pakistan. It was anticipated that Trump's Afghanistan strategy would emphasize preserving stability in Afghanistan and containing Pakistan.

Trump's proactive posture

Trump's pre-election rant against Pakistan for fanning terrorism and cheating the US created considerable buzz about his official take on Pakistan. The face value analysis of Trump's statement suggested that he would not prolong Obama's carrot-and-stick policy in dealing with Pakistan. In the past, Trump had tweeted, 'We've given them billions and billions of dollars, and what did we get? Betrayal and disrespect, and much worse.'[55] Trump, who has flaunted himself as the ultimate dealmaker, was anticipated to take a drastically different approach to deal with Pakistan than his predecessor. He was expected to act tough, in order to coerce Pakistan to dismantle terrorist sanctuaries and further tame

---

[55]Northam, Jackie, 'Trump Gushes about Pakistan in Call with Its Prime Minister', npr, 1 December 2016, https://www.npr.org/sections/parallels/2016/12/01/504010662/trump-gushes-about-pakistan-in-call-with-its-prime-minister. accessed 16 June 2021.

ISI from fanning strategic unrest in Afghanistan. It was further assumed that the ongoing US military aid to Pakistan would be put under tight scrutiny, and even terminated in case the Pakistan army failed to toe the red line, drawn by the new White House occupant. President Trump may have even resorted to arm-twisting top Pakistani leadership to compel the Taliban into coming to the peace table, in order to reignite the stuck peace process. Whether the Pakistan army, heavily drunk under the influence of China, adheres to the new Afghan manual of the White House was up for an acid test.

The US backing of India's strong role in Afghanistan was another bone of contention for Pakistan. Any explicit US support for joint efforts between Afghanistan and India to contain Pakistan could trigger Pakistan further to strengthen its strategic alignment with China and upgrade its nascent security partnership with Russia. Russia and Iran were also aggressively playing out the Afghan void. Balancing the key interests of major players in Afghanistan was expected to be an exceedingly daunting task for the new US administration. The challenges in Afghanistan were not militarily alone. Afghanistan's NUG was neither united nor did it deliver good governance. And corruption remained at an all-time high. In order to pressurize Afghan officials to prevent the misappropriation of US financial assistance, Trump could threaten to cut foreign aid to Afghanistan. But such extreme action would only increase the suffering of the Afghan people and aid his anti-Islamic image, further. The US has little to show for the $8.5 billion it has spent on counternarcotics efforts since 2002.[56] It still continued to fund the Taliban and their nefarious

---

[56]Dawi, Akmal and Noor Zahid, 'Afghanistan's Deadly Poppy Harvest on the Rise Again,' VOA News, 16 May 2017, https://www.voanews.com/extremism-watch/afghanistans-deadly-poppy-harvest-rise-again, accessed 16 June 2021.

designs in Afghanistan. Afghanistan still leads the world in opium production and is growing poppy at near record levels. Breaking the current stalemate in Afghanistan was going to be tough. The Taliban had momentum heading into the following year's fighting season (2017), and they would leave no stone unturned to press the initiative, once the snow starts melting (from the start of April). The Trump administration had to hit the ground running in Afghanistan. Any fatigue would severely increase the magnitude of the Afghan crisis.

President Trump was not complacent either. After his initial preoccupation with the immigration flare-up, he got down to the table with his new set of advisors to resolve the looming Afghan crisis. He announced the long-awaited new Afghan strategy for resolving the nearly 16-year-old conflict in Afghanistan on 21 August 2017. Among other things, it called for an unenumerated troop increase, an open-ended commitment to station American forces in the country, greater leeway to US commanders in making military choices, a warning to Pakistan to end its support to various terrorist organizations operating from its soil and an exhortation to India to enlarge its presence in Afghanistan. This was more or less on the expected lines. In announcing his plan, Trump deepened American involvement in a military mission that has engulfed his predecessors and that he once called futile.[57]

He was frank enough to openly admit it. 'My original instinct was to pull out—and, historically, I like following my instincts. But all my life I've heard that decisions are different when you sit behind the desk in the Oval Office; in

---

[57]Davis, Julie Hirschfeld and Mark Landler, 'Trump Outlines New Afghanistan War Strategy with Few Details,' *The New York Times*, 21 August 2017, nytimes. com/2017/08/21/world/asia/afghanistan-troops-trump.html, accessed 16 June 2021.

other words, when you're President of the United States.'[58] He further made it clear that the purpose of the US military presence is 'not nation building, but killing terrorists.'[59] 'Ultimately, it is up to the people of Afghanistan to take ownership of their future, to govern their society and to achieve an everlasting peace. We are a partner and a friend, but we will not dictate to the Afghan people how to live or how to govern their own complex society.'[60] It was another U-turn for the US as it withdrew from a nation-building role after funnelling billions of US dollars into it. He was non-committal on the date of the US military departure from Afghanistan, unlike his predecessor Obama. He said, 'Conditions on the ground—not arbitrary timetables—will guide our exit strategy from hereon. America's enemies must never know our plans or believe they can wait us out. I will not say when we are going to attack, but attack we will.'[61] In retrospect, the Obama administration erred in setting artificial timelines for US troop withdrawal from Afghanistan. After 16 years, the war with Afghanistan remains the longest one in the history of America, at the cost of $800 billion and death of nearly 2,400 soldiers. President Trump had to end on an optimistic note so he characteristically promised, in the end that the US will win.

The denunciation of Pakistan was for the first time put on the official strategy document of the US. In a way, Trump's speech attempted to correct the erroneous official White House

---

[58]Ibid.

[59]Ibid.

[60]In escalating America's longest war, Trump acts against his 'original instinct.' *The Washington Post*, 21 August 2017.

[61]Dobbins, James, Jason H. Cambel, Sean Mann and Laurel E. Miller, 'Consequences of a Precipitous U.S. Withdrawal from Afghanistan,' Rand.org. 2019.

narrative on Pakistan, a country that has for 16 years benefited from US financial largesse while continuing to undermine US interests in the region. It was hardly a revelation that Pakistan has long been playing a double game in Afghanistan. While drawing on substantial American military assistance, Pakistan has been very selectively pursuing Taliban unrest in Afghanistan by allowing them to operate within its borders and further providing mentoring through deep state. Trump's speech was a marked departure from his predecessor, Obama. President Trump viewed Pakistan as a core contributing factor to the Afghan quagmire, while his predecessor viewed Pakistan as having convergent objectives with the US in Afghanistan and even drew equivalence between Afghanistan and Pakistan as fellow victims of terrorism. Though in the last phase of his White House days, Obama too was found losing his patience with Pakistan.

The hit out at Pakistan also suggested that the US has run out of levers to persuade Pakistan to alter its policies towards the Taliban and its extended network of terrorists. Besides these, greater emphasis on India for rebuilding Afghanistan ignited Pakistan's deeply entrenched fears of being enfolded by India. This, in turn, made them gravitate more towards China. In the new policy, it was amply clear that the Trump administration would not sign a blank cheque for Pakistan. It was not rhetoric anymore. The US meant it seriously for the first time. Just two days after his boss announced the new Afghan policy, the then Secretary of State, Rex Tillerson, warned that the US funding for Pakistan would be cut if the Pakistan government did not cooperate with the US president's strategy in Afghanistan. 'Obviously, we have some leverage that's been discussed in terms of the amount of aid and military assistance we give them, their status as a non-

NATO alliance partner', Tillerson told reporters. 'All of that can be put on the table.'[62]

It was open and loud that Pakistan's role in Afghanistan would be strictly reviewed with ground-based performance metrics. Trump's articulation that Pakistan was part of the problem rather than the solution did not go down well both in Rawalpindi as well as in Islamabad. But Pakistan's brazen duplicity is not something that the new US president chose to ignore either. The Trump administration was keen to toe a harder line on Pakistan than its predecessors. Islamabad rejected the charges and in turn accused Washington of trying to make Pakistan a scapegoat for US military failures in Afghanistan. Ties between the US and Pakistan were strained after the aggressive posturing by President Trump.

Along with the tough posturing against Pakistan in the media, President Trump initiated a series of back-room negotiations and sent regular feelers to Islamabad and the army headquarters based in Rawalpindi for course correction. This was the last-ditch effort to enlist active support of Pakistan in order to contain the Taliban in Afghanistan. He wanted to reboot ties with Pakistan based on ground performance and not blank talk and self-certification by Islamabad, anymore. However, his constant acerbic rant coupled with the new Afghan policy angered Pakistan. This came on the top of fledgling Pak-US ties, left by his predecessor Obama. President Trump's policy of humiliating Pakistan for cheating the US and further blaming them for the present Afghan turmoil was the final nail in the coffin. Pakistan was in no mood to

---

[62]McLeary, Paul and Dan De Luce, 'Trump Administration Threatens to Cut Aid to Pakistan. Does It Matter?' FP, 23 August 2017, https://foreignpolicy.com/2017/08/23/trump-administration-threatens-to-cut-aid-to-pakistan-does-it-matter/, accessed 16 June 2021.

oblige Trump's new manual on Afghanistan. Pakistan had successfully blunted Obama's pressure with the tacit support of China, during his last days at the White House.

Heavily under the influence of China, Pakistan was not keen to subscribe to the Afghan agenda floated by the newly elected President Trump. The immediate financial need for creating jobs in Pakistan was taken care of by the multibillion-dollar CPEC under the BRI of the red dragon. Hence, Pakistan was not in any immediate hurry to work on the red line marked by President Trump, in Afghanistan. On the contrary, their tacit support to the Taliban continued and the terrorist sanctuaries flourished inside Pakistan. The Taliban also placed a large number of their fresh recruits in jihad training camps operating with an anti-Indian focus. This was part of a larger strategy to train Taliban terrorists under the guise of the Kashmir movement in order to escape the radar and wrath of the US intelligence agencies.[63] Soon, President Trump ran out of patience and opened the dawn of 2018 with an acerbic tweet, 'The United States has foolishly given Pakistan more than $33 billion in aid over the last 15 years, and they have given us nothing but lies and deceit, thinking of our leaders as fools. They give safe haven to the terrorists we hunt in Afghanistan, with little help. No more!'[64] It soon became clear that Trump's tweet was more than an idle threat. On 4 January 2018, the State Department announced that the US was freezing most military aid to Pakistan. The administration

---

[63]'Pakistan Army and Terrorism; an unholy alliance,' European Foundation for South Asian Studies (EFSAS), https://www.efsas.org/publications/study-papers/pakistan-army-and-terrorism;-an-unholy-alliance/, accessed 2 July 2021.

[64]Scroll Staff, 'US has "foolishly" given Pakistan billions of dollars in aid over 15 years, but no more, says Trump,' Scroll.in, 1 January 2018, https://scroll.in/latest/863448/us-has-foolishly-given-pakistan-billions-of-dollars-in-aid-over-15-years-but-no-more-says-trump, accessed 16 June 2021.

declined to specify the exact amount of funds it would cut off, but the suspension froze up to $1.4 billion in aid. The military equipment transfer too was put on hold.

The move infuriated Pakistan. The then Pakistan's Foreign Minister, Khawaja Asif, was the first to react in the popular Geo television series. 'We have already told the US that we will not do more, so Trump's "no more" does not hold any importance. Pakistan is ready to publicly provide every detail of the US aid that it has received.'[65] He didn't stop here. In his interviews to the US media, he said that the US had turned Islamabad into a 'whipping boy'[66] to distract from its own failures in the war in Afghanistan. He also implied that the US's move could end up terminating cooperation between the US and Pakistan on issues like intelligence sharing. 'We do not have any alliance with the US,' Asif said. 'This is not how allies behave.'[67] There was a lurking fear in the Pentagon that the faltering US-Pak ties may cut off intelligence sharing by Pakistan, putting the lives of US soldiers stationed in Afghanistan under a great deal of risk. It may further block the US from using supply routes via Pakistan that are crucial for its ability to conduct its military operations in Afghanistan. The US believed that Pakistan could be made to act in Afghanistan by suspending a security grant. It would hit them where it hurt the most. Hence, President Trump pressed the lever of frozen grant, once again, in September 2018. In a jolt to Pakistan, the Trump administration announced that it

---

[65]"Trump's "no more" holds no importance: Khawaja Asif,' Geo News, 1 January 2018, https://www.geo.tv/latest/174836-trumps-no-more-is-not-of-any-importance-asif, accessed 16 June 2021.

[66]Shah, Saeed, 'Pakistan Foreign Minister Says U.S. Has Undermined Countries' Ties,' The Wall Street Journal, 5 January 2018, https://www.wsj.com/articles/pakistan-says-alliance-with-u-s-is-over-1515155860, accessed 16 June 2021.

[67]Ibid.

had cut $300 million in military aid to Pakistan, increasing pressure on the country to crack down on militant groups that have jeopardized the ongoing US war in Afghanistan. The Pentagon further announced that more cuts are in the offing if Islamabad does not start doing what Washington wants it to do in Afghanistan.

With the frozen aid and recurrent rants against each other in full public domain, the US-Pak ties soon slipped to a historic low, amid no hope of improvement in the near future. In the meanwhile, a few things changed fast in Pakistan, viz. the beginning of an economic meltdown and a new government being voted to power in Islamabad. The ascendancy of Imran Khan was an exciting development as Pakistan voted above bipartisan politics, for the first time. Riding a strong anti-incumbency factor, star cricketer-turned-politician and Pakistan Tehreek-e-Insaf (PTI) Chairman, Imran Khan was elected Pakistan's 22nd prime minister on Independence Day (14 August 2018), in a disputed general election. This marked the pinnacle of his 22-year-long struggle to ascend the forefront of Pakistan politics. Nicknamed 'perennial opposition leader',[68] Khan was never considered a serious contender to be able to break and make his way in Pakistan's strong two-party system.

The involvement of Pakistan's powerful army in the all-parliamentary election is well-documented and 2018 was no different. His growing image as an army-backed candidate besmirched his political credentials. The Opposition termed him as a 'selected Prime Minister'[69] due to allegation of mass

[68]Nasir, Abbas, 'The many challenges awaiting Pakistan's Imran Khan,' *Dawn*, 26 July 2018, *Al Jazeera*, https://www.aljazeera.com/opinions/2018/7/26/the-many-challenges-awaiting-pakistans-imran-khan, accessed 16 June 2021.

[69]Inayat, Naila, 'In Imran Khan's Pakistan it's not the economy, stupid. It is a dreaded word keeping PM awake,' *The Print*, 27 June 2019, https://theprint.in/

rigging by the Pakistan army. In his first speech after being elected as Prime Minister of Pakistan, Khan vowed to work towards creating a naya (new) Pakistan—that was a cardinal part of his election manifesto and months long electioneering. He portrayed himself as the poster boy of anti-corruption and vowed to fix accountability of those who plundered Pakistan. 'We have to have strict accountability in this country; the people who looted this country, I promise that I will work against them,' he asserted. 'The money that was laundered, I will bring it back—the money that should have gone towards health, education, and water, went into people's pockets.'[70] He further offered himself as accountable for creating a corruption-free society and vowed for people-centric policies to pull the poor out of endemic poverty. The united opposition dubbed PM Khan's 'Naya Pakistan' as a pure fantasy play to keep the urban voters excited.

Prime Minister Khan inherited a nation tottering on the edge of an economic collapse. Long before the elections, Pakistan's downward economic trajectory was becoming apparent. This was from the very start of 2018. At the end of the fiscal year in June 2018, the Current Account Deficit peaked at $17.994 billion, which accounted for 5.7 per cent of Pakistan's GDP. On 27 July 2018, the foreign exchange reserve stood at $10,349.7 million, not enough to outlast the import bills for more than a month. The balance of payment was standing at a precarious level with both the International Monetary Fund (IMF) and the World Bank (WB) raising red flags about the alarming unfolding economic situation

---

opinion/letter-from-pakistan/in-imran-khans-pakistan-its-not-the-economy-stupid-it-is-this-dreaded-word/255041/, accessed 16 June 2021.

[70]Chaudhry, Fahad, 'Imran clean bowls Shahbaz to become PM,' *Dawn*, 17 August 2018, https://www.dawn.com/news/1426772, accessed 16 June 2021.

in Pakistan. Prime Minister Khan assumed power in August 2018 with an almost empty treasury. He did not even have money to run the daily affairs of the country. He faced tough challenges in the economic and service sectors too, as most of the Pakistani institutions were in the red. The Pakistani rupee was on a free fall with the inflation going through the roof. The state of the Pakistan economy was deplorable. As the country was on the brink of a balance-of-payment crisis, China announced a $2 billion loan to Pakistan, as a first hand of relief. China was neck deep invested and the slippage of Pakistan's economy would eventually hurt China. Pakistan's all-weather ally, Saudi Arabia too pledged $6 billion as soft loan to rescue Pakistan from payment default. However, the magnitude of the crisis was far bigger than the much timely financial help.

The grave issue of youth unemployment was raising its head. Pakistan is currently experiencing massive growth in its youth populace, making it one of the youngest countries in the world. As per economists, there is a need to create almost 1.3 million jobs annually to match the swelling employment demand. Any economic regression will create a very undesirable human capital challenge by way of shrinking employment and education opportunities, potentially setting back an entire generation and countering even greater socio-economic challenges. The PTI government was elected on the plank of youth voters. It was expected that Khan's ability to placate the youth with jobs would chart his political course and survival. Hence, the economy has to be grown, not just by dealing with the immediate balance-of-payment crisis but addressing macroeconomic stability in Pakistan. It was his stance on the economy that will determine his political fate and Pakistan's future. Khan did not waste any time in approaching the IMF for the country's second economic bailout in five years.

But the US, one of the IMF's biggest donors, raised fears that Pakistan would use any bailout money to repay debts to China, a suggestion Pakistan refuted strongly. Another pressing problem greeted Khan at the (Prime Minister's Office [PMO]). How would he get Pakistan off the FATF? The FATF had put Pakistan on the grey list on account of suspicions that some militants are able to game its banking system and further launder money. The US had the power and economic might not only to help Pakistan on the above fronts, but also bolster investment in the Pakistan economy. Releasing the blocked fund against security cooperation with the US was playing behind the mind of the newly elected prime minister. In the past, Khan, while in the Opposition, has been responsible for stoking up anti-Americanism in Pakistani society.[71] That phase seems to be over now. It was time to have a tryst with reality. It was time for Pakistan to reset its ties with the US. Nonetheless, there was one stumbling block. Throughout his political career, Khan had advocated for Pak-US ties based on the principle of mutual respect and dignity. The constant twitter rant of President Trump against Pakistan was playing the spoilsport.

But it was an opportune time for Khan to forget the past and play the present to the advantage of Pakistan. His 'Naya Pakistan' too required him to bring some fresh perspective into the foreign policy domain. Reorienting its foreign policy, especially with regard to the US in solving the Afghan deadlock carried the risk of enhancing friction with the Pakistan military

---

[71]Ali, Idrees, 'Pakistan's Khan talks of U.S. ties, but anti-American rhetoric has many wary,' Reuters, 27 July 2018, https://www.reuters.com/article/us-pakistan-election-usa-analysis-idUSKBN1KH21N, accessed 16 June 2021.

establishment. Historically, the Pakistan military has enjoyed highhandedness in the foreign policy of Pakistan. And at the time, when the Afghan crisis was at its peak, it was impossible for the military establishment to give unrestricted leeway to Khan to redefine the contours of the Pak-US ties. Khan knew well that he would not get a clean slate to retune the Pakistan-US ties, as per his vision. Nevertheless, the Pakistan military too knew that the bilateral ties need realignment in light of the growing attack of President Trump. It was also imperative to counter the growing perception of Pakistan as a terror-friendly state. Being in the bad books of the US would not serve the interest of Pakistan. The core question here was, 'Who will make the first move?' President Trump and his Pakistani counterpart did not make an ideal beginning of their friendship with exchange of barbs against each other over social media.

There was no doubt that the two countries needed each other. The US knew well that without Pakistan's support, there would be no exit from Afghanistan. On the other hand, Pakistan also needs the US for the revival of its struggling economy. It needs the IMF, World Bank and Asian Development Bank to improve its economy, and the US has considerable leverage in all these institutions. Pakistan cannot antagonize the US anymore with inaction on the Afghan front. And Washington cannot ignore Pakistan anymore due to its strategic relevance in the context of the Afghan war. They cannot be incommunicado about the Afghan war in a changed geopolitical and geostrategic environment. However, it was going to be a relationship of mutual compulsion, than one based on trust and choice. It was strategically compelling for both the countries to reset their bilateral ties. There was no doubt that Khan was better placed than his predecessor with the glamour and panache to bolster ties with the US. The real challenge before the Pakistani policymakers was to smoothen the rough edges before the relationship begins to show some promise.

President Trump knew that in 'Naya Pakistan', under the leadership of Imran Khan, there lies an excellent opportunity to reset the bilateral ties and further impress upon Pakistan to work out a peace settlement with the Taliban in Afghanistan. He did not lose any time in reigniting back-door diplomacy between Washington and Islamabad. He employed another tactic to put Pakistan under some pressure to play the role of a peace angel in Afghanistan. In July 2018, American officials secretly met Taliban members at their political office in Qatar. This was more to put pressure that the US might bypass Pakistan in establishing communication with the Taliban, directly. This, in turn, would make Pakistan irrelevant, further leading to its marginalization by the US.

Another smart move by the US was to engage Saudi Arabia and the UAE, Pakistan's supporters and friends in the Arab world, to pursue Pakistan. This created considerable pressure on Pakistan. Islamabad had to act this time and they concurred to the long US play to influence the Taliban to join the peace talks. The convergence of Pakistan's and the US's policy on Afghanistan rekindled sincere hope for the first time for resolution of the long and protracted Afghan conflict. The future Afghan stability was made contingent on Pakistan's good behaviour and further employing their leverage to make the Taliban discuss a political settlement with the US authority. President Trump was desperate to fix Afghanistan and ready to walk the extra mile, than the half-hearted attempt made by his predecessors in the White House. On 5 September 2018, Khalilzad joined the US State Department as President Trump's special adviser on Afghanistan. His appointment was crucial to open peace dialogue with the Taliban directly. The president deserves credit for having authorized the peace negotiation between special envoy, Khalilzad, and the Taliban.

After years of discord over Afghanistan, Pakistan started cooperating with the US to move the peace process, with the aim of extricating the US from its longest war. For its part, Pakistan was instrumental in making the Taliban agree to explore a political solution in Afghanistan, and more importantly to share the high table with the US. Pakistan belatedly received some muted recognition for its peace overtures and facilitating the delicate negotiation with the Taliban. On 12 October 2018, talks between the US envoy led by Khalilzad and the Taliban took place in Qatar. Russia hosted separate peace talks in November 2018 between the Taliban and officials from Afghanistan's High Peace Council. The first round of Doha talks was more about breaking the ice and defining the contours of the peace process. The peace talks that US envoy Khalilzad initiated with the Taliban were gaining momentum and broke some initial barriers. For the first time, it was made to believe that a political settlement was possible to end the conflict in Afghanistan. The US kept the pressure over Pakistan for higher cooperation in the peace process as their effort was suboptimal as per the Pentagon officials.

This was understandable, given the fact that Pakistan was refraining from putting all the eggs in one basket. In his interview with Fox News on 18 November 2018, President Trump attacked Pakistan again. 'And we give Pakistan $1.3 billion a year. ...(Laden) lived in Pakistan, we're supporting Pakistan, we're giving them $1.3 billion a year...which we don't give them anymore, by the way, I ended it because they don't do anything for us, they don't do a damn thing for us,' he said.[72] This time Khan had to respond in order to defend Pakistan and refused to be the perennial punching bag for President Trump. Khan fired back, telling the President on Twitter that he 'needs to be informed about historical facts'.[73] Khan said that the US aid to Pakistan was a 'minuscule' $20 billion, while the country lost 75,000 lives and more than $123 billion fighting the US war on terror.

By the end of 2018, the UN put the civilian casualties at 3,804 deaths and 7,189 injured in the fight between the Afghan government, US forces, the Taliban and the new entrant ISIS. The war in Afghanistan drained $45 billion from the US exchequer in 2018 alone, as per most conservative estimates. And there was nothing to cheer about on the poppy front either. The total area under opium poppy cultivation in Afghanistan was estimated at 3,28,000 hectares in 2017 (report released in 2018), a 63 per cent increase of 1,27,000 hectares or more compared to the previous year. This potentially means despite funnelling billions of American dollars, poppy continues to grow and fund the Taliban. The Taliban were growing stronger, organized and more sophisticated in their design and attack. None of these developments was aligned to what President Trump promised to his voters and above all his much-hyped 'America First' policy. Sign of any progress in Afghanistan was sparse and escaping.

The dawn of 2019 witnessed a much-worried Trump. His

---

[72]PTI, 'Everybody in Pakistan knew Bin Laden was there, and we gave them $1.3 billion a year: Trump,' Wion, 19 November 2018, https://www.wionews.com/world/everybody-in-pakistan-knew-bin-laden-was-there-and-we-gave-them-13-billion-a-year-trump-178099, accessed 17 June 2021.
[73]https://twitter.com/imrankhanpti/status/1064556017881686021?lang=en, accessed 18 June 2021.

patience was running out. Frustration was palpable in his public and media outburst, whenever he was grilled about Afghanistan. On 2 January 2019 while disparaging his resigning defence secretary during a cabinet meeting, Trump raised a legitimate question: 'Why didn't America win in Afghanistan?' Trump provided a curt response, 'You can talk about our generals. I gave our generals all the money they wanted. They didn't do such a great job in Afghanistan. They've been fighting in Afghanistan for 19 years. ... I want results.'[74] Slowly, the realization was sinking in the mind of President Trump that the war in Afghanistan is not winnable. It has engulfed two of his predecessors and his credentials too were on the line. Political settlement with the Taliban was the only way forward. And Pakistan is the only country that enjoyed the influence over the Taliban to upgrade the peace process after the initial momentum.

The peace process was progressing well. But it was confronted with two serious threats, which had the potential to derail it. The Taliban were not keen on abjuring violence, rather they were stepping up attacks in Afghanistan to gain more leverage on the peace table. This means that the civilian casualties were on a constant rise. And the black bags containing bodies of US soldiers killed by the Taliban were reaching Washington with an unfailing regularity. It was getting increasingly difficult for Trump to explain the Taliban's approach of 'talk and kill' at the same time. The media was questioning the submission of the US military to the Taliban. Scholars and analysts in Washington who have been following the Afghan war for decades critically questioned the leeway

---

[74]Young, Stephen B., 'Why America Lost in Afghanistan,' *Foreign Policy*, https://foreignpolicy.com/2019/02/05/why-america-lost-in-afghanistan-counterinsurgency-cords-vietnam/, accessed 2 July 2021.

provided to the Taliban, while the peace process was moving. The Taliban were further insistent on their long-stated approach of no dialogue with the Ghani government and even termed it as a puppet regime of the US. A higher cooperation was required from Pakistan than the half-hearted attempt in the ongoing peace process. And it was an opportune time for Pakistan to make a kill by riding their position of advantage. Saddled with the grim Afghan reality, President Trump extended an invitation to Khan for a talk on 22 July 2019 at the White House.

By accommodating the Pakistan PM's visit, the US has sent a message to Islamabad that the door is open to improve the relationship and build an enduring partnership for the future. This was even when the security assistance remained suspended. Pakistan has facilitated contacts to the Taliban, and met some of the critical milestones with regard to the peace process. The peace process was at a critical juncture and the White House aspired for enhanced cooperation from Pakistan. Pakistan was encouraged to use their full leverage in the peace endeavour and impress the Taliban to abjure violence, till there is an affirmative conclusion of the peace process. The White House also used the visit as an opportunity to incentivize Pakistan to use its leverage in order to step up the momentum of the peace process, which was stuck in its critical stage. A considerable amount of blocked security aid was released even before Khan boarded his return flight to Islamabad.

This was on the top of the US government's listing of the separatist Balochistan Liberation Army as a terrorist group and the IMF's agreement to lend Pakistan a badly needed $6 billion, announced as a precursor to Khan's meeting at the White House. The White House officials did not spare any time in suggesting that more grants are in the offing for Pakistan. Such grants are subjected to the fulfilment of roles and expectations set by the White House. The most coveted reward, however, was the expression of interest by President Trump to mediate the seven-decade-old Kashmir conflict between India and Pakistan. India was quick enough to throttle the bid much to the dismay of Pakistan, keeping only the blocked security aid as the adhesive for Pakistan to advance the peace momentum in Afghanistan.

US officials touted the meeting between Trump and Khan as a critical moment for both sides, while playing down perceptions that the US is rewarding Pakistan or, as Islamabad wants broadening bilateral ties beyond the current focus on terrorism issues. Khan boarded his return flight with his self-admission of euphoria, like winning the World Cup for the second time. He promised to play an extended role in the Afghan peace process by encouraging the Taliban to abjure violence and accept a peace deal in the overall interest of Afghanistan. However, it was not known if the influential Pakistan army was on the same page. Historically, the Pakistan army has remained closer to the Taliban and a web of other terrorist networks and further employed them as a strategic lever for fanning unrest, aimed at neighbours. It was to be seen if Khan would walk the talk or the Pakistan army would muscle the peace process and let the status quo extend in Afghanistan to tire out the US. After all, the Pakistan military was all set to gain from the extension of the status quo in Afghanistan, both financially and strategically. Prolonging the peace process suited their interests better than settling the same.

On the part of the US, their dependence on the same Pakistan, rejected multiple times from playing the double game in Afghanistan, was another U-turn. Washington for years blamed Pakistan for providing a haven to insurgency, making it impossible to defeat the Taliban. In an attempt to coax Pakistan to support America's Afghan war, the US ramped up military and economic aid, but Pakistan saw it as against its interests to fight the Taliban to the fullest and ties soured every now and then. Besides playing its part in convening the peace process, Pakistan was never found to be serious about fixing Afghanistan. President Trump was found no different than his predecessor in dealing with Pakistan. He too was slipping into the set groove of his predecessor, when it came to dealing with Pakistan.

The former chief of intelligence of Afghanistan, Rahmatullah Nabil, once suggested, 'If you eliminate 15–30 tier one Taliban leaders that were living in Quetta of Pakistan, and place another 15–30 Pakistan Generals on the sanctions list, the Afghan problem would be solved, for the immediate future. Please explain how one wins a war without hitting an enemy's command and control? The Taliban command and control is in Quetta, which you have left untouched. If the Pakistan Government wants, NDS can share the GPS coordinate of these leaders.'[75] It was reported in the media that Amrullah Saleh, the former National Directorate of Security (NDS) chief (and the current Vice President), had shared the presence of Taliban militants and their point-wise locational details with former President Musharraf in a bilateral security meeting. He had further explained to Musharraf as to how the ISI is helping the Taliban in planning and executing terror attacks in Afghanistan, with tangible evidence.[76] This peeved President

---

[75]Naibkhel, Farhad, 'Reactions over President Trump's Remarks on Afghanistan,' *Afghanistan Times*, 23 July 2019, http://www.afghanistantimes.af/reactions-over-president-trumps-remarks-on-afghanistan/, accessed 5 July 2021.

[76]'Interview: Amrullah Saleh, Return of the Taliban,' https://www.pbs.org/wgbh/

Musharraf along with his army. After a few months, the intelligence chief was asked to leave by the former President Karzai for the reason better known to him. A large number of top Afghan leadership have confided that targeting the top leadership of the Taliban is a better strategy for making them join the peace process rather than relying on untrustworthy Pakistan to do the job in the interest of the US.

Since the resumption of direct US-Taliban talks, Khalilzad has made no secret of his rush to reach an agreement. After nine rounds of direct negotiations, spanning over 10 months, the US and the Taliban finally reached an agreement in principle. According to the terms that were reported, Washington would cut the presence of US troops from Afghanistan against an assurance that Taliban-controlled areas will not be used by transnational terrorists to plot attacks against Americans. Khalilzad, a former US Ambassador to Afghanistan and the Trump administration's point-man on the Afghan conflict, explained to TOLO News that over 5,000 US troops would depart from five bases within 135 days of the agreement's signing. As his interview was being aired, Kabul witnessed a huge blast. The Taliban said it was behind the attack, which used a bomb strapped to a tractor to kill at least 16 people and injure at least another 119. The target was a residential compound housing foreigners, which was just outside the city's heavily fortified Green Zone. The attack—the third in as many days—highlighted fears that the US negotiations with the Taliban will not end the daily violence in Afghanistan and its terrible toll on civilians.

There were media reports that even after the closure of the formal channel of peace overture, the informal channel

pages/frontline/taliban/interviews/saleh.html, accessed 2 July 2021.

of peace talks with the Taliban were kept open. Khalilzad kept persuading the Pakistan army to arm-twist the Taliban and made them accept some of the terms and conditions that the US placed under the peace deal, the primary being a temporary ceasefire. This would have made the optics look good and further enable President Trump to placate the domestic audience. The international media scrutiny could also have been managed to a certain degree. President Trump is known for springing surprises all the time. And he does it with such consummate ease. At a time, when the world was contemplating the future of Afghanistan after the cancellation of the peace deal, President Trump in a press briefing after the end of his two-day visit (24–25 February 2020) announced that he is expecting a peace agreement with the Taliban very soon to formally end the war in Afghanistan.[77] This stunned all, especially the top leadership of the Indian government. The US Special Representative Khalilzad and the head of the Taliban, Mullah Abdul Ghani Baradar, signed the potentially historic peace agreement in Doha, Qatar on 29 February 2020, where the two sides spent months away from the glare of the international media hashing out the details. Under the terms of the peace agreement, the US committed to withdrawing all its military forces, including those of allies, within 14 months. The US was expected to reduce its troops to 8,600, in the first 135 days, from five bases located within Afghanistan. The rest of the forces were expected to leave within the remaining nine and a half months. The Afghan government was expected to also release up to 5,000 Taliban prisoners, as a gesture of goodwill against the release of 1,000 Afghan

---

[77]Kar, Sharmita, 'Trump India Visit Day 2: "Everybody Happy About US-Taliban Peace Deal," Says President Trump at Press Briefing,' India.com, 25 February 2020.

officials lying under the custody of the Taliban. The Taliban, on its part, agreed to negotiate with the Afghan government for a long-term political settlement after vehemently opposing any dialogue. Even though the much-awaited ceasefire was not explicitly mentioned in the press coverage, there was a tacit understanding about the same between both parties.

And the Taliban did not attack any target in the following week. This not only generated good press for the Taliban but also ignited peace hopes, though potently for the first time. The swapping of prisoners was the bone of contention between the US and the Afghan government. President Ghani after being neglected by the Trump administration in the ongoing peace negotiation was not in a mood to warm up to the peace deal. While keeping the media optic and presentation right, he put a spanner in the work. 'The Government of Afghanistan has made no commitment to free 5,000 Taliban prisoners,' President Ghani told reporters on 1 March 2020, a day after the peace accord was signed in Doha. He further reiterated that the Government of US was no authority to make such promises on behalf of a sovereign country that has an elected government as well as a functioning parliament. However, after weeks of pressure by the US, President Ghani signed a decree to facilitate the release of Taliban prisoners languishing in various Afghan jails. Consequently, the first batch of 100 Taliban prisoners was released on 8 April 2020. The process is in progress till today. The Taliban have made it amply clear that there will be no intra-Afghan dialogue, unless 5,000 Taliban prisoners are released under the signed peace deal. In the meanwhile, the Taliban continue to attack Afghanistan intermittently to keep the pressure on the top leadership of Kabul to expedite the release of prisoners. The peace process still looks fragile and one doubts if this would hold in the long term.

The US arrived in Afghanistan to weed out the Taliban and irreversibly degrade their capabilities in Afghanistan. A series of lofty goals such as nation building, eradicating poppy, enhancing the capacity of the Afghan military, fixing governance, etc. were added on with the passage of time. This further complicated the already complex Afghan war. None of these conditions have been met on the ground. The planned US withdrawal is an admittance of failure. Most Afghans with money have an exit plan; and the rest face the evolving future with fear and fraught. The sudden movement towards ending the war in Afghanistan in the backdrop of the peace process was not entirely due to President Trump's determination to withdraw all US troops from that country. American negotiations with the Taliban are driven by a painful admission buried in the Pentagon's most recent report on the war. Quietly, it acknowledged that after 19 years of struggle, the investment of $2 trillion, the loss of 2,400 Americans and 20,000 wounded, and the sacrifice of millions of military families, the war is at an impasse.

The US has achieved precisely nothing in Afghanistan. It may have generated vast amounts of data in terms of the number killed but the military operation has largely proven counterproductive and led to a resurgent Taliban in Afghanistan. The Taliban are on their strongest plank, after being bombed out of Afghanistan in November 2001. They control more than half of Afghanistan and are seriously threatening to take over Kabul. They have further moved out from their traditional bastion of southern provinces and registered their sphere of influence all over Afghanistan. Their attacks even extend to the heart of Kabul with consummate ease. There are many reasons behind the inevitable failure of the US forces towards neutralizing the Taliban. Time and again, NATO military personnel in Afghanistan have claimed to be chasing a lost cause in Afghanistan. The safe sanctuaries of the terrorists were nestled in the tribal belts of Waziristan, on the other side of the Durand Line that separates Afghanistan from Pakistan. It was a ripple effect that was being addressed in Afghanistan. How can one rely on a strategy that gives free licence to the US forces to go in for the complete kill on the Afghan side of the border, leaving the ever-doubtful and reluctant Pakistan army to deal with the Taliban on the other side? The Taliban resting in the Pak-controlled side of the Durand Line should have been dealt with an iron hand to make any sense of the war on terror.

A large section of the security forces, in informal discussions, was also candid about the flawed and haggard military strategies employed by the US and NATO. It is well-known how a British General lost his job in 2009, when his personal e-mail leaked such reality to the international media.[78] General Stanley A. McChrystal of the US Army raised serious questions with regard to the military strategy adopted by the US in Afghanistan. He went to the extent of questioning the US leadership over their overall Afghanistan strategy. He may have lost his highly prized military job due to his outburst, but there was a considerable section within the US forces subscribing to his assessment. The fate of the war was a foregone conclusion. The chorus of the US chasing a fault and flawed military strategy in Afghanistan only grew louder with time. Six months before, in August 2017, President Trump announced that he would send additional troops to Afghanistan. General John Nicholson, the then commander of the US forces in Afghanistan, testified before the Senate Armed

---

[78] Sarkar, Sujeet, *In Search of a New Afghanistan*, Niyogi Books, 2012.

Services Committee that 'the current security situation in Afghanistan is a stalemate.'[79] Five months later, Laurel Miller, who was the acting special representative for Afghanistan and Pakistan till June 2017, said in an interview, 'I don't think there is any serious analyst of the situation in Afghanistan who believes that the war is winnable'.[80] A year after that, Lisa Curtis, Deputy Assistant to the President and Senior Director for South and Central Asia at the National Security Council, told an audience at the US Institute of Peace that 'no one believes that there is a military solution to this conflict'.[81]

The US also did very little to tame the ISI to stay away from strategic matters concerning Afghanistan. The role of ISI in fanning Taliban unrest is well-documented in the public domain. The US officials, including its three presidents have widely criticized the complicity of ISI in fuelling the Taliban insurgency in various parts of Afghanistan. Every time, the top leadership of Afghanistan, including the incumbent President Ghani briefed the White House about the heavy-handedness of ISI, the US leadership failed to work on the actionable intelligence. While a war on terror was being carried out by the US on the soil of Afghanistan, the perpetrators of terrorism were being offered safe sanctuaries and political mentoring on the other side. ISI continued to march with their time-tested and dividend-yielding policy of 'double game' in Afghanistan. And when the US really wanted to put a break on ISI, it was perhaps too late. Cutting the aid was again too

---

[79]Glaser, John and John Muller, 'Overcoming Inertia: Why It's Time to End the War in Afghanistan,' CATO Institute, 13 August 2019, https://www.cato.org/policy-analysis/overcoming-inertia-why-its-time-end-war-afghanistan, accessed 2 July 2021.

[80]Ibid.

[81]Ibid.

little. The ISI should have been dealt with an iron hand right from the word go, after the US marines landed in Afghanistan to vanquish the Taliban. Islamabad, on its part, also played the China card well to blunt the US pressure for toeing its line in Afghanistan. The dependence on the same Pakistan to pursue the peace process by three successive US presidents, including incumbent Trump, to varying degrees, only portrayed them in a good light, and in more ways than one absolved them of their evil act in Afghanistan. President Trump in a way tried to toe a different path and throttled Pakistan for quite some time. However, like his predecessor, he too ended up distributing the 'Good Samaritan' certificate to Pakistan in order to lure it to solve the Afghan deadlock.

A majority of Americans turned against the war a long time ago, viewing it as a futile and expensive conflict with little to show for all. But a significant proportion of Americans simply cannot envision a complete US military departure from Afghanistan, and most of them buy into the conventional wisdom that successful counterterrorism policy is impossible without boots on the ground. Even retired General David Petraeus, who failed to win the Afghan war under his leadership, but accredited with the success in Iraq, wants his successor to keep trying in Afghanistan. He still believes that America's longest military war should extend and exit is not an option. According to him, victory is possible.

It remains doubtful if the Afghan forces can survive the Taliban attack without combat air support help from the US. There are lurking fears that the rudimentary Afghan forces cannot protect the country from the onslaught of the Taliban for a long time. Eventually, Kabul may fall to the Taliban within a few years, if not a year without the US support. It would be a disaster for the reputation and credibility of the US if Kabul fell in a manner similar to Saigon in 1975.

Money down the drain?

This brings up the question of the billions of American dollars poured by the US military to build the nascent armed forces, especially the Afghan army and police. The Taliban are nonchalantly preying upon Afghan cadets at their isolated checkpoints and executing a wide range of bomb operations deep in the heart of Kabul at their free will. The Afghan military forces are facing high casualty, and the Afghan government refuses to disclose the numbers. The largely understrength and untrained Afghan armed forces are sitting ducks in such an environment, and there is not much they can do but help the Afghan government manage what seems like an ongoing stalemate.

Afghanistan's security sector is perennially confronted with lack of training, equipment and technology, attrition, and growing insider attacks. Given the high frequency and spread of the Taliban attack, the Afghan security forces are overstretched and, in most cases, exhausted. Afghan forces have been fighting hard to stop the Taliban's expansion. Questions have been raised about the lack of robust and inspiring military leadership, the timely supply of logistics and endemic corruption in the armed forces. And on top of it, filling the casualties gaps is a constant challenge, as the security sector job is not a priority for the bulk of the Afghan youths. SIGAR has repeatedly pointed out these issues in its report. It has been a gargantuan task to create capable Afghan security forces; one that the US command cavalierly assured was within their capabilities. It proved not to be so. In his memoir in 2010,

President George W. Bush acknowledged, 'The task turned out to be even more daunting than I anticipated.'[82]

Take just one recent illustration. American taxpayers supported the gift of 159 Blackhawk UH-60 helicopters to the Afghans, at a cost of over $7 billion. Most of the choppers have already been delivered—but there are not enough trained Afghan pilots to fly the helicopters. The country doesn't even have enough trained Afghan aircraft engineers to maintain the aircraft. As a result, US contractors will be hired to keep the choppers flying, at a cost of over a couple of billions. And the aircraft will only fly from limited secure locations, because contractors are not allowed to work in dangerous places (i.e., where the Afghan helicopters will be needed to transport troops, ammunition and the wounded). It also turns out that Afghan generals are misusing the helicopters they have, carting around VIPs and ordering other non-combat sorties. Astonishingly, the US command resorted to imposing fines of $100,000 per flight hour on Afghan generals in a last-ditch effort to stop the malpractice. It did not stop, so the fines were raised to $150,000 for every hour the choppers were sent off on non-essential missions. Even though records are available in the public domain, one doubts if even one hour of penalty fee has been collected, after the steep penalty clause was imposed.

There is no end to such misadventure. The direct training by US commanders has been curtailed to a larger extent after insider attack influenced by the Taliban ideology. The army-to-army contact has been kept at a bare minimum in light of the growing attack, and more importantly widening trust

---

[82]Miller, Paul D. 'Bush on nation building and Afghanistan,' *Foreign Policy,* https://foreignpolicy.com/2010/11/17/bush-on-nation-building-and-afghanistan/, accessed 2 July 2021.

deficit. In such circumstances, the cost as well as quality of the military training is seriously questionable. It is worth remembering that handing over responsibility to a competent and trustworthy government that is able to provide security and justice for its citizens became the whole point of the war in Afghanistan. The ground conditions do not even remotely align with the laid goals. It rather appears more threatening than pre-2001. A 2019 report from SIGAR states that despite 18 years of trying to quell the Taliban insurgency and to build an independent and competent Afghan government, army and police force, 'Afghanistan remains one of the world's poorest and most dangerous countries,' with the security forces still 'not able to protect the population from insurgents in large parts of the country.'[83]

Wherever the blame lies, the American failure to stand up to the Afghan security forces will inevitably cast a dark shadow over Afghanistan's future, as it struggles to provide security to its own people. There are budgetary challenges too in maintaining security in Afghanistan. The Pentagon estimated Afghanistan's security funding requirement to be around $6.5 billion for the fiscal year 2020, of which the Afghan government pledged to cover only $500 million. This stands out to be a meagre 7.69 per cent of the overall security expenses of the Afghan government. And that too when the Afghan security forces remain grossly inadequate when compared with the gravity and the magnitude of the security challenges. How the security forces will stand on their own when the US stops doling out the green packs running into billions is difficult to comprehend. Perhaps it needs to be mentioned here that the $6.5 billion is on top of an annual $45 billion of military

---

[83] Aamir, Omer, 'Analysis of Afghan Situation,' SSRN, 24 March 2020, https://papers.ssrn.com/sol3/papers.cfm?abstract_id=3545132, accessed 2 July 2021.

expenses incurred by the US directly.

The nation-building effort too hardly produced any tangible dividends. A legitimate Afghan economy barely exists. The nation's total merchandise exports in 2018 was well short of a billion dollars. At present, international aid accounts for approximately 60–70 per cent of all public expenditure, making the government in Kabul heavily dependent on foreign aid for running the show in Afghanistan. All international efforts to make aid conditional on Afghan performance have so far met with only limited success. The public services are weak and excluded vast segments of Afghan citizens, especially those nestled in the remote and inaccessible regions of Afghanistan. The recurrent cut of foreign aid is further impeding the quality and reach out of public services. Corruption remains a serious problem with Afghanistan indicted as fifteenth most corrupt country, as per the latest ranking of Transparency International. Governance challenges have plagued the counterinsurgency operations too. The Afghan national police are largely viewed as corrupt, incompetent and often loyal to the regional warlords. The criminal justice system is perennially weak and almost non-existent, crippling the legal and institutional mechanisms for speedy prosecution of insurgents and criminals. The status of the criminal justice system has failed to pick up despite wholehearted efforts of multiple players, including USAID and UN agencies.

Poppy cultivation shows no sign of coming down. Since 2002, the US has invested over $9.6 billion in counternarcotics programmes, to no avail. Afghanistan continues to remain the global leader in poppy cultivation. In 2019, even if the country witnessed a decline of 28 per cent in the net sown area, the potential pure opium production increased by 21 per cent to 6,700 metric tonnes, when compared with the figures of 2018.

Poppy has remained stable at higher levels in 2019 and going into 2020. The newly released data mocks the whole poppy eradication campaign of the US military. The US efforts have proven counterproductive and swelled the Taliban coffers for a more organized and coordinated fight with the Afghan army. It has been widely accepted that the Taliban insurgency cannot be defeated so long as the poppy persists.

Afghan democracy is likewise on life support, with the controversial presidential elections throwing another power-sharing government with its legitimacy severely contested within the country. The unity government arrangement worked out by the White House in the past too failed to deliver in Afghanistan. The government was found neither united in its vision, nor in conduct. The unity government of President Ghani witnessed a dual stream of political ideology and vision, derailing the development process due to lack of coherence and convergence. Both camps folded under the fabric of an uneasy unity government. They spent their position and power in attacking each other, rather than jointly dealing with the challenges that were engulfing Afghanistan. The first term of the unity government was full of indecision and policy inertia. The White House remained a mute spectator to the drama of the unity government unfolding in Kabul. The US again played its role through diplomacy and aid cut to cobble the second instalment of the unity government after a prolonged standoff between President Ghani and his estranged ally Abdullah Abdullah. Can Afghanistan unite under the new president? Can it survive its gross failures in governance and the rule of law, poppy eradication and economic development without receiving billions of dollars in US civil aid? A detailed analysis of the civil aspect of the war shows that all indicators point towards the equivalent of a failed State.

The White House expected that all its military efforts would have at least won them civilian and political goodwill in Afghanistan. Ghani was not on talking terms with Trump; so much so that, according to insiders, the former's calls to the White House largely remained unanswered. This is an extension of a similar status quo between Karzai and Obama during their last few months in office. There has been no end to the awry aerial attack by the US Air Force in Afghanistan. The spate of aerial bombings in the civilian areas of the restive south and eastern provinces, which led to large-scale deaths of civilian population including women and children, fomented huge public resentment. Barring a few incidents, the US forces failed to fix responsibility for those awry air attacks. Civilian death is a deeply emotive issue amongst ordinary Afghans and every such awry air raid has turned the civilian populace against the US military.

The premise of killing the Taliban fighters hiding in community locales, through air raids, cut no ice with the public and the political leadership of Afghanistan. And if that was not enough, the obnoxious comment of President Trump to finish the Afghan war in a week did the rest of the damage. During a White House meeting with Pakistani Prime Minister Imran Khan, Trump said, 'If we wanted to fight a war in Afghanistan and win it, I could win that war in a week. I just don't want to kill 10 million people. Does that make sense to you? I don't want to kill 10 million people. I have plans on Afghanistan that, if I wanted to win that war, Afghanistan would be wiped off the face of the earth. It would be gone. It would be over in literally 10 days. And I don't want to go that route.'[84] This was

---

[84]Ward, Alex, 'Trump says he could wipe Afghanistan off face of the earth in 10 days,' Vox, 22 July 2019, https://www.vox.com/world/2019/7/22/20704248/trump-afghanistan-10-days-war, accessed 17 June 2021.

hugely criticized in Afghanistan from all quarters, including the top political leadership. The US and Afghan relationship has turned out to be a love-hate one in Afghanistan, with no option of a divorce.

There are two streams of thought in the White House with regard to the Afghan war. Proponents of continuing the war in Afghanistan maintain that the US must fight the war till it achieves a clear victory because anything less would derogate the steep costs in blood and money that it has already devoted to the mission. However, they advocate presence of light military footprints along with a lean air power, including drone fleet, to counter any overt aggression of the Taliban to capture Kabul or any other strategic province. Concerns about their global image and reputation have been their primary impediment to withdraw. Inadvertently, they want to justify the sunk cost and sacrifice by continuing in Afghanistan.

The second camp is keen on working out a political settlement with the Taliban through the propped-up prime minister Khan and make a face-saver exit deal from Afghanistan. President Trump has switched over from the former camp to the latter last year, when he made the peace overture to the Taliban. The Americans are stuck with a tar baby after their hasty entry into Afghanistan almost 20 years ago. They would love to declare victory and run for the exit. But they cannot. In that context, President Trump's strategy of harping on the failure of his predecessor, making a face-saving exit deal, running away from Afghanistan and not looking back too has failed in Afghanistan.

Unfortunately, the botched-up Vietnam war draws a tragic parallel with today's US war in Afghanistan. In Vietnam, Washington wasted 58,000 lives for nothing. In Afghanistan, the US has lost more than 2,400 troops, and still counting, for nearly nothing. In 1973, policymakers in Washington were counting on the Army of the Republic of Vietnam (ARVN) to hold off communist forces. In 2019, the US expected the weak Afghan security forces to hold off a combined threat consisting of both the Taliban and ISIS. Back in 1973, North Vietnamese forces occupying parts of South Vietnam neither disarmed nor withdrew. It would be a colossal mistake to assume that under any foreseeable peace deal, the Taliban, controlling more provinces of Afghanistan than at any point since 2001, would agree to disarm. In a final insult, just as the Saigon government was excluded from US negotiations with the North Vietnamese, the Ghani government in Kabul too has been excluded from US negotiations with the Taliban. In the Vietnam war, the US got commitments from North Vietnam in return for its withdrawal. But once US troops were gone, North Vietnam reneged on those commitments and invaded South Vietnam. The political settlement-cum-peace deal floated by the US relies heavily on the anticipated good behaviour of the Taliban—which has never come, since its formation.

Could Afghanistan become another Vietnam? The questions may be premature now. But they are not irrelevant, given the state of the Afghan war and scars of the US defeat in Southeast Asia. Is the US facing another stalemate on the other side of the world? Like Vietnam, the US intervention seems to produce another black hole of geopolitical instability, which one doubts would ever be sealed or healed.

In various ancient Indian tales, the aggressive kings would capture small kingdoms by killing people and wreaking havoc in order to avert potential future threats. They would then leave other people to clean up the mess. That description applies to the US, especially when it dives into misguided war. In Vietnam, the US smashed up things and human beings with abandon, leaving others to clean up the mess. Afghanistan looks like following suit. Sooner or later!

Had the US negotiated with the Taliban in 2003, 2009 or 2017, it could hardly have got a worse deal than it stands to get today. Was there a better way to get Osama bin Laden with a light military action and little more patience? Was a different approach required to deal with Pakistan and its powerful army? Did the US stretch its Afghan goal more than what was achievable? There are more questions than answers. Yet, with over 2,400 American troops killed and more than $2 trillion squandered in an attempt to fix one of the most volatile countries on earth, the US is further than ever from building a better Afghanistan. It would leave a far worse Afghanistan than it took over in 2001.

5

The UK's Helmand Misadventure

The British military chose the unruly Helmand to display their heroics against the Taliban, partly to erase the stain of Basra (Iraq) and retain the closest possible link with their all-weather ally, the US. They ended up turning a silent and sleeping province into a volatile volcano spurring the Taliban movement across the entire southern Afghanistan. What led to their pathetic show once again, after Basra?

In a historic moment in the Afghan desert Helmand, Britain lowered its flag in Camp Bastion on 26 October 2014 in an end of military operations ceremony signifying the finish of the longest and most torturous British military campaign in modern times. To mark the occasion, Prime Minister David Cameron had to say some encouraging words about the longest military mission for the British taxpayers and the marines who gave it a fight with the Taliban in

Helmand. Unlike his predecessors, Cameron was known for his politically astute and vigilant speaking, especially on matters pertaining to war against terrorism in Afghanistan, while being at 10 Downing Street. He awfully overstretched his political brief in claiming that British combat troops accomplished their mission after 13 years of fierce fighting in Afghanistan. The then defence secretary Michael Fallon was also toeing the line of his boss.

He told the BBC that troops were coming home with their 'heads held high', having helped make Afghanistan a 'much better place'.[85] He added that the country was no longer a 'safe haven' for the extremist group al-Qaeda and the Afghans now had a 'chance of a better future'. But he kept everyone in a fog by saying that there was 'no guarantee' that Afghanistan would 'be safe and stable forever', but the Afghan government now had 300,000 soldiers and police officers to defend. However, his military point man Brigadier Rob Thomson, the senior-most British officer in Helmand, was found guarded in his response, when asked if UK had won or lost the war, after the conclusion of the UK's military mission 'Operation Herrick' in Afghanistan on 26 October 2014. He said that in today's wars there is not a simple 'defeat' or 'victory' like there was with the Second World War. Deep inside, he knew that the British war on terror in Afghanistan was nothing more than an academic closure, and did not resonate around the claims made by the then Prime Minister Cameron.

The British people were certainly expecting more affirmative responses from their political and military leaders. After all, the war against terrorism was massive in blood and money—the loss of 453 service personnel and more than £27 billion

---

[85]'Troops' Afghan sacrifice never forgotten, David Cameron says', BBC News, 27 October 2014, https://www.bbc.com/news/uk-29782465, accessed 2 July 2021.

spent. Five thousand more British soldiers were wounded, with many hundreds of them losing their limbs or mutilated in other life-changing ways. And almost all psychologically battered. Afghanistan will remain with them for the rest of their lives. Despite funnelling huge cash coupled with troop loss, the frontline soldiers never had any sense that the British army was in control of the situation or even remotely close to winning it.

After 13 years of unabated war, is Afghanistan a better place and has British security improved? The public sentiment in the UK was not echoing the war fantasy of their prime minister; rather they were depicting a jaundiced view. The BBC telephone poll of 1,000 UK adults, carried out between 24–26 October 2014 found that 68 per cent believed that the war in Afghanistan was not worthwhile. About 42 per cent felt that Britain was 'less safe' as a result of the 13-year-long campaign. And a decisive 58 per cent respondents did not feel that the presence of the UK military aided Afghan stability and security at all. After 13 years of relentless military operations and colossal expenditure coupled with a heavy death toll, the British were no nearer to victory over the Taliban. Nor could they claim to have brought good governance and security to the province of Helmand. A few anonymous British commanders confided to the media that the influence of the British military was never felt beyond the range of their machine-guns surrounding the highly fortified Camp Bastion in Laskhar Gah, the capital of Helmand where most of the UK soldiers were based. A majority of them confided that they held tiny areas of influence, barely some 500 meters from their military bases, within Helmand.

The end of British combat operations was announced on Sunday (26 October 2014), which is a working day in

Afghanistan, with Camp Bastion handed over to the Afghan military. As British forces left their watchtowers, their Afghan counterparts were left to guard Bastion and fight the Taliban on their own. A fight that the British military failed to win with all their military might and precision, ably backed by uninterrupted flow of money from London. The exit plan was carefully drawn up over several months ahead of what was called as D-day in military parlance, the departure of all military personnel. The British military did not take any chances. Amid high threat perception that the Taliban would resort to attack, the British patrolled the skies like never before. The US fast jets, armed drones and attack helicopters were doing the sorties in tandem to thwart any remote possibility of a Taliban-led attack. In all, around 300 British soldiers and more than 500 US Marines departed in a cautiously choreographed fleet of 18 flights flying everyone to a US airbase in neighbouring Kandahar province, in transition to their exit from Afghanistan.

Getting it wrong

As before midday on Monday (27 October 2014) the final wave of UK helicopters left Camp Bastion for Kandahar, and perhaps for the last time, the hyperactive British media started doing the anatomy of the UK's Afghan war. The Afghan analysts were not to be left behind. The latter saw the UK's withdrawal as a ploy to avert the mounting fatality and largely looming defeat in Helmand. Under the NATO's declaration, the UK found the perfect cover to put their faulty and haggard Afghan military mission to rest. The legacy of Britain's involvement in Afghanistan too was complex, and anything but gratifying. Perhaps it needs to be mentioned here that the

Afghan fighters inflicted massive casualties, including large-scale deaths of British soldiers in both the First and Second Anglo-Afghan Wars fought in 1839 and 1878, respectively.

This was the second drubbing of the British military after their abysmal patch in Basra, Iraq, in recent history. British forces, hailed as one of the best in the world, had suffered 'heavy and tragic' losses in one of the longest military campaigns, in the history of the human race. When it comes to hitting precise targets, Britain's Armed Forces are second to none in this world. They are as good as any, and often better than the rest. So, what went wrong with one of the most powerful military in this world? The first and foremost question arises about their very engagement with the Afghan war. The UK had no cardinal reason for taking the Taliban head-on in Afghanistan; unlike their all-weather ally, the US. The threat emanating from the Taliban via the al-Qaeda on the soil of UK, was not even a secondary premise. The primary reason for the top leadership of Britain to deploy the marines in Afghanistan was to demonstrate to Washington that Britain remained its principal ally and the military bond is unconditional.

Senior figures within the British army had their own reasons for supporting military action in Afghanistan. Stained and battered by the humiliating British retreat from Basra in 2007, they saw the continuity with their combat mission in Afghanistan as a means of restoring their tarnished credibility, especially with their disillusioned US allies. The Afghan battle was the perfect pitch to reclaim the lost glory in Iraq. They viewed the Afghan war as a platform to redeem their pride and valour. And they also had to win it to justify their unbridled ability to stand with the US military, irrespective of their own merit. They kept expanding the objectives of their military mission time and again, in their bid to stay the course. Even the powerful opposition in London was not brave enough to challenge the continuous presence of the British military in this distanced and prolonged war in Afghanistan. Afghanistan occupied the top priorities of successive governments' foreign affairs in London. They kept pursuing the electorate that violent extremism in Afghanistan poses a threat to the UK's interests and to regional stability, and may claim the lives of thousands of civilians and security personnel. Thus, military boots are required. In fact, they prepared the case for the troop surge in the Afghan war with an unfailing regularity since the inception of the Afghan war.

The overenthusiastic and ambitious British military grossly misread the Afghan situation, especially their base province Helmand right from the start. It was the same Helmand that remained one of the locales of the Anglo-British war in the eighteenth century. History had to repeat itself. This time too, the British military failed to decisively win an Afghan war for the third time in a row. This time though they had the haze and lack of neatness of knowing who had won or who had lost, to escape, unlike the two previous times. The UK was countering a typical catch-22 situation in Afghanistan. Staying the course in this theatre of war would inflict more damage and dent their image further, but leaving would add another blot in their military history, after their escape from Basra (Iraq). Cameron finally resorted to live with the latter.

What drove them to withdraw from Afghanistan? Could they have done differently in Afghanistan? Was it required for the British military to step into Helmand and narrow down their conflict? And was it a case of biting more than they could chew in Helmand? Above all, has their Afghan misadventure served any purpose other than the political imperative of retaining the closest possible links with their all-season ally, the US? There are many questions about the failure of the British military, and a deep probing is required to get to the bottom of their military fiasco in Afghanistan, in general, and Helmand, in particular.

In the aftermath of the 9/11 terrorist attacks, the US accused the Taliban—then the ruling power in Afghanistan—of protecting the mastermind of the attacks, Osama bin Laden and declared an open war. Operation Enduring Freedom was launched on 7 October 2001, following the Taliban's refusal to extradite bin Laden. The US, UK and allies launched military strikes against the al-Qaeda training camps with the objective of weeding out the al-Qaeda and its chief from Afghanistan. The first UK ground troops were deployed to Afghanistan following an operation by 40 Commando Royal Marines to secure the airfield at Bagram (near Kabul). The Northern Alliance forces launched an attack on the city of Kabul on the dawn of 13 November 2001 and made rapid progress against the Taliban. The Taliban were weak after being massively damaged by American and British air strikes. There was no resistance, and Kabul was freed from the clutches of the Taliban in no time. It was a cakewalk, which even the US forces did not expect. The British embassy was reopened in November 2001, indicating the long play of the UK in Afghanistan after the fall of the Taliban. The Taliban were driven out from their last bastion of Kandahar on 7 December 2001. The then British Prime Minister, Tony Blair, hailed it as a victory, calling it 'a total vindication of the strategy we have worked out from the beginning.'[86] He further committed UK's support for long-term stability and reconstruction of Afghanistan. It was a test of the

---

[86]'UK troops in Afghanistan: Timeline of key events,' BBC News, 22 December 2015, https://www.bbc.com/news/uk-35159951, accessed 17 June 2021.

alliance's political will and appetite for the war-ravaged nation. The UK was leading the chart after the US. The UK became part of NATO-led operations, ISAF, in 2002.

This was in addition to the ground forces already assisting the US military in stabilizing Afghanistan. The first contingent of foreign peacekeepers comprised personnel from 18 countries. The forces had a mandate that extended only to helping the Afghans maintain security in Kabul and its surrounding areas. By April 2002, UK forces were concentrated in Kabul, with 1,700 soldiers working alongside other allied units. In January 2004, a British soldier was killed in a suspected suicide attack, the first to be killed in a combat role in the Afghan conflict. The active British media raised some serious questions, including if this was a precursor of a bigger devastation. The top leadership assuaged the media suggesting it as a one-off unfortunate attack rather than a structured insurgency attack.

The British embassy opened the floodgate of development aid to the interim Afghan government through their overseas development arm, Department for International Development (DFID). The goal of the UK in Afghanistan was now stretching beyond weeding out the al-Qaeda and the Taliban. Having achieved its limited aim of punishing the al-Qaeda for 9/11, and dislodging the Taliban from power, their aim overarched into a full-scale military intervention for enhanced security, along with a comprehensive effort to reconstruct a nation riddled with conflicts. Besides fighting insurgency, the scope of the military mission was soon enlarged to winning those elusive Afghan hearts and minds with development bounty, espousing democracy and women's rights, fixing governance along with building a western-style civil society. The list did not end here. The UK military further pitched them as a think tank on poppy eradication efforts in Afghanistan and volunteered to lead the same under the G8 security sector reform process in April 2002. Following the donor's conference in London in 2006, the role was renamed 'partner nation' with the anticipation of the Afghan government taking up greater responsibility. However, the change of title did not bring a change of role at the ground level. The counternarcotics efforts were mandatory to cut the chief source of funds for the Taliban and deny them any chance to regroup. The UK was now donning many hats in Afghanistan.

In January 2006, NATO announced that Britain would lead ISAF in Helmand province in the south of the country with a 3,300-strong force after fresh outbreaks of violence. It was perceived as no less than riding a tiger by the local media. Camp Bastion was built near the provincial capital, Lashkar Gah as the headquarter for 28,000 ISAF personnel. It was built in the desert as the launch pad for thousands of British service personnel stationed in the south. By May 2006, the UK military also assumed the lead for the Helmand provincial reconstruction team paving the way for the large-scale development programme along with training Afghan forces. The role of the British military was articulated well by the then Defence Secretary, John Reid, during his visit to Afghanistan in April 2006. He said, 'We would be perfectly happy to leave [Helmand] in three years without firing one shot.'[87]

Helmand choosing to concentrate all military efforts by Britain surprised even the military experts of the UK. After all, it was no ordinary province. It marked not just the most torturous phase of the British military, but also led to large-

---

[87]Borger, Julian, 'Why we went into Helmand,' *The Guardian*, 23 April 2012, https://www.theguardian.com/world/julian-borger-global-security-blog/2012/apr/23/afghanistan-helmand-deployment, accessed 16 June 2021.

scale death and devastation. Helmand is the heart of Pashtun culture, with a history of nursing hatred against any West-led invasion. Though a backwater of the country, Helmand is the epicentre of domestic opium production. The Taliban were eyeing Helmand to generate big and fast money through the opium trade to finance their resistance against the US invasion. But the lure of Helmand went beyond its opium money. Helmand was at the centre of the Taliban's long-term comeback strategy to expand their reach in the south, after their defeat.

They saw it as a stepping stone to other areas and hoped to make Helmand the first province they 'liberated' from the ISAF. They even dreamt of turning Helmand into a safe haven for leaders based in Waziristan, to save Pakistan from the wrath of the US. Helmand boasts good exit routes across the border to Pakistan or through neighbouring Nimruz province to Iran, and strong supply lines to other parts of Afghanistan. All the provinces surrounding Helmand have a strong Taliban footprint, making it easier for waging a high-intensity conventional war, by calling for extra reinforcements. And it would be extremely difficult for foreign military forces to besiege all of Helmand amid multiple exit routes. Military intelligence downplayed all warnings from the British embassy in Kabul that Helmand was likely to be a very dangerous hotspot. Military intelligence wholly misjudged the danger of sending troops there.

Helmand's population was scattered and highly dispersed along the land, on either side of the Helmand River and its many tributaries. It was very backward, largely lawless and corruption was endemic, with a limited presence of governance. The Taliban-backed drug lords called the shots. There was a single-tarmac road as the sole sign of modern development. As reported by the British military, the bulk of the top provincial officials, including its police chief, were illiterate. It was set to become a terribly tough and the most challenging environment for the British military to tame the Taliban.

Zeroing in on Helmand, about which the British military knew very little, was also conceived as a way of redeeming the army's damaged reputation in the eyes of the Americans. Stabilizing Helmand would be the toughest military assignment in Afghanistan. The British army initially approached Helmand with an inkblot strategy, often referred to as an effective strategy to stabilize volatile regions in military parlance. The strategy calls for subduing a large hostile region with a relatively stable military force. This approach to warfare is actually a tactic. The military force starts by establishing a number of small safe areas dispersed over the region. It then pushes out from each area, extending its control and making the areas larger till they eventually join up, leaving only pockets of resistance. The strategy was quite successful in Africa, countered with civil strife and ethnic conflicts. The British military established small bases all over Helmand with central command and large reinforcements lying at Camp Bastion in Lashkar Gah. The UK's initial approach was not to challenge the Taliban upfront. This was echoing with the original plan of the then ISAF chief commander General Stanley McChrystal. Its mission was to avoid combat and concentrate on protecting the population by providing basic security and fostering development to win the hearts and minds of local Afghans. The Taliban saw this as an opportune moment to suck them into the entire province by waging multiple, but limited wars. It was part of their overall strategy to inflict casualties, tire them out and further throttle all development efforts. Failure after British troops were deployed in Helmand province in 2006 came even more quickly than expected.

The rebellions spread 3,300 military personnel over nine platoons, scattered across the district centres of Helmand. The number of bases of the UK's military stretched to 137 in no time. While being pinned down in small and limited conflicts across multiple locales, the British military were far too scattered and thinly spread out to make any impact on the ground. The strength of the British troops along with their Afghan partners turned out to be insufficient, in any one place to dominate the ground effectively and provide the kind of basic security required to implement the central elements of an effective counter-insurgency approach. The process of development got derailed and nosedived. The so-called unified application of both civil and military power—the slogan of the British military—was not visible on the ground. Repeatedly, urgent cables were sent to London for additional deployments. And the political masters in London obliged them without asking any questions, as the dent in the image of the British military for the humiliation faced in Basra was fresh. And for all practical purposes, there was no option of quitting a mounting war. It would have made the UK look ugly, while NATO's mission was at its mid-stage in Afghanistan. Britain's Task Force in Helmand almost tripled in size, with an all-time high of 9,500 personnel.

But the additional reinforcement was also outstretched by the fast-spreading rebellion spearheaded by the Taliban. The Taliban too were facing the heat. It was time for the Taliban to change the strategy of war in Helmand. After waging a small and limited war against the British military, the Taliban resorted to a protracted and long conventional war in places like Sangin, Majra, Musa Qala, Laskhar Gah, Garmsir, etc. The Taliban would arrive with a large number of fighters and launch full-scale conventional attacks against the ISAF forces at a place and time of their own choice. The war would last for weeks and even months, in some cases. In most of the cases, they would retain control of these places for a considerable period, until driven out by additional deployments from ISAF, and US-supported air strikes from Kabul. The game of capturing and ceding control of key strategic districts and towns by the Taliban continued with an unfailing regularity. This included the seizure of Musa Qala for almost seven months after the controversial withdrawal of the British military in December 2006. It was reported in the Afghan media that the British military had a tacit deal with the Taliban to withdraw their forces from Musa Qala. The Taliban fighters were again forced out of the city of Musa Qala with a comprehensive military campaign code named 'Operation Snake Pit', after nine months of seizure.

The war in Helmand was heading for the worse. At the peak of the campaign in Helmand alone, 9,500 UK troops were stationed at Camp Bastion supported by 600 aircraft and helicopter movements a day. It was the busiest airport of Afghanistan in terms of aircraft movement. The British military resorted to aggressive air strikes to block the advances of the Taliban and inflicted considerable damage. The use of air strikes and heavy weapons rubbled the centres of towns like Sangin, Musa Qala, Majra and wreaked havoc on the lives of the local populations. Bombs ranging from 1,000–5,000 pounds were dropped at regular intervals. Civilian casualties were on the rise, and the local population started leaving the region for safer locales, risking their already fragile livelihoods. British troops in Helmand have killed at least 500 non-combatants. About half of these have been officially admitted and Britain has paid compensation to the victims' families. A quote of a local farmer saying, 'the Taliban do not even have a bakery that they can give bread, but still most people support the Taliban—that's because people are sick of night raids and being treated badly by the foreigners'[88] went viral epitomizing the effect of the night raids and air strikes in Helmand. The British military would often resort to raiding the houses of locals, pulling wives and daughters out of bed.

Night search would continue with the assistance of the Afghan ground forces in an effort to flush out Taliban fighters seeking refuge in the civilian populace. The development process was moving at a snail's pace with the whole military apparatus consumed in the full-fledged war. Air strikes were the only asymmetry that the British military enjoyed over their rival Taliban. And the British military was not in any mood to surrender their sole strength to placate the uprising Helmandis. This alienated the local population to the extent that they started viewing the British military as a foreign invader, and in turn drove them closer to the Taliban. The disenchantment of the local population served as a fecund ground for the Taliban to recruit fresh sergeants to scale up the war further. The local population was not the only 'friend-turned-foe' in the UK list of misery in Helmand. The civil society too questioned as to how the British military could win the hearts and minds of the Helmandis by bombing in their township/villages and consequently driving them out of their houses. The support for the Taliban started growing in Helmand. Little account was taken of growing local dissent and consequent reaction to British occupation that was aggravating death and destruction.

---

[88]Boone, John, 'No friendly waves only hatred for British troops in Afghan town,' *The Guardian*, 23 April 2021, https://www.theguardian.com/world/2010/apr/22/afghanistan-british-troops-hatred, accessed 17 June 2021.

The step up in military operations coincided with a sharp rise in the death toll at both ends. Thirty-nine UK military troops died in 2006, compared with five between 2001 and 2005. There were 42 deaths in 2007 and 51 in 2008. In total, 453 military personnel lost their lives in the Afghan war till their exit from combat operation in Afghanistan. The death rate was much higher than that of the conflict in Iraq. The bloodiest year was 2009, when 108 troops died. Operation Panther's Claw was launched in Helmand, a British-led offensive involving over 3,000 troops in June 2009. Following five weeks of fierce fighting, the Taliban were driven from their stronghold, key strategic crossings were secured and a considerable ISAF presence was established in the area. By 2010, a sizeable number of the strategic crossing and places with considerable influence went back to the Taliban again. More than 100 UK military personnel died in 2010. Helmand was witnessing a seesaw battle right from 2006 to 2010, with no decisive gain for the British military. The UK military was showing signs of fatigue.

The irony was that even the uninterrupted flow of money and machines coupled with the sacrifice of the British soldiers was not winning them any friends in Helmand. The local populace of Helmand was uprising against the presence of British troops in Helmand. The inability of the British military to tame the Taliban was producing a political antibody to repel their presence. Surprisingly, even the local government started questioning the military tactics of the UK for their inability to vanquish the Taliban. On the contrary, their presence had turned Helmand into a violent quagmire, after being a sleeping province for several decades. It was proving counterproductive to the core. The Afghan media too questioned the presence of the British military and wondered if the assembly in large numbers had given a lifeline to the Taliban inadvertently to regroup and revitalize their larger mission in Afghanistan.

The usually taciturn Helmand governor, Gulab Mangal, told a visiting US delegate led by the then US vice president, Joe Biden, in January 2009, that American forces were urgently needed as British security in the volatile Sangin was less than adequate and did not even extend to the town's main bazaar. (According to a cable sent from the US embassy in Kabul.) 'I do not have anything against them [the British] but they must leave their bases and engage with the people,' Mangal said.[89] He did not stop here. In another cable in January 2009, the governor, who had received strong backing from the UK and the US, is reported to have delivered a scathing dressing down to British officials on the state of security in the district of Sangin. 'Stop calling it the Sangin district and start calling it the Sangin base—all you have done here is build a military camp next to the city,' he said.[90] The same cable reported that the British troops told US officials that immediately outside the town 'cowboy country begins'.

The British military was of the opinion that it was even delusional to think that Helmand could be held with a force of 9,500 while all reliable estimates of the minimum needed for a region of that size and population was 30,000 at least. The Government of Afghanistan was holding another view, quite contrary to the British military. The problem was not the lack of troops, according to Governor Mangal. Even if they brought in thousands more, 'they would need a new plan and shift of focus to connect with people,' he told Biden during his

---

[89]HT correspondent (London), 'British Afghan effort criticized in WiKi leaks,' *Hindustan Times*, 3 December 2010.
[90]Sengupta, Kim, 'Key ally in Helmand privately criticised British Policies,' *Independent*, 2 December 2010.

official meeting.[91] At a meeting with Senator John McCain in December 2008, he said he was relieved that US marines were being sent to reinforce the British-led mission in Helmand and related an anecdote in which a woman from Helmand asked him to 'take the British away and give us the Americans.'[92] In another meeting with US officials, Rangin Dadfar Spanta, the then foreign minister, expressed disappointment at the ordering of an extra 2,000 British soldiers to Helmand, arguing 'they were not ready to fight as actively as American Soldiers.'[93] Everyone in Helmand was criticizing their inability to stabilize Helmand after a considerable period of military action.

It was not only the Afghans who criticized the British troops. The British operation also attracted criticism from Dan McNeill, the commander of NATO forces, in 2007–08, for its failure to deal decisively with the drug trade in Helmand. In mid-2007, McNeill said, 'particularly dismayed by the British effort. They had made a mess of things in Helmand, their tactics were wrong, and the deal that London cut on Musa Qala had failed,' of a ceasefire agreement with the Taliban that allowed the British to pull besieged troops out of the town of Musa Qala in late 2006.[94] The decision to 'surge' troops was doomed to fail because the British military was pursuing a wrong strategy in Helmand. Completely disconnected from the locals, they were operating in an island of their own. They lacked the strategy, structures, oversight and culture to converse and make things work.

---

[91]'WikiLeaks cable exposes Afghan contempt for British Military,' *The Guardian*, 2 December 2010.

[92]Suroor, Husan, 'U.K. Afghan mission a failure,' *The Hindu*, 3 December 2010.

[93]'WiKi Leaks cables citicise UK military in Afghanistan,' BBC News, 3 December 2010.

[94]HT correspondent (London), 'British Afghan effort criticized in WiKi leaks,' *Hindustan Times*, 3 December 2010.

While the UK trumpeted its 'comprehensive approach', it was never to be seen working in tandem even 500 metres away from the heavily fortified and patrolled military base camps. The real intent to fight with an apropos strategy was lacking. Brigades were sent on six-month tours, far too short in understanding a war as complex as Helmand. And before they could get a wind of the war, their Helmand tenure was over. Commanding officers seemed to want their stints to be marked by a career-advancing military effort, with little connection to actions before or after. The prime goal of the British military was to provide security to the people, but not more than 5 per cent of their total strength would be on patrol at any given point of time. While the British-led Task Force could cling to the major towns like Sangin, Gereshk and Lashkah Gah, with intermittent gaps, real population security depended on securing the land that stretches between them. And the British military was no way near the task.

There were other important reasons too for the British military failure. Despite mounting casualties, they failed to alter their strategy and their fighters fast both from conventional war to counterinsurgency; and secondly to tailor resources to what was achievable and not what they aspired for. The resources were finite and hence the action too had to be finite. Chasing the Taliban to the last mile and overstretching their resources was not a feasible option in Helmand.

There was very little to cheer about on the development front either. Nonetheless, under the guidance of civilian advisors, the British military made considerable investment in the province of Helmand, but most of them were aimed at arresting the growth of poppy production. The list of development misadventures in Helmand is long. One typical example of this approach was the transport of a huge single electric turbine through 100 miles of hostile Taliban-held territory to the Kajaki dam on the Helmand River, apparently to provide electricity for the region.

The task, involving 1,000 troops, mainly British, was accomplished, but the turbine was never installed, partly because there was no local engineer to operate it, partly because no high-intensity cables existed to transmit the electricity from the dam to southern Helmand. The projects had the elements of winning the support of the local population, but it went haywire tarnishing their image further in the public eye. The projects undertaken under the development campaign were not feasible as very little community opinion was sought in the process of designing them, and the cost-benefit ratio was a disaster. The outcome of the development exercise was miserable, given the resources and human power deployed.

The fact checks on poppy too does not look impressive. British troops were initially deployed in Helmand, under grandiose plans hatched by the then prime minister, Tony Blair, to take on local drug lords whose product ultimately ended up as heroin on the streets of Britain. The larger aim, however, was to give a death blow to the Taliban by cutting off their chief source of finance. But the move faced fierce resistance from a deal of convenience between the district's opium barons—who used to sell the product openly in local markets—and a resurgent Taliban, which profited from the trade. A hope of stamping out the drug trade was quickly abandoned, with British forces fighting a pitched war simply to stop Taliban forces over-running their bases. The war on drugs was converted to war against the Taliban in no time.

Though they had something to show about the progress on the poppy front in the initial years, it did not sustain. The UK boasted that poppy cultivation in the province of Helmand, where they had run the military and development effort since 2006, had fallen considerably since 2008, from an estimated 103,590 hectares net sown area to 75,105 hectares in 2012. Despite the metrics being in favour in Helmand, the UK was in a great hurry to leave the lead role of poppy eradication. With the first sign of success, British officials reassured themselves that they had demonstrated a more 'comprehensive' counternarcotics strategy and now the Afghan leadership should take it forward. By the end of 2012, the UK had all but completely abandoned its involvement in counternarcotics in Afghanistan and was barely on speaking terms with its former partner in the Afghan Ministry of counternarcotics. Forever the optimists, UK officials consoled themselves with the fact that while things were far from ideal on the counternarcotics front, they could not get much worse. Deep inside, the British military knew that opium reduction could not be contained in Helmand with more and more areas slipping under Taliban control.

The transient success provided them the best window to escape the 'crown of thorns'. It was better to leave now, rather than face greater humiliation for their poppy eradication policies later. The critics were proven true. The limited success of opium eradication was short-lived. The opium production in Helmand went up by 34 per cent to 1,00,693 hectares in 2013; cultivation was at a new all-time high. This punctured the UK's narrative of poppy control in Helmand. The erosion of their poppy control narrative continued even after they left Helmand. To the great dismay of the UK government, the poppy production rose to a historic high in 2017 with a net sown area of 1,43,973 hectares in Helmand accounting for almost half of the opium production in Afghanistan. The net sown area of opium was assessed at 69,324 hectares in the year 2006, when the British military stepped into this backwater to eliminate poppy. The billions of British pounds, along with the military, to arrest poppy have actually contributed to a more than double-fold increase in opium cultivation. It was reported that all the training and inputs to maximize agriculture production coupled with investment around improving irrigation infrastructure were put to good use for maximizing opium production. In a way, the British military strategy inadvertently aided the transformation of Helmand—from the breadbasket of Afghanistan to the world's largest source of opium.

On the war front, it was getting tough for the British military to withstand the growing assault of the Taliban. It was no more confined to guerilla tactics. The Taliban were now waging long and fierce attacks in almost all districts and townships of Helmand. By the dawn of 2010, Afghanistan was witnessing two changes in the stance of the US and the UK. Finding a resurgent Taliban and the US-led war in Afghanistan on the brink of a failure, the all-weather duo of US-UK overnight turned into an apostle of peace. The proposal of talks with the Taliban was put on the table. The UK was proposing talks with the Taliban, the same Taliban whom they have vowed to uproot from Helmand. The then Foreign Secretary, William Hague, openly admitted the prospect of parleying with the Taliban as key to stabilize Afghanistan, in general, and Helmand, in particular. Peace talks after loss of precious lives and billions drained from the state exchequer found more takers in the top political leadership of the UK than prolonging the military action in Afghanistan.

The exit plan

The NATO summit in Lisbon (19–20 November 2010) for the first time agreed to gradually withdraw combat forces from Afghanistan with a completion date of 2014. NATO reaffirmed its commitment to remain in Afghanistan to provide training and advice to Afghan forces and police, as a part of their overall state building. The appetite of Cameron for Afghanistan was no way close to that of Blair, and further not even to his most immediate predecessor, Gordon Brown. Brown was looking for an exit route without tarnishing the UK's global reputation. The military failure of the UK in Helmand was widening with every passing day. It was a staple for the British tabloids to criticize his government 24/7. For every soldier killed in Helmand, the Opposition's Labour Party would corner Cameron. And more importantly, like the US, the people of UK too were tired of the Afghan war. And for Cameron, these developments were a perfect backdrop to withdraw from Afghanistan. By 2011, demands were growing for the British to pull out, and Cameron pledged to end combat operations by 2014, saying, 'I believe the country needs to know there is an end point to all of this.'[95]

The winding down of the military role started soon after the announcement and British troops handed over responsibility for security of the capital of Helmand province, Lashkar Gah, to Afghan forces. In December 2012, Cameron announced that 3,800 troops, almost half of the force serving in Helmand Province, would be withdrawn in 2013 with numbers to fall to sub-5000. The UK ceased all combat operations in Helmand and withdrew the last of its combat troops in the early hours on the 27 October 2014. Task Force Helmand was closed, and Camp Bastion was handed over to local Afghan security forces. About 450 personnel were retained in Afghanistan to train, advise and assist local Afghan forces under their state-building

[95]'Uk Troops in Afghanistan, Timline of key events,' BBC, 22 December 2015.

mission. The last UK commander in Helmand, Brigadier Rob Thomson, expressed his pride and sense of relief when they all arrived safely.

In Parliament, Cameron said, 'Our incredible servicemen and women have driven al-Qaeda out and they have built up and trained the Afghan forces, none of which even existed in 2001, so that the Afghans can take control of their own security.'[96] The British media continued with its unsparing tirade against the prime minister. The British and other foreign troops were dispatched to Afghanistan to kill al-Qaeda operatives posing a threat to Britain's national security. Not a single Taliban/al-Qaeda operative or UN/US designated 'international terrorist' who could conceivably have threatened the UK is recorded as having been killed by the British military in Helmand. On the contrary, the threat itself has multiplied and further moved to the safe terrorist sanctuaries of Waziristan region, where neither the NATO, nor the British military forces, enjoy any access. And it is anyone's guess to determine if the threat perception on the streets of UK has been eliminated even by an iota of the killing of Taliban militants in Helmand or for that matter if Afghan-produced heroin is not available on the streets of the UK anymore.

Defence Secretary Michael Fallon told BBC's Andrew Marr show on the eve of UK military forces leaving Helmand that 'mistakes' had been made. 'I think the generals have been clear that mistakes were made,' he said.[97] 'Mistakes were made militarily and mistakes were made by the politicians at the time.' He said the UK was not 'walking away entirely' and

[96]Prime Minisiter's statement on European Council, www.gov.uk, 17 October 2014.
[97]Holtz, Michael, 'British Troop exit from Afghanistan stirs questions at home over mission,' *The Christian Science Monitor*, 21 October 2014.

would continue to give help and support, including financial aid and military training. The British military think tank renewed the importance of training and coaching the Afghan army to protect the growing onslaught of the Taliban. The irony was that the British military failed to stop the Taliban with all their military might, precision and air power. And now, it was expected from the rudimentary Afghan army to stop the Taliban sans air power. Asked if the Afghan army might collapse, as parts of the Iraqi army did in the face of Islamic State militants, Fallon said Iraq's forces were 'seen as sectarian' while the Afghan army had the 'support of the whole population'. He was found tentative and evasive in his response.

As expected, the situation in Helmand was not improving despite a large number of reinforcements of local Afghan forces. The Taliban were more aggressive with no air power of the British military to check their advance. By 2016, Helmand had fallen almost entirely to the Taliban. The first to fall were contested cities like Sangin. On Sunday, 20 December 2015, some 14 months after the departure of the British combat troops from Afghanistan, Helmand's Deputy Governor, Mohammad Jan Rasulyar, was pleading with the Afghan government to send reinforcements, after the deaths of some 90 members of the Afghan security forces in the previous two days. In an extraordinary public message posted on Facebook, he said, 'Your Excellency, Helmand is standing on the brink and there is a serious need for help to come.'[98] An MP from Helmand, and resident of Sangin, Hashim Alokozai, said the Taliban had captured all security posts in the district,

---

[98]Harooni, Mirwais, 'Afghan official warns Helmand province may fall to Taliban,' Reuters, 20 December 2015, https://www.reuters.com/article/uk-afghanistan-taliban-idUKKBN0U30DK20151220, accessed 18 June 2021.

including key buildings in the Sangin district centre. 'Since last night Sangin district centre is almost completely under Taliban control,' he said, adding that all remaining police were holed up in one building and were 'completely beleaguered'. He warned that if reinforcements did not arrive soon, all lives would be lost. The same Sangin that witnessed more than 100 British soldiers laying down their lives to defend was 'on the verge of collapse' due to the bloody onslaught from Taliban forces. And the newly trained Afghan forces were no way near to defend it. They were like sitting ducks being hunted in pairs by the Taliban in the outpost and beyond.

One district after another started falling to the Taliban in the province of Helmand. Soon after the fall of the districts and town, the local Afghan army forces would cry for additional reinforcements from Kabul and the top Kabul leadership would call for more US air strikes. The city would be rescued from the Taliban with the help of US air strikes. But the military success would be short-lived. It was reported that the UK military too sent some of their expert commanders to guide the Afghan army in Sangin, when it was on the brink of a collapse, in a purely non-combatant role.

The strategic cities and district headquarters were trapped in a vicious cycle of capture-liberate-recapture. The Taliban would challenge the writ of the state and capture a city, followed by a fierce fight from the state forces coupled with US air power to liberate it. The Taliban would leave for a while and recapture the strategic district and cities again, after a short gap. This game continued for a while. With no imminent fear of air strikes, the Taliban had to concentrate on the ground forces only. And the Taliban casualties were limited in absence of air strikes providing them with the edge of regrouping quickly after any resistance from state-led forces. The US air power was also overstretched with rescue calls coming from the entire length and breadth of the country. The element of asymmetric military war was no more visible in the air of Helmand. This made the Taliban overtly aggressive in their war design and execution. The guerilla tactics were completely shunned in the province of Helmand, with more emphasis on full-scale and protracted conventional military war. Hence, more and more important and strategic districts, townships and cities started falling permanently to the Taliban. And this was not making breaking news in the international media, anymore. The strategic district of Marjah was next in line. Marjah was long regarded as a 'festering sore' by senior NATO officers. The NATO forces recovered Marjah in February 2010. Led by the US Marine Corps, a joint force of 15,000 American, British, Canadian, Danish, Afghan National Army (ANA) and other ISAF units cleared Marjah with an all-out assault against the Taliban. Around 60 coalition troops lost their lives, hundreds wounded and an unknown number of ANA and civilian deaths.

But after five years of fighting, since the 2014 withdrawal of most NATO troops, changing administrations in London and Kabul and countless more killed and wounded on both sides in this seemingly never-ending war, the Taliban's white banners were flying over Marjah, once again. Marjah, being a centre of poppy cultivation, was also notoriously infamous for mass manufacture of roadside bombs, affecting the stability of all districts and cities within the province of Helmand. Its continued anarchy and instability posed a greater threat to the regional capital, Lashkar Gah. It has further put the capital on a virtual seize.

Helmand was the epicentre of war against the Taliban and had become totemic as the place that had claimed the lives of most British soldiers and massive investments. And the Afghan army was on the brink of losing the battle in Helmand. Violence continued unabated across Helmand in 2019, as the Taliban continued to march forward and make territorial gains. They kept attacking the Afghan national security forces bases and outposts, relentlessly. As per latest reports, 10 out of the 13 districts of Helmand province lay under the Taliban control. The Taliban heavily contested the rest. Even in the government-controlled districts, the writ of the Afghan state was openly challenged. Government forces abandoned their positions, retreating again and again until only Lashkar Gah was under government control. The fate of Lashkar Gah, once referred to as 'little UK' by the Helmandis due to the heavy presence of UK military forces, also hangs in critical balance. The Taliban were attacking the city with an unfailing regularity and ferociously pushing the war into government capital enclaves.

The white flags of the Taliban were seen flying across the highway just after a 10-minute drive from the city. The Taliban were releasing victory songs and appointing district administration to provide public services and security to the local Afghans. They were moving freely even in government-controlled areas. The Taliban have made repeated attempts to capture Lashkar Gah, the city of 200,000 people and the last hold of the Afghan government. The city was the scene of heavy fighting between the Taliban and NATO-led forces before their withdrawal in 2014 and as recently as September 2019. Perhaps it needs to be mentioned here that in 2016, US Marines returned to Helmand and helped the beleaguered Afghan army and National Police forces to push the Taliban back. Today, the Afghan army, still supported by US Marines and occasional air support, holds a tenuous line of territory in the province, and Lashkar Gah is no longer surrounded. With the stagnant peace process and an emboldened Taliban, it remains ever doubtful if the Afghan forces can hold the city for long. The Taliban have deployed highly trained shock troops and struck isolated outposts with overwhelming force. The Taliban commanders laid out guidelines for their ground fighters on how to wage their final assault and bloodletting. The fall of Lashkar Gah is inevitable. It is only a matter of time.

The failure to protect Helmand not only questions the ability of the Afghan army to neutralize the Taliban onslaught, but also questions the training and mentoring support provided by the UK forces to groom their Afghan counterparts. Despite billions of pounds being poured into creating an Afghan army and police force capable of fighting the Taliban in Helmand, none of the Army units have displayed their ability to operate independently.

UK soldiers did not get along with their Afghan counterparts in 2010, or in 2014 at the time of their departure. The Marines were frustrated by the Afghan soldiers' inability to fight like the British. They did not stop to care that their training lasted for a fraction of time, or that they lacked an established cadre of experienced professional officers, or that they were unpaid, grossly under equipped and deployed in their own backyard. Corruption, poor leadership, desertions and 'ghost soldiers' (the practice by some commanders of producing inflated numbers and pocketing the extra salaries) have plagued the Afghan forces. They are challenged not only by lack of heavy military machines, but also their inability to use the existing resources to full scale and effect. The widening trust gaps have further affected the quality of the military training.

Insider attacks, where an Afghan soldier would kill NATO personnel, have witnessed a sharp rise in Afghanistan. In

2012, more than 60 NATO service personnel, including a considerable number of British troops, were killed in such attacks. The trust gap was so wide that the Afghan army was allowed to take a position inside Camp Bastion only after the British soldiers were escorted out of the camp in four-wheel-drive bullet cars and a veering fleet of military trucks. After heavy security check, the Afghan troops were allowed to drive out of the gates of their base, which sits adjacent to Camp Bastion, before meeting at 'friendship gate', the point that connects the two camps. The data released by the US forces are more threatening. There were almost 100 of these attacks between 2008 and 2017, but 2012 was the worst year with 44 reported incidents. The so-called insider attack has significantly restricted the effective face-to-face military training and are more reliant on video materials and virtual training. This has dented the quality of military training along with the outcome.

The Afghan army is facing large-scale death and injuries in their fight against the Taliban. Over five Afghan soldiers are killed every day in Helmand alone, with no ready replacement. The mounting death toll is further triggering desertion. This also means the replacement is not as well trained as the deceased soldiers, thus further diminishing the ability of the Afghan army to take on their fight with the Taliban. They are also ill-prepared and demoralized. They remain a cannon fodder for the Taliban, who are hell-bent on capturing the whole of Helmand under all cost and probabilities. They are unable to withstand the brutal force of the Taliban.

Despite glaring challenges, the Afghan military is fighting to the best of their valour. There are no air strikes to save the ANA soldiers, no MRAPs—large anti-mine vehicles—to provide cover. The ANA was left to fend for itself. Helmand would have fallen long ago to the Taliban, immediately after the withdrawal of the British military. The intermittent US air support is holding the Taliban off from complete capture of Helmand. If Britain joined the Afghan war to retain its closest possible ties with the US, it is payback time for the latter. After Iraq, once again, Britain's military was out of its depth and needed to be rescued by the far better-resourced Americans.

But has the UK learned from its mistake? It does not seem so. In another bid to punch above weight, the then prime minister Theresa May announced sending another 440 British troops to Afghanistan to train the Afghan army and police in the second half of 2018. This has doubled the UK troops in Afghanistan. Surprisingly, the decision came at a time when the NATO leadership started pinning their hopes on a political settlement with the Taliban, with its past effort of building the Afghan forces falling flat. The British media viewed the decision of May and Trump's announcement of unnumbered troop surge in Afghanistan almost during the same period, from the same prism. It was not a mere coincidence, but a well-calibrated move to bolster their slipping ties. Now, May wanted to hold hands with the US. She dug deeper into the Afghan mess in her bid to portray a strong international image.

The UK continues to reward irrational optimism, investing more troops and money, all these years, in a mission which was doomed long back. All attempts to continually redefine the Afghan goal were to hide its failure. Constrained by the political imperative to portray an ever-rosy but false picture of relentless progress, and the need to do more, the UK continues on the path of an endless muddling in Afghanistan. Critical questions have never been raised even by Parliament to ascertain the true picture on the Afghan progress. Part of the answer, however, lies in the UK Parliament. Parliamentary committees should have asked more critical questions. For instance:

'General, you and your predecessors have described 2004, 2005 and each year through to 2014 as "the decisive year" in Afghanistan. Why should we believe you this time?'

'Minister, explain to me what does good governance and Rule of Law actually look like in the district of Sangin infested with the Taliban?'

'General, please explain how the rookie Afghan army would protect Helmand after your exit, if the British military, with all its sophistication and might, have failed to do so?'

'General, explain to me some tangible indicators for assessing your new-found obsession for building the Afghan army.'

'General, explain to me what does women empowerment looks like in Helmand.'

'General, explain to me if the poppy eradication result would sustain with the growing insecurity and influence of the Taliban in Helmand.'

'Minister, what is our exit strategy and how would you ensure the sustainability of progress in Helmand after your departure?'

'General, how can we weed out the Taliban from Helmand, when they find a safe haven and support in neighbouring Pakistan?'

'General, is it possible to defeat the Taliban in their own backyard when there is an interrupted flow of arms, money and militants from the other side of the border?'

Parliament owes soldiers on the ground respect, support and trust. It should never be in the job of questioning tactical decisions and operational intelligence. However, Parliament was very much within its rights to keep a strict check on the political and strategic priority of the UK in Helmand. The British parliament perhaps erred on the same as their US counterpart. One seriously doubts if adequate reforms have been undertaken by the UK Parliament to prevent another humiliation like Afghanistan/Helmand in the future.

The goal of 'state-building' while fiercely fighting with the Taliban in Helmand was misplaced and, so was the development journey. The military think tank was hypnotized by the idea of creating 'governance, civil society and the rule of law'. These themes may have earned traction in the press conferences of London, but there were no takers in Helmand. Afghanistan continues to linger as one of the most corrupt countries in the world. But with violence at record levels, a dysfunctional government plagued by corruption, a police and army riddled by the resurgent Taliban and public services coming to a grinding halt, Helmand is anything but better. Helmand is no more stable now than when thousands of British troops were deployed there in 2006. And on top of it, only three districts come under government control, that too if we trust Kabul's version.

Since 2006, on a conservative estimate, the UK has incurred a cost of £15 million a day to maintain Britain's military presence and advance other development agenda in Helmand province. The equivalent of £26,666 will have been spent for every one of Helmand's 1.5 million inhabitants. Even a primary school student in both Afghanistan and UK would say it is not worth the cost after looking into the fragile state of affairs in Helmand today. The amount is more than what a Helmandi would make in his/her entire lifetime. The story does not end here. The uninterrupted supply of money and military has turned a silent and sleeping province into a volcano, spurring the Taliban movement across the entire southern Afghanistan. The headless chicken act of the British military has emboldened the Taliban, like never before. More dangerously, it has imparted a cardinal lesson for the Taliban. If Helmand can be won from the jaws of the British military, Kabul too can be won from the US. The underlying lesson remains that before you engage in a war, understand the environment and its implications from the local perspective. Is it one goal that you are trying to achieve? Will it be worth the cost?

The British forces in the nineteenth century were faced with the delicate task of explaining to their empire the repeated failure of forces to quell the spread of revolts in light of an awakened independence movement in India. To avoid embarrassing questions, they adopted the simple device of describing them all as victories. The British army has adopted a similar approach in explaining its failure in Afghanistan again. They cultivated myths, blamed their predecessors and highlighted their limited and temporal poppy success in Afghanistan. And now they are all hiding under the garb of the peace process.

Barring the exception of the assassination of Osama bin Laden—carried out 10 years later in another country sans any UK role—none of the goals have been achieved after funding one of the most lethal and expensive wars, draining the UK state exchequer by £40 billion and still counting. The UK's military role in Afghanistan since 2001 has brought with it a heavy human toll, with 456 British soldiers killed and thousands lying injured and psychologically battered.

Britain went to Afghanistan partly to erase the stain of Basra and retain the closest possible link with the US. The effort was to bolster the initial hubris that the UK can conduct counter-insurgency better than the US. This met its own nemesis. They returned from Afghanistan with their ego battered and their credibility diminished. Their image and reputation were dented further. The failure in Helmand, after Basra, will remain a blot in the annals of history. As the local media put it, 'Britain has lost the third war in Afghanistan' after the not-so-successful, previous two 'Anglo-Afghan wars'.

The Indo-Pak Proxy Battle

After Kashmir, India and Pakistan have locked horns in
a proxy battle in Kabul. Both countries are competing
with each other to exercise influence over Afghanistan
in order to gain more strategic leverage and prominence
in the region. Who is winning this race?

Afghanistan's history is long and checkered with many invasions and foreign meddling. It has always been a playground of diplomatic games, with different nations battling to strategically control and influence Afghanistan, in order to checkmate their rivals for greater influence and authority in the region. While some of the players have changed over time, India and Pakistan remain the two constants, bent on marginalizing each other, in a third country. Afghanistan is known for an abundance of natural resources, but India and Pakistan have expanded their relationship with the embattled nation owing to various other strategic factors. A stable Afghanistan is critical for India and the region at large, but it doesn't suit the strategic interest of Pakistan. Both countries feel that exercising their influence in Afghanistan will enhance their strategic space and significance in the region. In the midst of competing interests, Afghanistan was set to emerge as a highly contested hotspot that Pakistan and India would attempt to assert strategic strength over. They were not averse to even undercutting each other in a third country. It was bound to become the new battlefield post-9/11, where both would seek to gain a geopolitical defence and promote their strategic agenda under the fold of affirmative development interventions. The stage was set to witness the second proxy battle, after Kashmir, where India and Pakistan have been fighting a proxy war for several decades.

India shared a 106-kilometre-long land border with Afghanistan along Kashmir. However, since 1948, that part of the border and the region has been under Pakistan-Occupied Kashmir (PoK) rule.[99] Prime Minister Jawaharlal Nehru, while welcoming his counterpart, Prime Minister Sardar Mohammad Daoud Khan of Afghanistan, on his visit to India in February 1959, had said, 'The partition of India separated direct boundaries and direct contacts between the two countries. But that made little difference to our age-long community of interests and our old friendship survived. And ever since then, we have grown closer to each other for a variety of reasons, among them being mutual interest.'[100] This holds true to the core. Despite Afghanistan not being an immediate neighbour of independent India, both share common history and interests, which have contributed to a proximate and mature friendship between the two countries.

---

[99]International Land Border, www.mha.gov.in.
[100]Foreign Affairs Record, 1959.

Bilateral ties between India and Afghanistan, spanning over decades, have always been more than cordial. Historically, both India and Afghanistan have maintained robust cultural ties, resulting in strong and stable relations between the two nations. Bollywood is at the heart of Afghan society, and has brought the two countries even closer. The immense popularity of Hindi films and Indian television soap operas has a significant cultural influence in Afghanistan, especially amongst Afghanistan's growing youth population. The Bollywood links have created a people-to-people bond that has had a lasting impact. In that sense, Bollywood and the Indian television industry have played the role of a true cultural ambassador in advancing the bond and cultural ties to the next level. Karzai went to a university in India, while another political heavyweight, Abdullah Abdullah, belongs to the old Indian-backed Northern Alliance. India has supported the Tajik-dominated Northern Alliance during the 1990s, as a counter to Pakistan-controlled hardline Pashtun factions, led by the Taliban.

The long-standing relationship has stood the test of time and further emerged stronger amid multiple crises that the war-ravaged country has witnessed, in its long, volatile history. India has refrained from treating Afghanistan as its backyard, like the other regional powers. However, India has rather carefully nurtured the ancient ties with Afghanistan in order to balance the adversarial nature of India–Pakistan relations.

India–Afghanistan bond

In the past, India and Afghanistan have played different foreign policy narratives, suiting their own strategic interest. While India harped on the Non-Aligned movement,

Afghanistan gravitated towards the erstwhile Soviet Union, in order to counter the growing proximity between the US and Pakistan. The Soviet generosity in providing extensive military and economic aid to counter the growing US interest, eventually led Afghanistan into the Soviet sphere of influence. This resulted in the Soviet occupation in 1979 and dawned an era of Cold War. The Non-Aligned movement was a divided house with no uniform view for or against the Soviet occupation. India was one of the few nations to openly come out in support of the Soviet Union. In fact, the Republic of India was the only South Asian country to recognize the Soviet-backed Afghanistan government in the 1980s. However, in the international arena, the move diminished the independent foreign policy credentials of India.

But it served a twin purpose for India. By supporting a Soviet-backed regime in Kabul, India retained the closest possible links with its all-weather ally, the Soviet Union, and further balanced the antagonistic relations with Pakistan. This was the first blow to the India-Afghan friendship as India's foreign policy stance was contrary to the popular public sentiment in the streets of Afghanistan. India failed to read the tea leaves properly. As the US-sponsored Mujahideen resistance against the Soviet occupation was gaining traction, India realized its foreign policy blunder. Perhaps it was too late for India to make amends and resurrect its foreign policy fiasco.

The chaos and pandemonium that resulted in Afghanistan following the Soviet occupation and its ultimate withdrawal in 1989 had far-reaching implications for global politics-cum-international relations. It was also time for realignment of foreign policies in light of the just-concluded Cold War. Afghanistan was at the forefront of foreign policy challenges that India was facing in the early-1990s after the Soviet withdrawal. As India was pondering over the apropos foreign policy posture for Afghanistan, the country slipped into a prolonged phase of civil strife, followed by the Mujahideen jostling for power. The writ of the government at Kabul was openly challenged in various regions within Afghanistan, making the Indian foreign policy think tank struggle to come out with a coherent foreign policy to deal with the conflict-ridden country. Spawned by the chaos and corruption that dominated post-Soviet Afghanistan, the Taliban ascended to power in 1996, with minimal resistance. India was once again at a loss to evolve a coherent and, more importantly, a pragmatic foreign policy response to deal with the new rulers of Kabul. New Delhi has historically sought to contain Islamabad's influence in Afghanistan, aligning itself with proxies and powers opposed to Pakistan or Pakistan-backed groups.

Following the withdrawal of Soviet troops from Afghanistan for instance, India, along with Iran and Russia, supported the Northern Alliance in the 1990s against the Pakistan-backed Taliban. The alliance, however, failed to contain the Taliban or stop them from seizing control of Kabul and much of Afghanistan by 1996. India's ties with Afghanistan were slipping dangerously through the Taliban's six-year (1996–2001) rule, when India continued to support the Northern Alliance by providing monetary aid and equipment. While India was losing its strategic stake in Kabul, Pakistan gained from the status quo because of its growing proximity with the Taliban.

India's ties with Kabul deteriorated significantly during the rule of the Taliban, which turned Afghanistan into a hotbed of terrorism, some of it directed against India and its strategic interest. Afghanistan was soon used as a backyard of Pakistan to prepare jihadis for the Kashmir battle. The already frail ties hit the nadir in late December 1999, when an Indian passenger airline was hijacked by Pakistani nationals and flown into Kandahar to secure the release of three dreaded terrorists, including the founder of Jaish-e-Mohammad, Maulana Masood Azhar. The umbilical cord of the Taliban linked to the ISI, made it impossible for India to approach the Taliban even through back-door channels. However, barring certain pockets of southern provinces, which are the traditional bastion of the Taliban, India was always a popular choice among the Afghans compared to Pakistan.

The Pakistan connection

Historically, Pakistan viewed Afghanistan as its strategic backyard and was piquantly uncomfortable with any Indian influence in the country. Islamabad has made great strides to check Indian influence in Afghanistan in the past. Pakistan supported the Mujahideen in chasing out the Soviets, who at the time were an important ally of India. Later, Pakistan supported the Taliban to keep the pro-India Northern Alliance out of contention. India, despite making its best effort to contain Pakistan, has failed with the Northern Alliance's inability to defeat the Taliban.

Pakistan and Afghanistan have much in common. Besides sharing a long common frontier, they also inherited the common cultural and religious tradition. Both declared themselves as an Islamic republic and enrolled as full members of the South Asian Association for Regional Cooperation (SAARC). Long-standing Afghan migration to the territories that now compose Pakistan makes them an integral part of the Pakistani society. Yet, the irony of the situation is that relations between these two countries, bound by linguistic, religious and geographical links, have remained far from cordial. The relationship between the two countries has been largely hostile since the independence of Pakistan in 1947. Afghanistan was the sole country to vote against the admission of Pakistan into the UN.

The primary cause of this hostility is the demand for Pashtunistan, which was put forward by the Government of Afghanistan immediately after the emergence of Pakistan as an independent state in 1947. The essence of this demand was that Pathans and Pashto-speaking tribes in northwestern Pakistan should be bestowed the rights to 'opt out' of Pakistan and carve out an autonomous state of their own. There was a greater degree of uncertainty about the future of Pakistan, after its independence from India. And the Government of Afghanistan's claims on Pashtunistan were based on this very belief that Pakistan would not survive as a state and was bound to fail. In anticipation of such an eventuality, Afghanistan wanted to claim certain areas in case of the failure of Pakistan to bind and hold as a state. The demand for Pashtunistan as an independent state also stems from the aspiration of Afghanistan to become a regional power. There were other reasons too. Afghanistan was nursing a long-cherished demand to get an outlet to the sea, as it remains a landlocked country. Afghanistan desperately needs an opening to the sea to reduce its dependence on transit routes to other countries and further reduce the cost of logistics to make trade and commerce more competitive. The Balochistan province of Pakistan was also included in the Greater Pashtunistan definition to gain access to the Arabian Sea.

The demand of Pashtunistan was not confined only to the peripheries of strategic discourse and political posturing. Afghanistan even armed the separatist movements in Pakistan to destabilize the country. With Pakistan showing its ability to hold as a state and its army establishing military superiority over Afghanistan, the idea of Pashtunistan was restricted to just political rhetoric, with each passing decade. However, this created deep mistrust and prevented the emergence of strong ties between the two countries.

There was another thorn in Pakistan's flesh. Since 1949, a series of armed skirmishes and firefights have occurred along the Durand Line between the Afghan National Security Forces (ANSF) and Pakistani Rangers. The two countries share a nearly 2,600 kilometre, largely porous border, which encourages illegal movement in both directions. The international border between the erstwhile British Raj and Afghanistan was established after the 1893 'Durand Line Agreement' between British Foreign Secretary Sir Henry Mortimer Durand of the then British Empire and Afghan representative Amir Abdur Rahman of Afghanistan for fixing the limit of their respective geographical spheres of influence. The Durand Line was reaffirmed as the International Border between Afghanistan and the British Raj in 1919 after the Anglo-Afghan war. The Pakistan side of the border area includes the provinces of Balochistan, the North West Frontier Province (NWFP), and the adjacent federally administered tribal areas (FATA). On the Afghan side, the frontier stretches from Nuristan province in the northeast to Nimruz in the southwest. The border region is predominantly inhabited by ethnic Pashtuns, who were divided by the Durand Line.

Pakistan inherited the Durand Line agreement after its independence in 1947, but all successive Afghan governments, including that of the Taliban, have never recognized the Durand Line as an international border. They further made claims on the Pashtun and Baloch regions of Pakistan. It has been long rejected by Pakistan and the border dispute remains a constant source of bilateral tension. Violence and fire exchanges have increased in recent years with Pakistan hell-bent on putting a barbed fence across the Durand Line disputed by the Afghan government. Pakistan is unilaterally installing a robust fence along most of the frontier, as it believes this would address mutual security concerns. The incumbent Afghan government vehemently opposes the move. And this is leading to recurrent fire exchange among the border forces of both countries and consequently the death of soldiers on both sides.

Afghanistan and Pakistan have had largely antagonistic relations under all governments. Pakistan's relations with Afghanistan have been largely characterized by mutual mistrust and devised through a narrow security prism. The deep-seated animosity and mistrust were bridged to a certain extent with Pakistan supporting the Mujahideen resistance against the Soviet occupation. The Pakistan army was heavily involved in training and further arming the Mujahideen under the aegis of the CIA. This created political goodwill for Pakistan, among considerable sections of the society, especially the Pashtu belt in the southern provinces of Afghanistan. Suddenly, Pakistan was in the list of well-wishers, if not friends of Afghanistan.

After the Soviets retreated, the different Mujahideen factions turned their guns against each other as they failed to agree on a power-sharing deal, which resulted in a prolonged civil war. Pakistan was in constant search for supporting a winning combination of Mujahideen leaders in order to wield power in Afghanistan and further treat it as its foreign policy backyard. The ISI and the Pakistani government of the late Prime Minister Benazir Bhutto became the primary source of support for Gulbuddin Hekmatyar in his 1992–94 bombardment campaign against the Islamic State of Afghanistan to capture Kabul. It was evident by the last quarter of 1994 that Hekmatyar was a spent force; they harped on the obscure Kandhari movement in their quest to establish proxy control over Afghanistan. The Kandahari student movement mostly comprised students educated in Pakistan-based madrasas. The ISI armed the student movement and provided them with the finance to gain prominence as the Taliban subsequently established control over Kabul in 1996. The Taliban ascended to power with both covert and overt support of the military and the civilian government of Pakistan. This created a permanent division of opinion for Pakistan, culminating in anger and frustration among the bulk of Afghanis with the growing misrule of the Taliban in Afghanistan. The military-devised interventionist policies, based on Pakistan's perceived national strategic interests, including controlling Afghanistan, mainly through their proxies i.e., the Taliban, have marred the relationship. Pakistan may have attained the military and foreign policy goal by fixing the Taliban in Kabul, but jeopardized the civilian goodwill to a larger extent.

Unlike the relationship with Pakistan, ties between India and Afghanistan are not hijacked by the legacy of distrust and a contiguous, and contested, border dispute. India's prolonged support for the Northern Alliance against the Pakistan-backed Taliban in the 1990s consolidated its position with Afghanistan, especially in the northern and central region of Afghanistan, including its capital Kabul. New Delhi silently aided the overthrow of the Taliban from Kabul in 2001. In many ways, the catastrophic 9/11 bombing and subsequent collapse of the Taliban regime in Afghanistan provided an opportunity both to India as well as Afghanistan to reset their bilateral ties in light of the new reality. India was in a position of distinct advantage with its growing economic stature.

The geopolitical position of Afghanistan, because of the various developments in the neighbourhood, had gradually emerged as a central piece of India's foreign policy. In light of India's deteriorating relationship with China, on one hand, and the constant threat of Pakistan's hostility, on the other, Afghanistan took an immediate importance for India to necessitate a change of emphasis in its relations with it. India's support for the Northern Alliance against the Pakistan-backed Taliban in the 1990s strengthened its position in Kabul after 2001. Many members of the same Alliance were members of the interim government in Kabul. Hence, it served as a lever for India to reboot Indo-Afghan ties, after the fall of the Taliban. The president of the interim government, Karzai, being educated in India, had a soft corner for India. He was quite vocal about it. It was another lever for India. India used the connection with Karzai to demonstrate its eagerness to revive its ties with the Pashtuns. India also wanted to restore the balance in its engagement with a range of different ethnic groups and political affiliations in Afghanistan, in order to gain greater relevance in light of the changing power equation and its growing stature, in the post-Taliban political set-up.

India did not waste any time and upgraded the Indian representation in Afghanistan from a Liaison Office to a full-fledged Embassy in 2002. Delhi immediately reopened its consulates in Kandahar and Jalalabad. It later opened consulates in Herat and Mazar-e-Sharif, the major commercial centres in the western and northern parts of Afghanistan, respectively. These diplomatic posts enabled India to build relationships with local leaders, facilitate trade and investment, and increase awareness of regional developments. Afghanistan was the second largest foreign outpost of India, after the US. This signalled the importance that New Delhi attached to Afghanistan in the post-Taliban era. India's engagement with Afghanistan readily became multidimensional after the installation of an Interim Authority in 2001. India actively participated in the Bonn Conference and was instrumental in facilitating the creation of a post-Taliban governing and political authority in Afghanistan. India's main focus was to support the interim Afghan government and the political process in the country as mandated under the Bonn Agreement in 2001. India has continued to pursue a policy of high-level engagement with Afghanistan through extensive and wide-ranging humanitarian, financial and project assistance, as well as participation in international efforts aimed at democratic consolidation and economic rebuilding of the country.

Soft power diplomacy

Since 2001, India has relied primarily on its 'soft power' to woo Kabul and enjoy a deep influence. Today, India is the third largest civilian donor to Afghanistan and the largest regional donor. After the fall of the Taliban, India has invested close to $3 billion in a surfeit of development and reconstruction projects spread all over Afghanistan. India is delivering critical humanitarian assistance as well as helping Afghanistan in addressing its infrastructure needs. It is also building core infrastructure, providing medical facilities, supplying high-value military equipment and helping with capacity-building programmes in an effort to develop and enhance long-term human capital. India's multifarious goals in Afghanistan aligns well with its regional and global interests. A major factor behind India's proactive Afghanistan agenda has been India's attempt to carve out for itself a greater role in regional affairs, more in consonance with its rising economic and military profile. Countering Pakistan's influence is certainly one of India's key goals, but New Delhi pursues a broad range of interests in Afghanistan that go beyond simply blocking its principal foe. New Delhi's most fundamental goal for Afghanistan is to prevent it from being used as a base for Pakistan-supported extremists to launch terrorist attacks in India and its interests in Afghanistan.

There are lurking fears that once US troops withdraw, Islamabad will move to dominate Afghanistan's political landscape, by fixing the pro-ISI Taliban in the new power structure of Kabul. This will enable Pakistan to use the country as a safe haven and training ground for breeding anti-Indian extremists. And the ISI will unleash this new breed of jihadists at its disposal on India with unfailing regularity. This not only means that Indian interests would be harmed within Afghanistan, but a likely spillover to Kashmir, and even beyond, is possible. To prevent such an alarming development, Delhi also invests in a stable, democratic, multiethnic Afghan government that can establish control over the whole country, maintain peace, prevent the return of the Taliban and mitigate anti-India extremism. Achieving such an arrangement, however, required India to counter Pakistani political influence. The best way to do it was to stop Pakistan from becoming the sole arbitrator of the Afghan political and strategic discourse, as this would not only reinforce the proxy war against India, but also fuel Islamic radicalism in the country.

India's Afghan interest also hinges on getting access to the energy producers of Central Asia to fuel the uninterrupted growth of its modernizing economy. The proposed 1,000-mile, $7.6 billion Turkmenistan-Afghanistan-Pakistan-India (TAPI) pipeline would carry 33 billion cubic metres per year (bcm/y) of Turkmen gas, with India receiving 14 bcm/y, almost

1.5 per cent of its annual energy consumption. Afghanistan would gain $1.4 billion per year in transit fees, besides a sustained source of cheap and clean fuel. However, the transport of Central Asian energy resources to India (and even Pakistan) requires stability in Afghanistan, whose territory the TAPI pipeline must cross.

India's high growth coupled with the global integration of its economy has enhanced the importance of commerce and trade objectives in New Delhi's foreign policy outreach. There is a growing perception among Indians that the country is a global power and should seek to shape the region around it, if not the world. In addition to advance economic influence in Kabul, Delhi also strives to integrate Afghanistan into regional economic structures, offers economic development through enhanced trade and commerce and hopes to win Afghans' hearts and minds. The Preferential Trade Agreement signed by India and Afghanistan gives substantial duty concessions to agricultural produce, including dry fruits when entering India, with Afghanistan allowing reciprocal concessions to Indian products such as sugar, tea and pharmaceuticals. Kabul wants Indian businesses to take advantage of the low tax regime to help develop manufacturing hubs in areas such as cement, oil and gas, electricity, and in services including hotels, banking and communications. These overtures bode well for future expansions of bilateral investment links in the coming years.

Afghanistan is also viewed as a gateway to the Central Asian Republics (CARs), where India hopes to expand its influence. India does not have a direct land passage towards CARs and hence Afghanistan remains its best bet to access CARs. The deep influence over Afghanistan has an advantage for India since it acts like a bridge for entering into CARs. India is set to gain in the long run by accessing and expanding the trade footprint in lucrative markets of Central Asian countries via Afghanistan.

India's efforts go even beyond the peripheries of the political and economic sphere have worked to bolster the capabilities of the Afghan security forces through India-based training. New Delhi is principally against any form of reconciliation that brings the Taliban into the Afghan government, and in effect Pakistan-backed extremists to resume using Afghanistan as a safe haven. India's security interest primarily revolves around denying any political or military space to the ISI-backed Taliban and other such fundamentalist groups. Hence, India aspired to emerge as a key player for any reconciliation talks for any peace process-cum-political settlement to keep Pakistan's interest of fixing the radical Taliban leaders at bay. However, most of India's assistance has primarily revolved around extending socio-economic development cooperation.

Asserting that 'social and economic development is the key to ensuring that Afghanistan becomes a source of regional stability,' the Indian government has used a range of economic policy tools—including development assistance, trade promotion and private investment—to promote stability and increase Indian influence in the country. Indian aid to Afghanistan focuses primarily on four main categories: humanitarian assistance, major infrastructure projects, small and community-based projects, and education and capacity development. Some of the notable development investment that generated tremendous civilian goodwill are stated below:

- Construction of Afghanistan's Parliament in Kabul (the complex includes a library).
- Construction of the Delaram-Zaranj Highway connecting the province of Herat and Kandahar. The

highway was designed and constructed by the Border Roads Organization (BRO) of India.

- Reconstruction of Salma Dam, now renamed Indo-Afghan friendship dam.
- The establishment of an electricity transmission line from Pul-e-Khumri to Kabul, ensuring almost 24/7 supply of electricity in the capital city of Kabul.
- Reconstructing the Indira Gandhi Institute for Child Health/Indira Gandhi Children's Hospital in Kabul.
- Financing the establishment of the Afghan National Agriculture Sciences and Technology University (ANASTU) in Kandahar and assisting it in various ways.
- Providing scholarships to 2,000 Afghan students to study in various Indian universities. It remains the most popular and sought-after student scholarship in Afghanistan.

Although India's reconstruction strategy was designed to highlight Indian benevolence, expand trade and seek political leverage in Afghanistan, it is also intended to undercut Pakistani influence there. By constructing a 220-kilometre road between the Afghan cities of Zaranj and Delaram in 2008–09, BRO connected the main Herat-Kandahar highway with existing routes leading to the Iranian port of Chabahar. It is no coincidence, however, that the road will significantly shorten overland journey appreciably to a commercial ocean outlet and will be much faster than the present network that connects Afghanistan to the Pakistani ports of Karachi and Gwadar. Perhaps it needs to be mentioned that India is the principal investor in developing the Chabahar port in Iran. Similarly, to facilitate Indian companies' access to Afghanistan's estimated $1 trillion in minerals and raw materials, Delhi is planning to build a rail link from Hajigak, a mineral-rich area in Bamyan province, through Zaranj, and onward to Chabahar. India is also working with Iran to build a 600-kilometre road from Chabahar to the Iranian city of Zahedan, near the southwestern corner of Afghanistan that would follow a similar route to the rail line. These transit routes will reduce the time it takes for Afghan goods to reach a major port, and Indian goods to reach Afghanistan. Considerable chunks of Pakistan exports' incomes come from Afghanistan and help them manage their slipping trade deficit. Indian design in progress would not only spur trade and commerce between India and Afghanistan, but also impair the Pakistan economy.

The new routes at work would facilitate faster Indian-Afghan trade and commerce and reduce the dependence on Islamabad for a transit permit for any export to Afghanistan by road. It possesses the potential to give a death blow to Pakistan's Gwadar port, which was built at considerable cost with significant Chinese investment. The aggressive investment in road, railway and port also depicts growing interest in minerals in Afghanistan, estimated at $1 trillion. Indian companies are not to be left out. Notably, in late 2011, no fewer than 14 Indian firms bid on an iron mining contract in Bamyan province that could generate $6 billion in investment. Eventually, an Indian consortium led by state-owned Steel Authority of India Ltd won the mining rights for three out of four iron ore blocks in Afghanistan.

The US, under both presidents, i.e., Obama and Trump, made a series of calls for India to send its military to Afghanistan. But the Indian government refrained from sending its military and harped largely on the soft power by opening up a generous bounty for Afghanistan. It was feared that sending the army, following in the footsteps of the US, would be counterproductive for India. The ISI would unleash their strategic arsenal to target India and impound a much greater damage. The attacks would lead to more instability in Afghanistan and dent India's image of goodwill and civilian generosity. There was a general consensus in India that it should not send troops to Afghanistan. And the military cooperation should not be extended beyond soft training of Afghan military personnel in India. Beyond this, there was minimal agreement about what policy options it has if greater turbulence in the Afghanistan-Pakistan region spills over to India. The traditional Indian stance had been that while India was happy to help the Afghan government in its reconstruction efforts, it would not be directly engaged in security operations. However, a small contingent of the Indo-Tibetan Border Police was posted by India to secure its properties and selected projects in India.

India has come to enjoy considerable soft power in Afghanistan. Indeed, ordinary Afghans have welcomed Indian involvement in development projects in their country. Indian films and television programmes continue to remain extremely popular among the local Afghan populace. India remains the favourite destination for Afghans, with the Indian embassy and four other missions issuing around 350 visas daily. India has further emerged as the favourite medical destination for the majority of Afghans. Every day, over 200 Afghans arrive for medical treatment in New Delhi.

New Delhi's success in projecting political, economic, commercial and cultural influence has been effective in advancing its strategic interests in Afghanistan. Since 2002, India's humanitarian aid and infrastructure projects in Afghanistan have provided the much-needed lifeline amidst the ongoing war, sectarian divisions and terrorism. The Karzai government responded positively to Indian initiatives by strengthening its political, economic and diplomatic ties with Delhi despite Pakistan's clear and overt displeasure. India's development forays were based on the assumption that the Taliban are dead and dull after their exit from Afghanistan, in October 2001. However, with the passing years, the Taliban not only emerged from the shadow, but also regrouped themselves into a resurgent group attacking Afghanistan at their free will. This was a major setback for India, and the cloud of uncertainty started looming on its development endeavours in Afghanistan. Not only is the Taliban getting stronger to threaten the development projects of India, but also overruns the elected government in Kabul.

Pakistan did not have the deep pockets to match the growing economic might of India in terms of aiding the reconstruction of Afghanistan. However, it was not to be left behind in the diplomatic race, either. Not to be outdone by India, Pakistan has extended development aid to Afghanistan and initiated a slew of measures promoting Afghan trade and commerce. The government has spent close to $500 million in bilateral assistance, most of which has been directed towards the construction of roads that would connect Pakistan to the energy-rich CARs. Islamabad and Kabul signed the Afghanistan-Pakistan Transit Trade Agreement, in which Afghanistan would permit Pakistani goods to transit enroute to Central Asia, and Pakistan would allow Afghan products to transit on the way to Indian markets. However, the limited bilateral philanthropic outreach was to camouflage the larger strategic design for Afghanistan. The primary goals in Afghanistan are mainly India-centric and focus primarily on undermining New Delhi's growing influence in Kabul, while promoting its own ulterior strategic agenda. Strong India-Afghanistan ties are essentially seen by Pakistan as detrimental to its national security interests, as the two states flank the two sides of Pakistan's borders. A friendly political dispensation in Kabul is viewed by Pakistan as essential to escape the strategic dilemma of being caught between a powerful adversary in India, in the east, and an irredentist Afghanistan, on the other side.

Pakistan has the residual Taliban, including the top leaders at its disposal after being thrown out of Afghanistan by the ISAF forces, post 9/11. They were hiding in various sanctuaries located in the lawless Waziristan belt of Pakistan. Pakistan retained considerable influence over the Taliban along with the Haqqani network even when they were flushed out of Afghanistan. Pakistan knew that this was their biggest asset. They would be on the reckoning in Afghanistan, as long as the Taliban remain potent and do not lose their teeth to bite Afghanistan. Hence, a greater degree of effort was deployed to rebuild the Taliban by providing them with finance and facilitation of training and operations by the ISI and even the Pakistan army-backed deep states. With the Taliban at work, the dual strategic agenda of keeping Afghanistan unstable and the relentless attack on Indian interests (in Afghanistan) could be achieved.

Hence, according to the new ISI manual for the war-ravaged country, the Taliban were overhauled. Islamabad aimed to maximize Taliban influence in a weak Kabul government to gain 'strategic depth'. Other important priorities were guided at keeping the government at Kabul weak thereby marginalizing the historical Afghan claims on Pakistani territory. Islamabad needed a weak Kabul government for another reason too. A friendly but weak regime in Kabul was necessary to keep India out from the thick of things. This was in line with the much-established Pakistan military doctrine that a weak, subservient government in Afghanistan is needed to ensure that Pakistan has sufficient strategic leverage.

A pro-Pakistani and weak Afghan state would also enable Islamabad to establish a rear base to train Islamist militants beyond the Taliban, such as Jaish-e-Mohammed and Lashkar-e-Taiba, for strengthening the supply line for jihad in Jammu, Kashmir and elsewhere in India. These strategic assets would be additionally deployed along with the Taliban, to attack Indian interests in Afghanistan. The use of jihadist proxies is an established tenet of Pakistan's foreign policy and one of the principal means by which the ISI has imposed significant damage on India. Presence of a safe haven outside Pakistani territory would allow Islamabad to sustain its proxy war against India, while enabling it to deny direct sponsorship of terrorism and escape the eventual international fallout. Pakistan's control over these jihadist networks would check Indian aggression and further deter India's outreach to Afghanistan.

Pakistan has long considered India to be an aggressive state that poses a fundamental threat to its territorial integrity. Not only does Islamabad blame Delhi for orchestrating the creation of Bangladesh out of East Pakistan in 1971, but it also accuses India for fomenting trouble in Balochistan through the consulate office in Kandahar.[101] The foreign ministry of Pakistan has asserted that 'Indian consulates in Jalalabad and Kandahar are a veritable base for Research and Analysis Wing (RAW), and its accessories' aimed to fan unrest in Balochistan.'[102] The

---

[101]Hanauer, Larry and Peter Chalk, 'India's and Pakistan's Strategy in Afghanistan: Implications for the United States and the Region, 2012,' Rand.org. https://www.rand.org/pubs/occasional_papers/OP387.html, accessed 2 July 2021.

[102]'RAW active in Indian consulates: Pakistan,' *Dawn*, 2 August 2003, https://www.dawn.com/news/133194/raw-active-in-indian-consulates-pakistan, accessed 18 June 2021.

Indian counterpart has denied the allegation and asked for tangible evidence to corroborate the same.

Balochistan remains a weak link for Pakistan and is even disputed by Afghanistan. And there could be overlapping of purposes with the Afghan government getting aggressive in claiming Balochistan. A strong Afghan government would further rake up the Durand Line debate. If India gains traction and enjoys greater influence over Kabul, the position of Islamabad in the country as well as in the regional front would be significantly weakened. This may even allow Afghanistan to flex its muscles and pose serious trouble for them.

Pakistan had serious fears that India's efforts to gain leverage in Afghanistan is a deliberate strategy of encirclement that is aimed at trapping and ultimately weakening Pakistan by opening hostile fronts. Islamabad's overriding objective in Afghanistan was therefore to block New Delhi's own penetration into the country by helping to foster a pro-Pakistani administration in Kabul. Hence, as India was aiming to undercut the influence of Pakistan in the post-Taliban makeover of Afghanistan, Pakistan was hell-bent on opposing anything that India does in Afghanistan, irrespective of merit and premise. The Indian outreach in Afghanistan had to be opposed in all its forms and manifestations, and Islamabad was open to both covert and overt means for doing so.

In addition to limiting Indian power projection in Afghanistan, Pakistan also pursues to limit the extent to which other states are able to extend their influence in Afghanistan. This is particularly true of Iran and Russia. Islamabad's relationship with Tehran has always been uneasy, reflecting the latter's alleged support of Shi'a militias operating in Balochistan. Moreover, Iran has managed to garner a relatively high degree of support among the Afghan Shi'a communities along the border with Pakistani Balochistan—an area in which Pakistan has traditionally enjoyed very little influence. From Islamabad's perspective, any further expansion of Iranian influence in this area could foster instability in the historically restive Balochistan province.

Pakistan views the growing Russian involvement in Afghanistan with a great deal of suspicion. The Pakistan army leadership is full of officers commissioned during the Soviet occupation. They still remain critical about the role of Russia in Afghanistan after the disintegration of the Soviet Union. But more than that, Islamabad is wary of Moscow's historical and strong ties with India. The lingering doubts and suspicions have only transferred to their Afghan policy, with the Pakistan army enjoying formidable clout in the foreign policy of Islamabad.

One of the central aspects of Pakistan's Afghan policy was to remain relevant and be an essential part of any process exploring the long-term political settlement of Afghanistan or even a rapprochement with the Taliban for creating durable peace. In that sense, both the civilian and military leadership would continue to impress the White House about the indispensability of Pakistan in fixing Afghanistan. Pakistan has successfully pressurized the US to protect its key strategic interests in Afghanistan, taking advantage of US dependence on Pakistan for sharing of intelligence and for permitting transit of NATO supplies through its territories. Pakistan has extracted substantial US military assistance, totalling more than $16 billion since 9/11 by cooperating with the US in the war against terror. The Indian army has expressed repeated concern that much of this aid has been redirected from the war on terrorism to ramp up the Pakistani military's capability for anti-Indian posture. Like India, Pakistan too aspired for bolstering trade and commerce with Afghanistan and further gain access to the lucrative energy market of the CARs.

Pakistan has had a great measure of strategic success in keeping the Kabul government weak and off-balance. Islamabad's support to the Taliban, particularly the provision of a safe haven to the group's leadership, has allowed the insurgency to continue and prevent the Afghan government from asserting its authority over more of Afghanistan. The Taliban have spread their tentacles and fomented unrest beyond their traditional bastion of southern provinces to the relatively stable northern provinces. Similarly, Pakistan's efforts to disrupt any attempt at reconciliation in which it is not a key player has undermined Afghan stability and obstructed Kabul from developing alliances that Islamabad does not control.

Pakistan has also been able to expand its bilateral trade relations with Afghanistan. Islamabad has managed to enhance overall economic ties with Kabul and currently stands as one of its most important trading partners. The inking of the Afghanistan-Pakistan Transit Trade Agreement was also a major boon. Although the agreement had much to do with US back-room lobbying and pressure on Pakistan, Islamabad was able to negotiate terms that enhanced its own commercial links with Afghanistan while limiting India from doing the same—at least for the immediate term. For a considerable part, however, Pakistan's various diplomatic forays into Afghanistan have been ineffective. It has failed to prevent Afghanistan's regional integration, expand its own reach into Central Asia, or undermine Indian political and economic influence. Pakistan's failures are largely of its own making. For one, internal rivalries between the civilian leadership and the security institutions prevent a coherent approach to achieving Pakistan's objectives. However, some of Pakistan's strategies, particularly its support for the Taliban may have worked in Afghanistan, but backfired at home with the emergence of the TTP, leading to internal instability and destruction.

Pakistan's rivalry with India and its ulterior motive had to aggressively show up in Afghanistan. The Taliban and the Haqqani network were employed in full force to attack Indian interests and targets in Afghanistan. As India's profile grew in Afghanistan, the ISI, intent on ridding Afghanistan of Indian involvement, also upped the ante in an attempt to rupture burgeoning India–Afghanistan relations. The preoccupation of the West with the war in Iraq also allowed the Taliban, with support from Pakistan, to bounce back and reclaim the strategic space from which it had been ousted. As the balance of power shifted in favour of Pakistan and its proxies, Indian interests, including personnel and projects, emerged as viable targets. In July 2008, the Indian embassy in Kabul was struck by a bomb blast, leaving 60 dead—including embassy officials. In October 2009, a suicide car bombing outside the Indian embassy left at least 17 dead, and scores of others wounded.

Afghanistan intelligence soon concluded that the attack was perpetrated by the Pakistan-based Haqqani group, and suggested that Pakistani ISI had also played a role. After the second attack on the Embassy in 2009, the Afghan envoy to the US too underscored the involvement of Pakistani intelligence. This was the second time that a top Afghan official was openly blaming the Pakistani intelligence agency (ISI) for a terrorist attack in the Afghan territory. The target of the Indian embassy on two occasions was not an isolated attack. Multiple attacks were further targeted against Indian aid workers and project personnel stationed in Afghanistan. The Zaranj-Delaram road constructed under the aegis of India was brought to a standstill by deploying the Taliban fighters and, presumably, its Pakistani backers to disrupt any commerce along the routes.

This was defeating the purpose and viability of such an expensive road project. For the transit links to be truly effective, therefore, security in the region would have to be significantly improved. New Delhi was also pondering to deploy additional security forces to protect its aid and investment projects from being constantly attacked. Eventually, New Delhi deployed 500 members of the Indo-Tibetan Border Police to secure Indian development workers and diplomatic facilities after a series of high-profile attacks. It was fairly inadequate when compared with the magnitude and gravity of the security challenge in light of growing attacks by the Taliban.

The attacks on US and Afghan targets were also on a constant rise and so were the casualties. Afghanistan was becoming unstable and volatile despite the presence of over a hundred thousand western forces, dominantly from the US, with the latest range of weapons and machines. This was clearly suggestive of the fact that the Taliban were on the rebound with a heightened sense of political uncertainty in Washington as well as in New Delhi about the future of the war against terror in Afghanistan. India was facing the heat and had much to consider. Despite India's intent to continue providing development assistance to Kabul, the poor security environment in Afghanistan was clearly affecting Delhi's willingness to start new projects. Even the old projects were getting choked. It has been India's deliberate policy to refrain from giving its support to an overt military dimension and majorly stick to civilian matters. New Delhi has so far shown an unusual tenacity in its expanding military footprints in Afghanistan beyond soft military training.

The first round of India-Pakistan proxy battle stretching up to 2009, in Afghanistan, threw a bag of mixed results. Between

India and Pakistan, the soft power game has played out clearly in favour of India, while Pakistan enjoyed an upper hand in the strategic game checkmating India. Ordinary Afghans, however, appeared to have welcomed Indian involvement in development projects in their country. In addition to winning the support of the Karzai government, Delhi has also earned the respect of ordinary Afghans. The extent of popular support for India—a by-product of promoting civilian and reconstruction assistance, soft power projection and outreach to all major Afghan ethnic groups—stands out, when compared with the Afghans' perceptions of Pakistan. A 2009 ABC News/BBC poll, for example, found that '74 per cent of Afghans held favourable opinions of India, while 8 per cent held favourable opinions towards Pakistan.'[103] Delhi's non-participation in military activities taking place in Afghanistan has helped cultivate India's image as a positive contributor to Afghanistan rather than as an outside meddler. This stands in stark contrast to Pakistan, which 86 per cent of Afghans believe plays a negative role in Afghanistan. Indian initiatives further promoted the legitimacy of the Karzai administration, both by offering programmes to enhance jobs and by focusing Indian support on President Karzai's development priorities—infrastructure, education, training, healthcare, agriculture, telecommunications, power generation and civil aviation.

However, the return of the Taliban is threatening what New Delhi has accomplished to date and further set to derail future initiatives. In that sense, Pakistan enjoys the upper hand, as their covert support has resulted in a resurgent Taliban threatening and attacking Indian interests in the war-torn country at will. This has left India unquestionably

---

[103]Howenstein, Nicholas and Sumit Ganguly, 'India-Pakistan Rivalry in Afghanistan,' *Journal of International Affairs*, Vol. 63, No. 1, pp. 127–40, 2009.

behind in the race to gain dominance and extend influence in Afghanistan.

Karzai was remarkably successful in harnessing and manipulating both India and Pakistan to advance Afghanistan's primary geopolitical and economic objectives. Karzai managed to reduce Afghanistan's reliance on Pakistani territory for trade. He further reduced (at least to some degree) Pakistan's influence over Afghan affairs by building ties with India, by shaping the reconciliation process and by participating in US-led COIN (counterinsurgency) operations. Yet, at the same time, Karzai downplayed the significance of such cooperation in statements aimed at assuaging Pakistan's concerns and taking steps to encourage Islamabad to see the benefits of collaborating with his government. Remarkably, President Karzai has managed to secure large-scale Indian aid and investment without causing Islamabad to retaliate by undermining his regime or stirring up even greater unrest. Key to his success has been his adept balancing of his outreach to both countries. While India and Pakistan were battling it out in Afghanistan, Karzai was milking the situation by keeping himself in the good books of both the countries.

In the India–Pakistan relationship, each side often thinks itself the victim of the other's machinations and diplomatic outreach. Pakistan's army generals viewed India's growing ties with Afghanistan as threatening and underscored the need to do more in Afghanistan to edge out India from the thick of things. The security situation was set to become more volatile with India and Pakistan focusing on the Taliban, albeit with cross-purpose, in the conflict-ridden set-up.

New Delhi has so far shown an unusual tenacity in its dealings with Afghanistan. However, with the rise of the Taliban, India started pondering if it needs to move beyond the binary of development cooperation and soft diplomacy, and develop a more comprehensive military engagement, that includes supplying arms and troops to the war-wrecked zone. Afghanistan is a tough country. Only those who are willing to fight on multiple fronts and levels will be able to preserve and uphold their strategic leverage. India's approach towards Afghanistan has, from the very beginning, been highly dependent on the benevolence of others. New Delhi continued to insist that it wants to invest only its soft power in Afghanistan to win civilian goodwill and further check Pakistan. But the fact is that it succeeded in the first leg due to the overarching US security umbrella. India has engineered some excellent work in Afghanistan—in being one of the largest civilian aid givers, in being a major source of cultural influence, in building capacities in various sectors of an emerging democratic polity and in training security forces. But when it came to the crunch, it had to rely on others for hard power projection, even when its own civilians and interest were recurrently targeted. With the Taliban penetrating the US security at their will, India's continual obsession for soft diplomacy targeted at civilian goodwill was under a great deal of risk. The position was becoming increasingly harder to sustain. Pakistan had the advantage of the Taliban and India was losing the strategic momentum in the war-torn nation. There were calls from all quarters, including the US and Afghanistan that India should start supporting its development endeavours in Afghanistan with a stronger military presence.

If Afghanistan was the most critical frontier in combating terrorism targeted against India, the critics asked, how long could India afford to continue with its present soft policy trajectory, whereby its civilians and interests were getting killed in pursuit of its developmental objectives? India's attempt to leverage its 'soft power' in Afghanistan became increasingly risky, in light of a growing Taliban offensive. The dilemma confronting Indian policymakers on Afghanistan was not merely limited to the country's specific interests and engagement, but stems from India's overall mission to play a larger role in regional and global affairs. Indian military strategy has increasingly called for more expeditionary forces that can project power throughout South Asia, while the political leadership wants to attain the said stature with soft and more economy-led diplomatic outreach. There are visible disagreements between the military and the political leadership, when it comes to projecting hard power.

Allaying all concerns and criticism, India decided to continue with its policy of soft diplomacy and development aid. However, to make a strong gesture, Indian stepped up the security cooperation with Afghanistan to the next level, and started supplying even lethal weapons to the Afghan military. India further stepped up the training of the rudimentary Afghan army. It was also a ploy to check the growing strategic leverage of Islamabad over Kabul, by arresting the spread of the Taliban without dispatching military boots directly on the ground. In the past, India has refrained from supplying lethal arms to avoid the wrath of the Taliban and abstain from joining the unpopular western military bandwagon. India feared that it might prove counterproductive. However, there was a slight moderation in the Indian standpoint now. Western observers, though, lauded India's policy of not sending troops to Afghanistan to counter the Taliban directly but opined that the move would significantly contribute to the growing volatility and deterioration of security in Afghanistan.

By the third quarter of 2009, Afghanistan was witnessing another fundamental change in the mood of the US and

NATO forces, which had the potential to redefine the future of Afghanistan. All forces and their political masters in the West, including the US started singing peace carols in a huddle. They were willing to talk to the Taliban, whom they had set out to eliminate. The 180-degree change in perception and view was a grim realization that the US war on terror had proven largely counterproductive and the Taliban were far from vanquished. It was also documented with clear evidence that Pakistan would not dismantle the terrorist sanctuaries flourishing in the unlawful tribal belt of Waziristan. The US officials started taking turns to blame Islamabad for fanning Taliban unrest in Afghanistan. The double game of deceit and duplicity played by Pakistan was up for open condemnation not only by the US leadership, but also Afghanistan. On one hand, Pakistan was posturing that it was with the US in supporting its war against the Taliban, while mentoring the same Taliban on the other hand. President Karzai vehemently criticized Pakistan for harbouring terrorist sanctuaries and further fomenting trouble in Afghanistan through their proxies.

When all the guns should have been trained on Pakistan to put them under pressure for not meddling in Afghanistan, the US toyed with the idea of dangling a peace process with the Taliban. Though pragmatic, the policy decision suggested that the US forces were on the verge of fatigue and signalling an US exit from Afghanistan for the first time after their entry in October 2001. The idea of good Taliban and bad Taliban was coined for the first time, along with building a case for engaging with the good Taliban. It was an unchartered territory for the South Block in India. India was shocked to say the least and caught completely off guard to deal with the peace outreach to the Taliban. The Indian foreign ministry never believed in the schism of terrorists into good and bad, irrespective of differing ideologies of ruling political dispensation.

The 60-nation London Conference on Afghanistan held in January 2010, for the first-time advocated talks and protracted engagement with the Taliban in quest for an enduring political solution. The development jolted India, as New Delhi viewed with alarm, its rapidly shrinking strategic space for diplomatic manoeuvring in Afghanistan. India damaged its position further when the then External Affairs Minister S.M. Krishna underscored the Indian policy of not making a distinction between a 'good Taliban and a bad Taliban'. He was completely out of sync with the popular mood at the conference. India was left out completely in the London deliberation with none subscribing to India's insistence of not making any truck with the Taliban under the garb of good and bad Taliban. The US-led western alliance had made up its mind that it was not a question of 'if', but of 'when' and 'how' to exit from Afghanistan, which the leaders in Washington and London felt was rapidly becoming a never-ending quagmire.

As the London Conference settled that the time had come to woo the 'moderate section' of the Taliban, a new political arrangement, inclusion of the Taliban in the new power structure of Kabul was a foregone conclusion. It was an indication that Pakistan seemed to have convinced the West that it could play the role of mediator in negotiations with the Taliban—thereby underlining its centrality in the unfolding strategic dynamic in the region. The proximity with the Taliban threw a potent possibility that Pakistan would cream the peace process in its favour and further succeed in lodging the radical pro-ISI Taliban leaders in the much-anticipated new power arrangement in Kabul. Such a possibility would be catastrophic for Indian security if remnants of the Taliban were to come to power with the backing of the ISI and Pakistan's military. These changing ground realities forced India to start reconsidering the terms of its involvement in Afghanistan.

Pakistan's paranoia about the Indian presence in Afghanistan had led the West to underplay India's role in the peace process in Afghanistan. India's largely beneficial role in the country, even as Pakistan's every claim about Indian intentions was being taken at face value, failed to earn them a place at the peace table. The Taliban militants who blew up the Indian embassy in Kabul in 2008 and tried again in 2009 have sent a strong signal that India is part of the evolving security dynamic in Afghanistan despite the country's reluctance to take on a more active role in the military operations. India's isolation at the London Conference underlined that its role in Afghanistan was not being fully understood and appreciated, even by the West. Islamabad and Kabul also managed to formalize a pact that would allow the Pakistani army a role in negotiating the reconciliation between Kabul and the Taliban, which was supported by the US. There was a sharp change in Karzai's stance and approach too. After blaming Pakistan of supporting and mentoring the Taliban, President Karzai was depending on the same Pakistan to find a lasting solution for Afghanistan. Though India did not like the change of stance, it was hardly in any position to resist it. India erred on another account too. India was heavily reliant on the US to safeguard its interests in Afghanistan. India thought that the US would keep India's concern at its heart in finding a solution for Afghanistan, even if that means engaging with the Taliban. It was diplomatically naive on the part of India's policy contingent to think that the US would compromise with its priorities, should it boil down to a situation of finding a better alternative suiting the larger interest of the US.

There was another visible change in the approach of the US with the launch of the peace process. The US started actively discouraging India from assuming a higher profile in Afghanistan for fear of offending Pakistan. But at the same time, it failed in getting Pakistan to take Indian concerns seriously. This has led to rapid deterioration of India's diplomatic muscle, with New Delhi having little or no strategic space to manoeuvre in Afghanistan. Not surprisingly, therefore, India was forced to reassess its priorities vis-à-vis Afghanistan-Pakistan, given the huge stakes that New Delhi has developed in Afghanistan over the past decade.

Not only did the US publicly endorse the idea of negotiations with the Taliban on a political settlement with Washington, they even started holding several back-door meetings with the representatives of Mullah Omar. Pakistan succeeded in convincing the West that the best way out of the present mess was to reach out to the 'good Taliban'. It was another diplomatic victory for them over India. Though the US and Afghan governments insisted that any settlement process should result in an end to Taliban violence and a willingness to conform to the Afghan Constitution, the possibility of a Pakistan-sponsored settlement between hardline elements of the Taliban and the Afghan government was a serious concern for India. The diplomatic cables released by WikiLeaks underscored that India was concerned about US plans to exit from Afghanistan and its possible repercussions on India's security. With the official launch of the peace process after the London Conference, Pakistan registered dual strategic victory over India. Islamabad was happy elbowing out India from the peace process and at the same time gain the driver's seat of the peace process. India may blame Islamabad and President Obama for its slide in Afghanistan; however, it was a self-inflicted failure. India's rigid stand of not making a distinction between the good and the bad Taliban, when the whole world was ready to make amends to their past standpoint was one of the reasons for finding themselves on the fringe.

As Indian hopes belied, New Delhi had to rapidly alter its approach towards the relation between Afghanistan and Pakistan. India has to align with the rest regarding the newly launched peace process in Afghanistan. Officially, India started advocating support for an Afghan-owned, Afghan-led reconciliation process. New Delhi wanted the Kabul government to be the key player in the talks with the Taliban. India expected that Karzai, being its close ally, would ensure India's interests are integrated in case of a peace resolution resulting towards creation of a new order political arrangement. India was seriously worried about the post peace process Kabul arrangement infested with the Taliban. Such a development would enable the Afghan territory to be used once again as a launching pad for militant attacks on India. It would place Kabul back in the Pakistani orbit, and effectively put an end to Indian aid, investment and trade in Afghanistan.

The 2010 multinational peace talks left open the possibility of a Taliban role in the future government, despite vociferous Indian opposition. India concluded that some form of reconciliation would happen with or without Indian support, and it accepted the idea of negotiating with insurgent leaders who were willing to abjure violence. India moderated its position in an effort to maintain some degree of influence. Such a radical change in stance represented an acknowledgement in New Delhi that it would need to have linkages with Kabul, whatever the composition and structure of government might throw up. While many Indians castigated their government for assenting to the Taliban's involvement in a future Afghan government, leaders in New Delhi were clear that they would be better positioned to counter Pakistani influence if they maintained a voice in the reconciliation process than if they opposed it from outside. Whether the moderation in stance towards the Taliban will earn India a seat at the high table, was anyone's guess.

The rolling of the peace process witnessed a sharp shrinking of the strategic space generated by India, with the generous development outlay, over a decade. The progress of the peace process also outlined the complete withdrawal of US and NATO forces from Afghanistan by September 2014. The US wanted to exit under the cover of the peace process. It was a foregone conclusion that the US is not winning the war against the Taliban. The war against the Taliban has only emboldened them further. The Taliban were not keen on abjuring violence, even when they were part of the peace deliberation. Stepping up the mayhem was part of their ploy to gain more strategic leverage in the peace negotiations. Hence, Afghanistan was witnessing an unprecedented surge in Taliban-led violence and attack, even when the peace deliberations were going on. The security cover provided by the US and NATO forces was outstretched. The situation was set to get worse with the approaching withdrawal of the western forces. India intended to play the security void even with the red line of 'no military boots' in Afghanistan.

To preserve its interests and further arrest its continual strategic slide, India took a number of policy measures, which included achieving greater policy coordination with states like Russia and Iran, and reaching out to prominent political leaders across the political spectrum, beyond Kabul. India was constantly upgrading its security ties with Afghanistan to regain lost strategic space and stay relevant. India agreed to train more Afghan security forces, under the landmark October 2011 Indo-Afghan Strategic Partnership Agreement and further supplying lethal arms, peeving Pakistan. Karzai offered reassurance that the agreement 'is not directed against any country' and called Pakistan his nation's 'twin brother'.[104] Similarly, even as Karzai was vocal about minimizing Pakistani influence in his country, he moderated his criticism of Islamabad with counterbalancing praise. In October 2011—merely a day after denouncing Islamabad for harbouring terrorists (while standing alongside US Secretary of State Hillary Clinton)— Karzai again stated that Pakistan was a brother and asserted that his country would side with it, under any circumstances. While Karzai fought back against Pakistani interference, at the same time he ensured that he keeps them in good spirits. He was trying to keep both India and Pakistan happy in the best interest of Afghanistan. In a way, Karzai was following a well-trodden path of Afghan leaders who have sought to balance Afghanistan's two more powerful South Asian neighbours— India and Pakistan.

After gathering initial momentum, the peace process began crumbling by the end of 2012. This was largely due to the mounting attacks by the Taliban. In between, the Taliban attacked the US embassy in Kabul twice, first in September 2011 and then in April 2012. The first attack inflicted serious damage with seven killed and 19 wounded, mostly Afghans. The source of both the attacks were tracked to the ISI-backed Haqqani network. The support of ISI was also clearly established in the first attack. The top military officials of the US said that Pakistan's spy agency played a direct role in supporting the insurgents who carried out the deadly attack on the American

---

[104]PTI, 'Partnership with India not targeted against Pak: Karzai,' *The Economic Times*, 5 October 2011, https://economictimes.indiatimes.com/news/ politics-and-nation/partnership-with-india-not-targeted-against-pak-karzai/ articleshow/10244202.cms?from=mdr, accessed 19 June 2021.

embassy in Kabul. It was the most serious charge that the US had levelled against Pakistan in the decade that it (the US) has been at war in Afghanistan. In comments that were the first to directly link the spy agency, the Directorate for Inter-Services Intelligence, with an assault on the US, Adm. Mike Mullen, the Chairman of the Joint Chiefs of Staff, went further than any other American official in blaming the ISI for undermining the American effort in Afghanistan.

President Karzai's patience was also wearing out with the crumbling of the peace process. He too openly started blaming Pakistan for supporting the Taliban in spreading unrest in Afghanistan. Pakistan's continuing support to the Haqqani network and other extremists had severely angered the Karzai administration. President Karzai charged that the Pakistani border and security units not only lack the capacity but, more intrinsically, the will to stem cross-border infiltration. Relations became so tense at times that Karzai even threatened to send troops across the border to attack militants operating from bases in Islamabad's tribal belt. He did not stop there and further made a series of efforts to impress upon the US to act tough against Pakistan.

The Pakistan muddle

The call for Islamabad to neutralize the Taliban operating from sanctuaries in Pakistan started growing louder. Pakistan was in no mood to surrender their strategic assets (in the Taliban), despite the US warning. Pakistan knew that the warning was nothing more than a blank threat, as Washington could not do away with Islamabad. The growing rant against Pakistan was, however, undermining its relationship with both the US and Afghanistan. Pakistan was becoming increasingly unpopular in Afghanistan. A few Pakistan-based prominent newspapers even alerted Islamabad that the policy of overt support to the Taliban would throw Afghanistan into the arms of India. But the Pakistan army was more than reluctant in acting against the Taliban. The Pakistani civilian leadership was also subscribing the military doctrine to its army. Sartaj Aziz, the national security adviser to Prime Minister Nawaz Sharif, told the BBC that there was no need for Pakistan to target militants who did not threaten the country's security. 'Why should enemies of the US unnecessarily become our foes? Some of them were dangerous for us and some are not. Why must we make enemies out of them all?' he said, referring to the militant Haqqani network.[105]

In one of his interviews, Pervez Musharraf, a former military dictator who ruled the country from 1999 to 2007, said, 'They (India) want to create an anti-Pakistan Afghanistan. If Indians are using some ethnic groups in Afghanistan, then Pakistan will use its own support, and our ethnic allies are certainly Pashtuns.'[106] Some Pakistani observers believe that the former general was still close to the current military leadership of the nuclear-armed state, and that he is probably only echoing his former institution's views on India and Afghanistan. The overlapping of these comments was not a mere coincidence, rather part of a coherent policy of Islamabad binding the top military as well as the civilian leadership on Afghanistan. The two different statements by two Pakistani leaders carried a

---

[105]Shams, Shamil, 'What prompted Pakistan to ban the Haqqani network?' DW, https://www.dw.com/en/what-prompted-pakistan-to-ban-the-haqqani-network/a-18199505, accessed 19 June 2021.

[106]Shams, Shamil, 'India and Pakistan "battle" for Afghanistan,' DW, 19 November 2014, https://www.dw.com/en/india-and-pakistan-battle-for-afghanistan/a-18073889, accessed 19 June 2021.

single narrative—Islamabad feels threatened by New Delhi's close ties with Kabul; hence, it will likely continue to support some faction of the Taliban as counterbalancing forces in its western neighbourhood. And there was nothing new about Pakistan's Afghanistan policy. The country's military and civil establishment considers the Taliban an important strategic ally, who they think should not be dispensed with, amid growing international call. They further viewed the Taliban to be an indispensable part of the Afghan government after the US and NATO pullout. Pakistan played the China card to its advantage to wither out the US pressure to handle the Taliban with an iron hand.

Sensing the non-cooperation from Islamabad for long, the US was gearing itself to a new strategy of dealing with Pakistan. The US moderated its support to Pakistan with a carrot and stick policy. The era of signing a blank cheque to the Pakistan army for its support in Afghanistan soon became a thing of the past. This, however, lifted the residual moral obligation and eventually released all pressure from Pakistan to act tough against the Taliban. The rising attack by the Taliban coupled with the continual reluctance of Pakistan resulted in the collapse of the London Conference-backed peace process completely by the beginning of 2014. This did not deter the West from furthering its plan in Afghanistan. The US and NATO forces moved ahead with the exit plan and Afghanistan was left at the mercy of a rudimentary Afghan army along with a leftover 14,000 US soldiers, mostly in non-combatant mode, in the last quarter of 2014.

The Taliban were emboldened and more resolute than ever in its aim to capture Kabul. The Pakistan support to the Taliban was now open and more forthcoming. Afghanistan was becoming more volatile than ever. Not only were Indian development endeavours coming to a standstill, but also there was a complete freeze on any new announcement of development projects by New Delhi. India was also opening up to a potent possibility of a Taliban-laced government in Kabul, either through a future peace and reconciliation process, or by capture of Kabul by the Taliban. The latter was a possibility with the complete withdrawal of the US and NATO forces. The situation in Afghanistan necessitated India to further soften its stand against the Taliban.

The road to success for President Obama's Afghanistan strategy had a strong Pakistan connection. It was critical for the US to reverse the Taliban's momentum, which required getting rid of the movement's sanctuary in Pakistan, along with the top Taliban leadership based in and around the city of Quetta. But while Pakistan was aggressively tackling its domestic Taliban (TTP), it has consistently declined to act against the Afghan Taliban groups based on its soil, because it sees the Afghan Taliban as a useful counterweight to India's presence in Afghanistan. Even freezing of grants coupled with recurrent rant against Pakistan was not yielding any dividends in Afghanistan. By the beginning of 2013, Karzai started making acerbic charges against Islamabad holding them solely responsible for the emboldened Taliban attacking Afghanistan.

His attack was not restricted to Islamabad only. He was even unsparing in his tirade against the US leadership, including the then US President, Barack Obama, for being soft on Islamabad. It was reported that Karzai shared the intelligence about the presence of Taliban leaders and wanted the US to attack them on the basis of actionable intelligence. The bilateral relationship between the US and Pakistan was on the slide. And President Obama did not show the courage to send drones to Quetta. It was reported that the White House was divided—while one section wanted to attack the Taliban leadership, the other was keen on pressurizing Pakistan through softer means like freeze of grants. Still, today, there are US security analysts who believe that the US should have handled Pakistan with an iron hand to make them cooperate in the war against terror in Afghanistan. The continual inaction by the US against Pakistan deteriorated its relationship with Karzai to the extent that the White House reportedly stopped taking his calls towards the end of his presidential term.

2014 also witnessed a change of political guard, both in India as well as in Afghanistan. Afghanistan elected the former Finance Minister of Afghanistan, Ashraf Ghani Ahmadzai as the successor of Hamid Karzai after a prolonged and controversial election. The election threw up the unity government with CEO Abdullah Abdullah and President Ghani sharing power. Abdullah Abdullah was from the camp of the Northern Alliance, whose relationship with Pakistan was antagonistic to the hilt. President Ghani, having served in the World Bank, was suave and diplomatic in his outreach. The international community, including the denizens of Afghanistan were interested to witness how the new government would approach India and Pakistan.

India too witnessed the election of Modi as the new prime minister, after a landslide victory in May 2014. The right-wing Bharatiya Janata Party was coming to power after a hiatus of 10 years. It was anticipated that their outreach to Pakistan and Afghanistan would be fundamentally different to that of its predecessor, the Congress. Pakistan also had a relatively new army chief (Raheel Sharif) appointed in November 2013.

India was keenly observing the election in Afghanistan, and so was Pakistan. Ghani's victory surprised India more than Pakistan. While India was harping on an Abdullah Abdullah victory, Pakistan had built a stake for the election of Ghani.

After an exhausting and contentious election process, Ghani, a US-educated economist-turned-reformist politician, took charge at the Arg, the presidential palace in Kabul, on 29 September 2014. As a first step, Ghani pledged to do what his predecessor, Karzai, refused to do, and signed a deal to secure a continuation of international military assistance to Afghanistan after 2014. This clearly reflected that he wanted to make amends to the Afghan–US relationship strained by Karzai, in the twilight phase of his political career.

The international community was excitingly watching the outreach of the new president to India and Pakistan. Within days of his succession to power, he made it clear that he would politically align with the Pakistan–China axis more in his prime endeavour to fix Afghanistan. President Ghani was walking the talk. In light of his new foreign policy priority, President Ghani visited China from 28–31 October 2014, after assuming office. The visit concluded with the ministerial meetings of the Istanbul process showcasing China's leadership in multilateral efforts to protect Afghan stability.

President Ghani chose China for his first official visit abroad to seek a closer partnership with his country's largest neighbour, as Afghanistan moved into a new, post-NATO era. Afghanistan needed China for extending its influence over Pakistan, but more importantly for economic assistance. Afghanistan could potentially receive a number of infrastructure and other economic investments from China as Beijing pushed ahead with its Silk Road Economic Belt connecting Western China with Central Asia and beyond. This project could help revitalize Afghanistan's economy and provide jobs to the growing youth population and, in turn, give the new government in Kabul more legitimacy. President Ghani's preference of China also suggested that Afghanistan

wanted to broaden its regional connection beyond the binary
of India and Pakistan. Afghanistan also desperately wanted to
partner with China to cut its dependence on aid and political
support. China too needed Afghanistan, though to a lesser
degree, to check the infiltration of terrorists in the already-
restive Xinjiang and Uyghur autonomous regions, in case of a
Taliban capture in Kabul. Beijing was greatly concerned about
the movement of foreign militants into Xinjiang; the regime
collapse in Afghanistan would deeply exacerbate this issue.

President Ghani's preference of Islamabad, over New Delhi,
as his second tour surprised many, including New Delhi. Ghani
had the option to either maintain the status quo by taking
no interest in improving ties with Pakistan, or to extend—
yet again—an offer of peace and cooperation. His actions
signified that he zeroed in on the latter. After being sworn-in
as President in September 2014, Ghani's first official visit to
Beijing, in October, and immediately thereafter to Pakistan,
in November, was making his intention clear. His thrust on
engaging Pakistan and China as part of his effort to carve out a
political space for the Taliban within the existing political and,
to some extent, constitutional framework, should not have
come as a surprise. His gravitating towards Rawalpindi and
Beijing was a concerted effort to find a negotiated settlement
to the conflict with Pakistan's proxy—the Afghan Taliban,
including some unilateral confidence-building measures to
fundamentally transform Afghanistan's traditionally strained
ties with Pakistan. Washington, with a suboptimal military
footprint in Afghanistan and greater occupation with West
Asia, was glad to let Kabul play up the Beijing–Rawalpindi
axis. Ghani's regional forays probably had the full backing of
the White House. In any event, Kabul did not really have much
to lose by way of reaching out to Beijing and Rawalpindi.

What was further surprising was President Ghani's decision to meet the Pakistani General Raheel Sharif at the army headquarters in Rawalpindi, during his first visit on 14 November 2014. Pakistani troops presented Ghani with a guard of honour. The Afghan delegation was also given a detailed briefing on the Pakistani army's efforts to secure border areas with Afghanistan. Ghani's visit to Pakistan's military headquarters was described as a significant development in bilateral ties, because many Afghans blamed that institution for security problems that Afghanistan was facing. Ghani's predecessor, Karzai, strongly accused the Pakistan army and its spy agency, the ISI, of supporting the Taliban insurgency in Afghanistan. It was amply clear that President Ghani would not go against Pakistan for the mess Afghanistan was going through. Rather, he would approach Pakistan to resolve Afghanistan. After the conclusion of the visit, Ghani announced that Pakistan was unconditionally ready to cooperate with Afghanistan in bringing the Taliban leadership to the negotiating table. The two countries were further open to explore a plethora of mutual cooperation measures, including security and training of the Afghan military. Officials in both the countries viewed the Afghan leader's visit as a fresh opportunity to improve bilateral relations that were historically marred by mutual suspicions and mistrust. This was seen as the first step towards building a relationship based on mutual trust and confidence between the two countries. For this relationship to work, Pakistan had to prove that it was a trustworthy ally, capable of fulfilling its promises to bring the Taliban to the negotiating table, deny sanctuaries to terrorist groups and not interfere in Afghanistan's internal affairs.

As a long-standing Afghan ally, India had legitimate concerns over the sudden shift in Ghani's foreign policy towards Pakistan. Improved relations between Afghanistan and Pakistan would allow the latter to harm India's interests in Afghanistan. The fate of billions of dollars in reconstruction and development aid to Afghanistan was also important. Indian generosity was based on a long-term strategic objective to keep Afghanistan on its side. This calculation was set to change with Afghanistan-Pakistan relations charting a new course and direction, which was beyond India's comprehension. In addition, thousands of Indian citizens were involved in development projects across Afghanistan. The safety of those citizens was a major concern for New Delhi. The diplomatic community argued that President Ghani's move of choosing Islamabad over New Delhi signified a shift in the leadership's view towards its nuclear-armed neighbour, while others said it had the potential to make New Delhi reconsider its strategic relations with Afghanistan.

The Pakistani media was flexing its muscles, sparing no time in attacking India's policy towards Afghanistan. President Ghani was aware of the growing anxiety in South Block. The newly elected president had to placate the growing concerns, but did not want to balance his strategic outreach to India, by visiting New Delhi as a next stop, immediately after Islamabad. Visiting India and Pakistan in the same leg of a diplomatic tour has been a popular approach adopted by western leaders, especially the US and the UK, to balance their strategic relationship with the two arch-rivals. In the past, Afghanistan too tried to walk the path of delicately balancing the two countries and keeping both happy and, more importantly, not annoying either of the two.

Though, for Afghan leaders, balancing the country's regional foreign policy between India and Pakistan has never been a cakewalk. President Karzai would refer to India as an all-weather ally,[107] but Pakistan as a twin brother, almost in the same breath. He maintained the balance well, except for the fag-end of his presidential years, when he squarely blamed and even threatened Pakistan to enter the border and attack the Taliban sanctuary. President Ghani was in an active mode to repair the relationship and certainly prioritize Pakistan over India. His strategic priority-cum-well-thought-out move was pinned around the fact that it was Pakistan who had the ability to stabilize Afghanistan by taming the Taliban. And if he gravitated too much towards India, Pakistan would employ the lever of the Taliban to further aid instability in Afghanistan.

But at the same time, President Ghani knew well that Afghanistan could not afford to upset India with the civilian largesse flowing into his country. The US reconstruction aid was dwindling. In this context, the Indian aid was further more important and potentially serving as a lifeline for Afghanistan. Hence, he had to make amends with India and placate growing apprehensions in New Delhi. Seven months into his presidency, President Ghani finally visited New Delhi with his entourage, from 27–29 April 2015. The spacing of the visit was a well-calculated move to avoid any dilution of his cardinal message to Pakistan. The Indian media started asking where exactly India figured in Ghani's vision of Afghanistan and what steps India needed to take in order to secure its interests even before he disembarked from the plane. Afghanistan acted smartly by sending Abdullah Abdullah, Afghanistan's newly elected Chief Executive Officer, to New Delhi in March 2015.

Even though he was on a private visit, his task was cut out for doing the groundwork for Ghani's visit later in April 2015

---

[107]*India Today,* 15 December 2013, https://www.indiatoday.in/india/north/story/hamid-karzai-afghanistan-india-manmohan-singh-terror-operation-pakistan-220827-2013-12-15, accessed 20 June 2021.

and also allay India's growing concerns about Afghanistan gravitating towards Pakistan. In his interactions in New Delhi, he expressed his disappointment, at the rising scepticism among a section of India's strategic affairs community on the future trajectory of India–Afghanistan relations. The Afghan strategic community held a different opinion. One could certainly question the viability of Ghani's diplomatic initiatives or have an opinion on its likely ultimate outcome in light of past experience with Pakistan, but not its relevance from Kabul's viewpoint, given the sheer magnitude of the challenge that Pakistan posed for Afghanistan.

In an interview to an Indian TV journalist prior to his India visit, Ghani repudiated the charge that India was not significant for him.[108] He said that India was one of his top foreign policy priorities. During his visit, President Ghani and Prime Minister Modi had a wide range of discussions on bilateral issues mainly centered around development. India was willing to make big-time security cooperation for enhancing its military footprint in Afghanistan, but President Ghani did not warm up to the idea. Ghani wanted Indian aid to flow in. He was keen to get Indian businesses to invest in a big way in the country's mineral sector. However, he wished to play to Pakistan by adopting a segmented approach and keeping India out of the security sector of Afghanistan. Modi also highlighted India's role in Afghan security, and the principles that needed to be the basis of reconciliation with the Taliban. Ghani chose to remain neutral on both accounts.

It was further evident from Modi's and Ghani's statements at the joint media briefing that while the former was more

---

[108]Katju, Vivek, 'Ghani and India: Circles of Separation', Gateway House, 29 April 2015, https://www.gatewayhouse.in/ghani-and-india-circles-of-separation/, accessed 2 July 2021.

forthcoming and dwelt on specifics, the latter revolved around generalities. Modi, while emphasizing connectivity, expressed a willingness to join the successor to the Afghan-Pakistan Trade and Transit Agreement. Ghani responded by outlining an impressive vision of regional connectivity and of Afghanistan's crucial place in it. He also spoke of Afghan transport reaching Wagah-Attari, but was silent on Indian goods going via Pakistan to Afghanistan from those points. India had invested a lot in Afghanistan, and the bulk of this investment was strategically aimed at minimizing Pakistan's influence. Modi was inclined to enhance India's partnership with Kabul in the security sector, but there was no taker in the new government in Kabul. President Ghani was refraining from overcommitting to India in the fear of rubbing Islamabad the wrong way. During his India visit, he uttered nothing that could raise an eyebrow in Rawalpindi. His gesture explained the lengths he had travelled, during his India visit to ensure that he did not jeopardize the new-found bonhomie with Pakistan.

And, more importantly, he was not in any mood to entertain any security-centric commitments to New Delhi, as this was bound to have a repellent effect in Rawalpindi. President Ghani though left no stone unturned in stepping up development cooperation with India. He was further keen on promoting trade and commerce without getting into specifics. By the end of his visit, it was amply clear that Ghani's approach of dealing with New Delhi would be vastly different from that of his predecessor Karzai. He was more than willing to tone down security cooperation with New Delhi to placate Islamabad. He was ready to trust Islamabad and test the hypothesis of persuading Pakistan to influence the Taliban for joining the political process, in his bid to stabilize Afghanistan. Washington fully backed President Ghani's strategic bet to see if it worked better for Afghanistan. Also, the White House was losing appetite for Afghanistan with the war against terror turning from bad to worse.

India was upset with the timid response of President Ghani. However, it was in no position to undertake any retaliatory gesture to balance the growing proximity of Kabul towards Islamabad. India was invested neck deep in Afghanistan. And staying out of the game from a highly relevant and strategic hotspot like Afghanistan was not an option, anymore. Islamabad, on its part, was keenly observing President Ghani's visit, and was pleased with the outcome of the same. It was aligning well with the strategic interest and priorities of Islamabad. It was yet another diplomatic victory of Islamabad over New Delhi, after elbowing out India from the peace process. It was a double blow for India, which did not augur well for India after having done everything it could to stay the course in Afghanistan.

Karzai, after a brief initial flirtation with Pakistan, realized that India had a crucial role to play in the security sector in Afghanistan. It is another matter that the United Progressive Alliance government's response was cold in expanding the military partnership. While the Modi government wanted the bilateral status quo to expand under the new government in Kabul, there was a clear lack of appetite at Ghani's end. Ghani's outreach towards India was in sharp contrast to that of his predecessor. In order to address Pakistani suspicions, he toned down Afghanistan's traditional alliance with India and stepped up unprecedented security cooperation with Islamabad, despite facing a volley of domestic opposition. To allay fears of Afghanistan's growing proximity with India, he even put the issue of ongoing security cooperation with India on the back-burner. This created a renewed hope both in Afghanistan, as well as the international community that Pakistan may amend its ways and assist Afghanistan in a political settlement. Afghan President Ghani had offered everything to expand the bilateral ties, providing Islamabad with fresh opportunities to improve the relationship.

It was an opportune time to recalibrate relations towards advancing the stalled peace process and further refrain the Taliban from spreading unrest in Afghanistan. The Afghan people were getting impatient with Pakistan's unwillingness to rein in the Taliban, make them abjure violence and further compel them to join the negotiating table. It was action time for Islamabad, with little room for complacency. The US too was looking at Islamabad with a renewed hope that the fresh diplomatic outreach to Islamabad and, more importantly, preferring Islamabad over New Delhi might influence Pakistan to make amends. The Obama administration once again relied on the powerful Pakistan army to help organize and kick-start reconciliation talks aimed at ending the war in Afghanistan, despite accusing the disgraced ISI of secretly supporting the Haqqani terrorist network—which had mounted sustained attacks on the US interest, in the past. Prime Minister Sharif wanted to respond positively, but the Pakistani military and civilian leadership's preferences towards Kabul were diverging, with the former enjoying the clout when it came to defining the path and intent of diplomacy with Kabul. The situation instead of calming down in Afghanistan, was on the spike.

The Taliban were getting hyperactive and were attacking Afghanistan at their free will. The Taliban wormed out from their traditional bastion of the south to the relatively stable northern provinces. They were massing on the outskirts of Kabul and attacking the city with an unfailing regularity. The civilian casualty was on the rise. With the US no more in a combatant role and the rookie Afghan army unable to check the advance of the Taliban, the situation was getting from bad to worse. The UN estimated that a quarter of all Afghan districts was now under the control of the Taliban, and another one-third was heavily 'contested' between government forces and the Taliban.

The ISI had little interest in bringing the Taliban, including the Haqqanis to the negotiating table, as it continued to view the insurgents as its best bet for maintaining strong influence in Afghanistan as the US reduced its presence there. Meanwhile, Afghanistan was falling into the grip of a resurgent Taliban. And now, even the Islamic State militants were raising its head to add to the mayhem in Afghanistan. Bilateral relations between Afghanistan and Pakistan started straining over continual ISI's support for the Taliban. Islamabad though made the right optics in forging the quadrilateral group—comprising China, the US, Pakistan and Russia—in the overall interest of the West, in quest for peace. But it was more of an academic gesture rather than any strong resolve for finding a political solution. Iran too joined the group at a later stage, with India missing the train once again to be in this strategic group. India was left out at the behest of Pakistan. Islamabad convinced the White House to keep India out of the latest round of the peace venture. Washington did not want to upset Pakistan, as it knew well that the US exit was improbable without the support of the Pakistan army. Hence, the US was left with no option but to adhere to Pakistan's request of keeping India out of the peace fold. Islamabad succeeded in rubbing the wrong end of New Delhi, once again.

India too did not do any favour to its case, with a waning relationship with Kabul post a heavy investment. New Delhi thought that a massive development cooperation would earn them a seat in any high table concerning Afghanistan. The established formulae predominantly highlighted in any diplomatic manual might work in normal settings, but not in a volatile context like Afghanistan. In such settings, the number and depth of strategic levers define the rules of the game rather than the magnum of money put in the pipeline of development. India had growing stakes in peace and stability in Afghanistan, and the absence of India in the quadrilateral peace group underlined its continual marginalization on the strategic front. India should have hedged its bets with Iran and Russia. They have been the traditional supporters of the Northern Alliance along with India, and driven by almost the same agenda of not letting the Taliban come to power. This would have boosted India's chance to board the peace process, instead of being on the sideline.

President Ghani harped on Pakistan, but it was based on certain conditions. He maintained that Pakistani commitments had to be judged by actions on the ground. He was unwilling to subject his diplomatic gesture-cum-new political investments made in Islamabad at the complete goodwill of the Pakistani generals. Ghani did everything he could to improve ties with Pakistan. His 'tilt' towards Pakistan was antagonistic to India's strategic interests. In addition to keeping India out of his immediate ring of foreign policy priority, he kept the security cooperation on hold. Under pressure from the Pakistani military, Afghan security forces clamped down on the TTP and also allowed operatives from the ISI to interrogate TTP prisoners in Afghan prisons. None of these favours, however, generated any returns in terms of reduction in Taliban insurgency nor did it open the possibility of direct talks between Kabul and the Taliban. Eventually, the signing of an MoU between Afghan and Pakistani intelligence agencies in

May 2015, for sharing intelligence, was the epitome of security cooperation, even with the ISI openly supporting the Taliban to aid and abet unrest in Afghanistan.

The Pakistan army confirmed that the two countries' security agencies had signed an MoU in which Pakistan would help train and equip Afghan intelligence officers take part in the interrogation of terror suspects and conduct joint operations. It was an astonishing step for Afghanistan's NDS, which has long accused its counterpart at the Pakistani military's ISI directorate of practically sponsoring Taliban insurgency. Despite professing loyalty, former president Karzai too sharply criticized the decision to send Afghan army cadets to Pakistan for military training. Karzai's willingness to send men to India while spurning Pakistan enraged Pakistan's generals, who believed the future leaders of the Afghan army were being indoctrinated by their mortal enemies. This was a serious setback for India. However, the unprecedented attempt to improve cooperation between Afghan and Pakistani spies caused a massive uproar in Afghanistan, where politicians and the media accused the government of selling out to Pakistan. The civilian mood against Pakistan was poisoned further with no action against the Taliban amid growing terrorist attacks within Afghanistan. It was seen as an insult to their national pride. It was becoming difficult for Ghani to ignore the internal situation and continue his march towards Pakistan. President Ghani's patience with Pakistan in the face of constant inaction was dissipating now. The spring offence (2015) by the Taliban saw an unprecedented surge in Afghanistan when it was expected to subside, given Pakistan's commitment to help stabilize Afghanistan by opening a new door of communication. Kabul witnessed three suicide blasts on 7 August 2015, which killed more than 60 people and injured over 300 others. This was followed with the siege of Kunduz by the Taliban for over a week, 28 September 2015 onwards. The ANA is believed to have lost over 8,000 men, killed and wounded in operations against the Taliban, in 2015 alone. It was amply clear now that Islamabad was least interested in committing to the pledges made to President Ghani.

At a press conference condemning the attack, Afghan President Ghani accused Pakistan of sending 'messages of war' and harbouring terrorist training camps.[109] 'The last few days have shown that suicide bomber training camps and bomb-producing factories, which are killing our people are as active as before in Pakistan,' the BBC quoted Ghani as saying. 'We hoped for peace, but we are receiving messages of war from Pakistan. We can no longer see our people bleeding in a war that is exported from outside.' Everyone in Pakistan knew that President Ghani's rancorous outburst was for the consumption of the domestic audience rather than Pakistan. He was invested neck deep in Pakistan and giving up on Pakistan would be tantamount to loss of face and his already waning credibility. This would further give an upper hand to CEO Abdullah Abdullah, his unity government partner, for an unsparing attack in order to up his political brand. But his outburst was certainly signalling that his patience with Pakistan was exhausting.

However, he was willing to give it another try. He surprised everyone by attending the Asia Conference hosted by Pakistan, from 8–10 December 2015, in Islamabad. He made many enemies back home by approaching Pakistan once again to

---

[109]Scroll Staff, 'Afghanistan is "receiving messages of war from Pakistan", President Ghani tweets in anguish,' *Scroll.in*, 11 August 2015, https://scroll.in/article/747680/afghanistan-is-receiving-messages-of-war-from-pakistan-president-ghani-tweets-in-anguish, accessed 21 June 2021.

help Afghanistan settle a political deal with the Taliban. Critics painted Ghani as kneeling to his hosts after his fresh outreach to a country which had been his chief tormentor. President Ghani had his own reasons to attend the conference. 'He feels we have no choice but to engage Pakistan, despite the long history of mistrust between us,' said one private adviser to the president, speaking on the condition of anonymity. 'He often says we are not teenagers who can fight and sulk. We have paid too high a price for this undeclared war with Pakistan, and we don't have the luxury of letting it go on. He will do whatever it takes to end it.' Afghan political leaders publicly warned President Ghani not to smile when he visited Pakistan for a global conference on 9 September 2015, but he soon found that to be hard. As the Afghan president stepped off his plane at the Islamabad airport, he was surprised to discover the Pakistani Prime Minister and the country's military chiefs on the red carpet along with many other dignitaries as an honour guard blasted off a 21-gun salute. It was hard for President Ghani to ignore, but there had to be a fall-out in Kabul.

Rahmatullah Nabil, the Afghan intelligence head, suddenly resigned after decrying the ongoing Taliban slaughter while Afghan leaders 'catwalked' on Pakistan's red carpet.[110] He was peeved at President Ghani's participation in the conference and his reaching out to Islamabad to stabilize Afghanistan. Nabil's embarrassing departure highlighted a broader problem of power struggles, policy splits and lack of leadership within Ghani's administration at a time of growing insecurity. It could not have come at a worse time. With Parliament balking at many of his appointments, Ghani's government had no defence

---

[110]Reuters, 'Afghan spy chief resigns after rows with president,' *The Guardian*, 10 December 2015, https://www.theguardian.com/world/2015/dec/10/afghan-spy-chief-resigns-after-rows-with-president, accessed 21 June 2021.

minister, no attorney general and now no intelligence chief.

Ghani enjoyed strong western backing, but he was facing an array of domestic problems that damaged his credibility as a reformer and modernizer while also estranging him from the Afghan populace. He could ill afford the evolving situation. Suffering from a frenzied response to the increasing terrorist threats emanating from Pakistan, President Ghani had to harden his stance over Islamabad.

By the end of April 2016, Ghani was attacking Islamabad vociferously for sheltering the Taliban and other terrorist groups in Pakistan and further orchestrating terror attacks in Afghanistan. In his symbolic speech to the joint session of the houses of Parliament on 25 April 2016,[111] after a deadly terror attack in Kabul, he pointed fingers at Peshawar and Quetta, from where he said the enemies send terrorists to shed blood and destroy Afghanistan. Later, he threatened to approach the United Nations Security Council and complain about Pakistan for supporting the Taliban in spreading terror in Afghanistan. This was the first severe crack in the Afghanistan-Pakistan ties, after Ghani made an unprecedented move to repair their ties with Pakistan and, more importantly, use their influence over the Taliban to stabilize Afghanistan. The 18-month rapprochement between Ghani and the Pakistani military leadership proved to be completely one-sided. The Afghanistan-Pakistan bilateral ties were on the verge of a collapse.

Ghani was getting frustrated with not just Pakistan but the US as well. He was constantly urging Washington to end its inaction against the long-existing sanctuaries for the Taliban and the Haqqani network in Pakistan. The US had to act against Pakistan in order to fix or capture the Taliban

---

[111]Faizi, Aimal, 'Ashraf Ghani's war strategy will fail,' *Al Jazeera*, 10 May 2016.

leadership. But the US was as vulnerable as Afghanistan. Under the NUG, the US forces enjoyed a free hand in conducting their military operations in Afghanistan by employing drone strikes, air raids as well as unlawful house searches. But it had done nothing to check the deteriorating security situation in Afghanistan. Rather, it proved counterproductive. The US had to produce something to add to their account and stem the rising anger in Kabul.

On 21 May 2016, the killing of the Taliban leader Mullah Mansour in a US drone attack in Pakistan further derailed the rudimentary peace process and created ripples in the US–Pakistan relationship. The attack, which took place a few miles from the Afghanistan-Pakistan border in Balochistan province, reflected the growing US frustration with the Taliban and Pakistan. After all, Pakistan not only failed to bring the Taliban to negotiate peace with the Afghan government under the QCG framework, but it had also continued to extend support to the Taliban, including providing shelter to their leaders.

President Ghani had invested nearly all his political capital on his much-criticized outreach to appease Pakistan. Not only did the president have nothing to show for his misguided diplomatic endeavour, but he also wasted a crucial period, which made the Taliban gain significant advantage, resulting in more destruction and deaths in Afghanistan. It did not take long for his hope—that Pakistan could make the Taliban come to the negotiating table, so as to arrive at a modus vivendi, ensuring security and stability in the country—to be shattered. At the home front, Karzai too was upping the ante against President Ghani. He alarmed President Ghani for his outreach to Pakistan, through various interviews. He expressed fear that this would push his country under Pakistan's thumb and reverse all critical gains. The view of the former president, who continued to enjoy political charisma, was not easy to ignore. The former president was in the thick of Afghan politics and had the ability to shape political opinions, despite semi-retirement. The rapprochement with Pakistan irritated India to a large extent. And there was a tap to the civilian aid to Kabul. It was no more as free flowing as it used to be in the Karzai era.

Pressure was building for President Ghani from all fronts. And it was an opportune time for him to make amends for the extra miles he walked with Pakistan, hoping to enlist its help in brokering a peace deal with the Taliban. His immediate priority was to repair its damage with India. Ghani visited New Delhi from 14–15 September 2016. The visit took place in the backdrop of two back-to-back tours by Prime Minister Modi to Kabul, the first in December 2015 to inaugurate the Parliament building, the symbol of Afghan democracy, constructed by India as a gift to Afghanistan, and again in June 2016 to inaugurate the Afghanistan-India Friendship Dam at Salma.

Ghani's visit raised the need for accessing more arms from India, including lethal weapons, more attack helicopters, transport helicopters, tanks, artillery and ammunition to deal with the growing insurgency and attacks by the Taliban operating from Pakistani soil. There was a 180-degree change in his approach this time. It may be recalled that just after coming to power, Ghani had withdrawn the request put in by his predecessor President Karzai for armaments from India. That was part of Ghani's strategy to put pressure on Islamabad to oblige its commitments. The atmosphere and vibes between the two leaders were starkly different from what was witnessed during Ghani's first tour. At that time, although Ghani was hosted as per diplomatic protocol, there was a certain coldness and aloofness in his approach.

As a healthy sign that India and Afghanistan were continuing to strategically converge, in September 2016, New Delhi committed to providing Kabul with a fresh $1 billion in economic aid. Prime Minister Modi reiterated 'India's abiding support for a unified, sovereign, democratic, peaceful, stable and prosperous Afghanistan.'[112] He conveyed India's readiness to consider further requirements of Afghanistan for capacity building in spheres such as education, health, agriculture, skill development, empowerment of women, energy, infrastructure and strengthening of democratic institutions. Although somewhat late in coming, the swiftly expanding cooperation with Afghanistan was a shot in the arm for the government's policy of winning back its key strategic ally. Ghani's visit heralded a new chapter in the bilateral collaboration and sent out a strong message of the enduring and growing partnership to the region and the world.

Ghani's trip to India came in the backdrop of both India and Afghanistan having seen their relationships with Pakistan deteriorate. Moreover, New Delhi's new-found support for Kabul came shortly after White House officials encouraged India to play a more active role in ensuring Afghanistan's stability. Both leaders expressed 'grave concern at continued use of terrorism and violence in the region for achieving political objectives'[113]—a veiled reference to common neighbour Pakistan.

Islamabad was at great discomfort with resurrection of

---

[112]'India-Afghanistan Joint Statement during the visit of President of Afghanistan to India,' PM India, 14 September 2016, https://www.pmindia.gov.in/en/news_updates/india-afghanistan-joint-statement-during-the-visit-of-president-of-afghanistan-to-india/, accessed 21 June 2021.
[113]Ibid.

India–Afghan ties. It was miffed with the bilateral ties slipping to an active mode and increasingly worried about the growing defence partnership between India and Afghanistan. It also meant that Pakistan was released of whatever little moral binding it had to act against the Taliban. The security analyst community warned that Pakistan would step up unrest and give an open licence to the Taliban to spread unrest in Afghanistan. President Ghani's gravitating towards India was to balance its relationship with Pakistan. It was also an opportune time for President Ghani to check the excessive leeway provided to Pakistan.

India was in no mood to let go of the new-found bilateral momentum. It was keen on seizing the initiative. India hosted the Sixth Ministerial Conference of the Heart of Asia-Istanbul Process (HoA-IP) on 4 December 2016. Fourteen partner countries and more than 30 supporting countries and international organizations attended the conference. Rarely in a multilateral meeting or conference does a participating country become the principal target of attack by a country that is the 'chair' or 'co-chair'. After the rupture of his outreach to Pakistan, Ghani became a virulent critic of Pakistan. He was unsparing in his attack against Pakistan and used the international platform to launch a fresh round of verbal assaults against Pakistan.[114]

Ghani opened the conference by snubbing a $500 million pledge from Pakistan for development projects in Afghanistan, stating that Afghanistan needed aid to fight terrorism. 'We need to identify cross-border terrorism and a fund to combat

---

[114]Nanda, Prakash, 'Heart of Asia conference: Pakistan "embarrassed" on terrorism, but policy will continue', *FirstPost*, 5 December 2016, https://www.firstpost.com/india/sc-reserves-verdict-on-pleas-seeking-rs-4-lakh-ex-gratia-to-kin-of-covid-19-deceased-9738511.html, accessed 21 June 2021.

terrorism. Pakistan has pledged $500 million for Afghanistan's development. This amount can be spent to contain extremism,' Ghani said, directly addressing Foreign Affairs Adviser Sartaj Aziz, who was in attendance at the two-day discourse.[115]

'Afghanistan suffered the highest number of casualties last year. This is unacceptable... Some still provide sanctuary for terrorists. As a Taliban figure said recently, if they had no sanctuary in Pakistan, they wouldn't last a month,' the Afghan president thundered.[116] He emphasized the need to 'confront the fifth spectrum in the room, which is terrorism' and called on Pakistan to 'verify cross-border activities.'[117] The Afghan president appreciated India's support to Afghanistan, which he said comes 'with no strings attached. The relationship is based in shared values and beliefs.'[118]

Adviser to the Prime Minister on Foreign Affairs Aziz, on his part, said, 'It is simplistic to blame only one country for the recent upsurge in violence. We need to have an objective and holistic view... Pakistan is ready to extend every kind of cooperation for lasting peace in Afghanistan,' he said, adding that Afghanistan should avoid levelling false and baseless accusations at Pakistan.[119] The adviser said that peace talks

---

[115]FP Staff, 'Heart of Asia summit: Afghanistan prez wants intervention on Pakistan; "no blame games",' *FirstPost*, 4 December, 2016, https://www.firstpost.com/india/heart-of-asia-summit-afghanistan-prez-wants-intervention-on-pakistan-no-blame-games-3138972.html, accessed 21 June 2021.

[116]Miglani, Sanjeev, 'Afghan president says Taliban wouldn't last a month without Pakistan support,' Reuters, 4 December 2016, https://www.reuters.com/article/us-india-afghanistan-idUSKBN13T0CM, accessed 21 June 2021.

[117]APP, 'Ghani, Modi lash out at Pakistan on terrorism at Heart of Asia moot in Amritsar,' *Dawn*, 4 December 2016, https://www.dawn.com/news/1300452, accessed 21 June 2021.

[118]Ibid.

[119]Ibid.

between the Afghan government and the Taliban had not produced positive results, adding that Pakistan was making a serious effort to facilitate peace talks through the QCG.

Although Modi did not refer explicitly to Pakistan in his speech at the Heart of Asia Conference, he had vowed to step up a drive to isolate Pakistan diplomatically following the Uri army base attack on 18 September 2016, which it blamed on Pakistan—an allegation that Islamabad denied.

After being marginalized in the strategic game for long, India was recovering its lost ground in Afghanistan. It was now Pakistan's turn to slip into rough waters in Afghanistan. Pakistan–Afghanistan ties were at its lowest ebb after the conference in December 2016. The US was showing all signs of a republican victory in the presidential election concluded on 8 November 2016. Throughout his presidential campaign, Trump was acerbic in his charges against Pakistan for fanning terrorism. He was clearly holding Pakistan responsible for aiding and abetting terrorism in Afghanistan. This was clearly indicative of a change of policy in the White House, while dealing with Pakistan in the Trump era. President Trump continued with his tirade against Pakistan even after assuming office on 20 January 2017. His recurrent and rancorous tweet against Pakistan made Islamabad more than worried. Walking the talk, Trump unveiled a new Afghanistan policy in the third week of August 2017. As expected, the policy exposed the deceit and duplicity game played by Pakistan in Afghanistan. While elaborating on the policy, President Trump said, 'Today, 20 US-designated foreign terrorist organizations are active in Afghanistan and Pakistan—the highest concentration in any region anywhere in the world.'[120] He further said, 'For its part,

---

[120]India TV News Desk, '"You have much to lose by harbouring terrorists": Trump warns Pakistan as he unveils new Afghan policy,' India TV, 22 August

Pakistan often gives safe haven to agents of chaos, violence, and terror.'

Armed with the US charge on Pakistan for fanning terrorism in Afghanistan, President Ghani further stepped up his attack against Pakistan. In a hard-hitting attack against Pakistan while visiting India in the last week of October 2017, Ghani said, 'the time has come for Islamabad to make a clear choice, suggesting the country may have to pay a price under the US' new South Asia policy if it does not stop backing terror groups.'[121] Hailing India's role in Afghanistan, he added, 'the new US policy was an important tribute to the importance of New Delhi in bringing peace and stability to the region, hit by the spectre of terror.'[122] This rubbed salt into the wounds of Pakistan. India finding traction in the new South Asia policy of President Trump upped the ante further. Pakistan was facing heat from all sides.

They were bearing the brunt for supporting the Taliban and other terrorist groups. In one of his first tweets of 2018, President Trump accused Pakistan of deceiving the US and harbouring terrorists while accepting billions of dollars in foreign aid, an equation that would no longer be tolerated. In his tweet he said, 'The United States has foolishly given Pakistan more than 33 billion dollars in aid over the last 15 years, and they have given us nothing but lies and deceit, thinking of our leaders as fools. They give safe haven to the terrorists we

---

2017, https://www.indiatvnews.com/news/world-trump-warns-pakistan-against-harbouring-terrorists-as-he-unveils-new-afghan-policy-397569, accessed 21 June 2021.

[121]PTI, 'Pakistan needs to make a choice: Ashraf Ghani on terrorism,' *The Economic Times,* 24 October 2017, https://economictimes.indiatimes.com/news/international/world-news/pakistan-needs-to-make-a-choice-ashraf-ghani-on-terrorism/articleshow/61207506.cms?from=mdr, accessed 21 June 2021.

[122]Ibid.

hunt in Afghanistan, with little help. No more!' The tweet was followed by the announcements that the US was withholding payments of more than $250 million in aid that it delayed sending to Islamabad in August, due to Pakistan's perceived failure to crack down more effectively on terror groups operating from within its own boundary. The US resorted to harsh tweets-cum-punitive action throughout 2018. President Trump suspended an estimated $2 billion in security aid to Islamabad after accusing it of continuing to give sanctuary to the Afghan Taliban, despite months of warnings that the US was losing patience. President Ghani too kept the pressure on from Afghanistan's end. It was not only India, Afghanistan and the US were also against Pakistan. Pakistan's policy on Afghanistan alienated NATO allies too, which still have troops stationed in Afghanistan, albeit in a non-combatant role. Only China and Turkey were behind Islamabad. Pakistan was on the verge of losing the Afghan game.

Pakistan had no scarcity of cheaper and committed terrorists in the Taliban and Haqqani network. The low-cost, abundant supply of these terrorists had served as an effective tool of foreign policy for the Pakistan military establishment, specially while dealing with Afghanistan and India. Reportedly, Islamabad was keen to change its approach in Afghanistan with the erosion of their international image. But the Pakistan army once again was vehemently against it and wanted an extension of the status quo in Afghanistan. As the Pakistan army enjoyed an upper hand with regard to the country's policy towards Afghanistan and India, the civilian government was not in any position to resist their military doctrine.

Getting clear signals from their masters in Rawalpindi, the Taliban and the Haqqani network continued their unabated violence and attacks in Afghanistan. The destruction and devastation touched alarming heights despite Pakistan being kept under pressure by the US President with his constant outburst and frozen grants. Was the new US policy in Afghanistan working in favour of the Afghan populace? This was anyone's guess. It was by no means stabilizing Afghanistan to help the US exit from the Afghan conundrum. On the contrary, it was emboldening the Taliban and making Afghanistan further unstable and volatile. More importantly, the status quo was generating greater confidence for Pakistan about its winning formula of supporting the Taliban and Haqqani network, despite all odds.

It was all clear that the new strategy of Afghanistan was not working. The spur in the war and destruction was eating away President Trump's carefully cultivated strong image of 'America first' policy. Reverting on the Afghan policy was not an option for President Trump. And Pakistan was hell-bent on continuing with their dividend-yielding strategy. President Trump increasingly realized that intensifying military operation in Afghanistan against enemies who were operating from Pakistan, and who were motivated to die as martyrs, was not the solution to the problem. A fresh approach was required to solve the Afghan quagmire.

Trump started sending feelers to the Taliban that the US was open to talks and rapprochement with the Taliban for fixing Afghanistan. Back-channel discussions were initiated with the Taliban by mid-2018. Pakistan was also going through the process of political change and leadership in Islamabad. Imran Khan was sworn in as the 22nd Prime Minister of Pakistan on 18 August 2018, after his party swept the controversial general election. After assuming power, he projected himself against terrorism and expressed his keenness in solving the vexed issue of Kashmir and Afghanistan.

Yet, the US was not keen on impressing upon Pakistan to help the US solve the Afghan mess. President Trump wanted to bet on his proposal for direct talks with the Taliban. He decided to approach the highly important task on his own. Khalilzad, who served as US ambassador to Afghanistan and Iraq and as UN ambassador during the administration of President Bush, was named President Trump's special adviser to Afghanistan in the second week of September 2018. His job was to try to bring the Afghan government and the Taliban to a reconciliation. Khalilzad's appointment was a sign that the Trump administration was serious about a political solution to the US's longest war.

Meanwhile, the Twitter battle shifted to Trump vs Khan. The tirade of acerbic tweets hitting Pakistan continued. From America's usual refrain to Pakistan of 'Do More', Trump tweet-jumped to Pakistan 'do[es] nothing for us'.[123] Nothing unites Pakistan quicker than a Trump tweet or blaming Pakistan for supporting terrorism. Khan was not to hide and let his barrage of cabinet ministers take on the Twitter battle with the White House. Khan too responded quite strongly to the tweet. Responding to President Trump, he tweeted, 'Instead of making Pakistan a scapegoat for their failures, the US should do a serious assessment of why, despite 1,40,000 NATO troops plus 2,50,000 Afghan troops and reportedly $1 trillion spent on war in Afghanistan, the Taliban today are stronger than before.'[124] This brought a chill to the US–Pak relationship for the rest of 2018. However, the US moved ahead with the peace plan. Peace ambassador Khalilzad was keen to seal the deal

---

[123]Tarar, Mehr, 'Imran vs Trump: Pakistan emerge as the victor', Gulf News, 21 November 2018.

[124]Chaubey, Santosh, 'Pakistan Army chief hits back at US President Trump', *India Today*, 21 November 2018.

with Pakistan in order to enlist their cooperation in the peace process with the Taliban.

The rancorous exchange between Islamabad and Washington subsided with the progress of the peace process in the first half of 2019. There was quite a chill in the bilateral relationship. However, both Washington and Islamabad realized the indispensability of each other. Officials in the Pentagon realized and subsequently accepted the centrality of Pakistan once again to advance and conclude the Afghan peace process. And Islamabad, on its part, needed the US to end its international isolation and come out of its worst economic crisis. The peace process was gathering momentum and unexpectedly moving at a much faster pace. Pakistan was more than helpful by delivering the Taliban leadership to the table for peace talks. Trump's close aides and team working on Afghanistan were impressed with Pakistan's extra enthusiasm in advancing the dialogue with the Taliban.

The officials' briefings pleased President Trump to the extent that he invited Pakistan for a one-to-one meeting at the White House on 22 July 2019. It was time for both the US and Pakistan to repair and reset the bilateral ties. The two first-term leaders met and had wide-ranging discussions mainly centred on Afghanistan.

Prime Minister Khan's visit to the US could be termed as a resounding success. Pakistan was able to converge its Afghan policy with that of the US. Primarily, the focus of Khan's meeting with President Trump remained on Afghanistan. However, Pakistan was successful in linking Afghanistan and the Indian part of Kashmir, with an analogy that the former cannot be solved without the latter. In doing so, Pakistan employed one of its greatest sources of leverage with the US, by agreeing to deliver the Taliban leadership to the table for the conclusive round of the peace talks, in lieu of US mediation in Kashmir. Prime Minister Khan impressed President Trump to the extent that the latter expressed willingness to mediate between India and Pakistan. What made the situation worse for New Delhi was Trump's reference to a conversation with India's Prime Minister Modi, where the latter allegedly asked for US mediation to resolve the issue of Kashmir.[125] Trump's statement, however, was denied by India, within hours, with New Delhi maintaining its long-standing policy that it does not accept third-party intervention on the issue of Kashmir.

While Islamabad was basking in the diplomatic victory, there were criticisms emanating from New Delhi, Kabul and even from their own proxy Taliban for linking Afghanistan with Kashmir. Quite unexpectedly, the Taliban urged both India and Pakistan not to turn Afghanistan into the 'theatre of competition,' Taliban spokesperson Zabihullah Mujahed said.[126] 'Linking the issue of Kashmir with that of Afghanistan by some parties will not aid in improving the crisis at hand because the issue of Afghanistan is not related.' President Ghani too chided Islamabad for linking Kashmir with the Afghan crisis. Pakistan's efforts to link Kashmir with the US-led peace process in Afghanistan was 'reckless, unwarranted and irresponsible', Kabul asserted as it also slammed Islamabad's 'sinister intention' to prolong the violence in the country.[127]

---

[125]The Wire Staff, 'Trump Says Modi Asked Him to Mediate in Kashmir Issue, India Denies Making Request,' *The Wire*, 23 July 2019, https://thewire.in/world/kashmir-issue-donald-trump-narendra-modi-imran-khan, accessed 21 June 2021.

[126]ANI, 'Don't link Afghanistan with Kashmir issue: Taliban rebukes Pak,' *Business Standard*, 9 August 2019, https://www.business-standard.com/article/news-ani/don-t-link-afghanistan-with-kashmir-issue-taliban-rebukes-pak-119080900065_1.html, accessed 21 June 2021.

[127]PTI, '"Reckless, unwarranted and irresponsible": Afghanistan slams Pakistan's efforts to link Kashmir issue with US-led peace process,' *FirstPost*, https://www.

The conclusion of the US visits certainly suggested that the US would rely heavily on Pakistan, in solving the Afghanistan issue through a peace-cum-political settlement. President Trump was careful about mentioning any role of India in the peace process, in the fear of annoying Pakistan. India had its sense of wariness, as Washington brought it into the loop much later.

Ever since the commencement of peace talks between the US and the Taliban started under the leadership of Khalilzad, India has again struggled to play an influential role in Afghanistan. Despite being one of Afghanistan's most valuable strategic partners, India remains a mute spectator of the US-Taliban peace talks as well as the nascent intra-Afghan negotiations. President Trump once hailed the Modi government as the US's number one partner in its South Asian strategy. India's journey from being central to Trump's Afghanistan strategy in 2017, to becoming marginal during the US-Taliban peace talks in 2018 and 2019 depicts its slipping strategic stake in the war-ravaged country. India's position of not having anything to do with the Taliban had done enough damage to its standing and stake in Afghanistan.

It was only in November 2018 that New Delhi decided to send two former Indian diplomats 'at a non-official level' to participate in the Moscow round of talks with the Taliban. The change of stance expresses its willingness to engage in discussions with the battle-hardened militants and is evidence that Delhi was open to adapt a more pragmatic stance. But perhaps it was too late, if not too little. In a regional setting, it also signifies that Pakistan has once again inflicted a heavy

---

firstpost.com/world/reckless-unwarranted-and-irresponsible-afghanistan-slams-pakistans-efforts-to-link-kashmir-issue-with-us-led-peace-process-7186961.html, accessed 21 June 2021.

defeat on India in the decades-old proxy war in Afghanistan. Pakistan outdid India once again in the peace process of Afghanistan. Pakistan is in the driver's seat of the Afghan peace process after elbowing India out of it.

As India finds itself increasingly ignored in Afghan affairs, it was pinning all hope on President Ghani to safeguard the Indian stake and strategic interest in Afghanistan. More importantly, stopping Pakistan from milking the peace process. However, New Delhi ignored other ground realities, such as the fact that the Kabul government was lacking legitimacy, that massive corruption was undermining the State and, importantly, that this was an unwinnable war and reconciliation with the Taliban was the only way out. The Taliban were not very keen on engaging in any thick dialogue with Ghani's administration in Kabul, constraining India's room to manoeuvre. The interest of Kabul was compromised by the US giving more leeway to the Taliban to define the contours and the confines of the peace process. Without doubt, Ghani remained politically weak, facing dissent from within the government and has been unable to quell the Taliban insurgency. He is no more in the good books of the US either. Nonetheless, he is going to be part of the peace process somehow at a later stage. For all the support poured from India for rebuilding Afghanistan, President Ghani must appreciate that India has genuine security interests in the entire region and these have to be safeguarded. And his tilt towards India after the initial flirting with Pakistan generates a degree of confidence in India that Kabul is unlikely to surrender the Indian interest. The only way in which the flailing Ghani government can retain and enhance its legitimacy is by bringing the Afghan economy back on track. For this it largely depends on other countries and India is playing an important role by laying the foundations for sustainable economic development in the war-ravaged country. At a time when international aid is dwindling in Afghanistan, Ghani needs New Delhi more than ever.

President Trump was increasingly upset with the relentless and unsparing attack by the Taliban, despite the ongoing peace talks. The US analyst with a keen interest for Afghanistan was critically questioning the US strategy, if the relentless killing by Taliban in the midst of the peace talk is acceptable. And is the Taliban really serious about peace? The attacks by the Taliban in the midst of peace negotiations was eating away the carefully built 'tough guy' image of President Trump, thus eroding his chances of a second stint in the White House.

Besides Pakistan and Taliban, no one was complaining either. This was a blessing in disguise for India. India was quick to welcome the cancellation of US-Afghan Taliban peace talks in Doha. In an expression of support for Kabul, which was ostracized from the talks, New Delhi asserted that any future process on the issue must include 'all sections of the Afghan society including [the] legitimately elected government.'[128] India reiterated a long-standing position of supporting Kabul against the Pakistan-sponsored Taliban. President Ghani and the entire top leadership also heaved a sigh of relief after being restricted to the sidelines from the peace process as a mute spectator. The reasons for India and Afghanistan were different though.

However, the sense of relief for both Afghanistan and India was short-lived. In a complete U-turn, the US signed a landmark peace agreement with the Taliban on 29 February 2020 in Doha in the presence of representatives of 50 countries. The deal

---

[128]The Wire Staff, 'Afghan Presidential Election Process Has India's Full Backing, MEA Confirms,' *The Wire*, 12 September 2019, https://thewire.in/diplomacy/afghan-presidential-election-process-india-mea, accessed 21 June 2021.

was signed by US special envoy Khalilzad and Taliban political chief Mullah Abdul Ghani Baradar with US Secretary of State Mike Pompeo as a witness. As part of the deal, the US, within the first 135 days of the US-Taliban agreement, would reduce its forces in Afghanistan to 8,600, which stood at 13,000, with allies also drawing down their forces proportionately. A full withdrawal of all US and coalition forces would occur within 14 months of this deal being signed, if the Taliban held up their end of the deal, the joint statement said. For Trump, the Doha deal represented a chance to make good on his promise to bring US troops home. The most contentious part of the deal was an agreement for prisoner swap.

Both parties started releasing prisoners and at the same time blaming each other on falling short of the promises made under the US-brokered peace deal. Some 5,000 prisoners, mostly Taliban have been released as part of the deal between the Taliban and the Afghan government in the midst of continual Afghan war. Both the government of Afghanistan and the Taliban had to engage in an intra-Afghan dialogue to thrash out the full scope and power-sharing arrangement under the peace deal. This looks very bleak given the constant attack against each other. At this time, Afghan forces and the Taliban are attacking each other and at the same time siting with each other after a pause to deliberate on peace. Both the US and the Taliban had wind of the tough path that lies ahead. There is a deep uncertainty and scepticism around the peace deal, about whether it would end the Afghan war.

While Pakistan was at the forefront of the newly signed peace deal, India was once again missing from the frame. Pakistan was again praised for bringing the Taliban to the peace table. Much to the worry of India, the US has further enlisted a role for Islamabad to provide backhand support to facilitate the intra-Afghan dialogue, and oversee the conclusion of the peace deal. The Indian analysts put the blame on the US, arguing that Washington ditched India after leading it up the garden path. Pakistan, its arch-rival, would step in more aggressively to hurt Indian interests in the war-ravaged country. New Delhi expects anarchy to intensify in the backdrop of an US withdrawal without a durable solution, as insurgents in Afghanistan would repeatedly attack and undermine local and international confidence in the viability of the extant political structures in Kabul.

After the controversial election in Afghanistan, the US was successful in making President Ghani sign a power-sharing deal with his political foe Abdullah Abdullah and present a coalition government, popularly referred to as 'Unity Government 2.0' to take forward the peace deal. Ghani and Abdullah have been in a bitter feud over the presidency for more than half a year after a presidential election that triggered dissent and rivalry. As the two leaders finally clambered out of the ditch and ended the long-standing political dispute, a big portion of the puzzle is solved and the country can move on—without encumbrance—with its peace plans. It is widely reported that Khalilzad's quick visit on 7 March 2020 was to placate growing concerns of India for being sidelined in the Afghan peace process and further enlisting the good office of Modi to agree to both the warring leaders of Afghanistan to sign a power broker deal.

Incidentally, India enjoys good influence over both Ghani as well as Abdullah Abdullah. India certainly played its part in cobbling the unity government in Kabul. The peace envoy mentioned that India had a significant role to play in Afghanistan's development, but paradoxically, does not play a role in the peace efforts. He further stressed that India must engage in the peace process and directly open a dialogue with the Taliban. This was largely said to placate India and generate good press coverage. Khalilzad knows it well that Pakistan will not allow a meaty role for India in the peace process. And the US cannot afford to annoy Islamabad when the peace process is set to enter its final phase.

The peace process has been paused for the time being, but the Afghan government will eventually try to seal the deal with the Taliban in some form or the other. Alternatively, the Taliban will run over Kabul at some point of time. And in both cases, the ascent of the Taliban to power in Kabul, in considerable form is pragmatically conceivable. India cannot set aside the probability of dealing with a Taliban-laced power structure in near term. As and when the Taliban come to be in a position of power following a political settlement (or otherwise), Pakistan's long-standing goal of fixing a pro-Pakistan, anti-India Afghan government would be achieved. India has to deal with an exultant Pakistan that is ahead of the strategic race compared to India. The return of the Taliban to Afghanistan would pose a major threat to India's interest in Afghanistan, along with its own borders. And this spectre is haunting Delhi the most—the strong likelihood of a Taliban takeover in Afghanistan, and of a Sharia State emerging in India's neighbourhood. Pakistan would continue to invest its strategic stake in advancing such a reality to push India back.

Epicentre of rivalry

Afghanistan is the new epicentre of extended India–Pakistan rivalry, after Kashmir. A conventional military reaction is probably too costly for Pakistan, given its struggle with precarious finances. With India's conventional military forces being far superior, Pakistan will always harp on asymmetrical means. Hence, Pakistan would continue to ride its most effective and time-tested strategies against India—using an array of militant groups as proxies to continuously bleed India. Once the US winds up in Kabul, a lot of Pakistan-based militant groups have an incentive to turn their focus and latent energy against India. These groups that were operating in Afghanistan will no longer have US troops to turn their gun, giving them the motivation to refocus their attention and pent-up energy on the Indian part of Kashmir. Their handlers in Pakistan would leave no stone unturned to motivate them with aid and equipment to target Indian interest. In the end, the brunt of Taliban-fuelled terrorism will be borne by India, which has already been described as 'the sponge that protects the West'.[129] It will take a lot to get Pakistan to change the calculus as well as its well-established and dividend-yielding track in Afghanistan.

India also has to deal with an aggressive China on its own. If China's overarching shadows stretch over the Hindu Kush and canvass Afghanistan as a hub of the BRI, which seem quite evident, the great game will resume. As the US vacates Kabul, China would seek to establish its dominant presence in the Hindu Kush. With the US losing its hegemony in Afghanistan for a foreseeable future, India's strategic relevance is bound to slide significantly in the region. The all-weather duo of Pakistan and China would restrict the strategic growth of India, along with its economic foray into the CAR too.

This is a seriously uncomfortable position to be in, after being one of the largest civilian donors of Afghanistan,

---

[129]Saxena, Sobhan,'Who will take out Lashkar-e-Taiba founder Hafiz Saeed?' *The Economic Times*, 8 April 2012.

and with a genuine intention to rebuild Afghanistan. Many in India would blame the Trump administration for the strategic slippage of India in the rapidly evolving situation of Afghanistan. But that is not a fair assessment of the situation. Washington has its own web of interests in Afghanistan that it intends to promote and safeguard. It is likely that in the process, it would preserve some Indian interest in Afghanistan. After all, the US needs India beyond Afghanistan to maintain a favourable balance of power in the Indo-Pacific and beyond. However, excessive dependency on the US and fragile Afghan government to bat for India, especially when India is aspiring to be a leading global power, looks impractical.

The long-running conflict between India and Pakistan has caused the US to be held hostage to the competing foreign policy goals between the two of them. The more aid the US gives to Pakistan to assist with counter-terrorism efforts, the more it is perceived as a threat to India by shoring up Pakistani military power. But when India stripped the Indian part of Kashmir of its autonomy, it was set to complicate the vexed issue of Afghanistan further. The US will further find it difficult to balance its Indo-Pak outreach. Pakistan, which has launched a major lobbying effort, would continue to impress Washington to reverse the move of India in Kashmir. Pakistan would even step up its engagement in solving the Afghan imbroglio, if the White House mediates the Kashmir issue with India. Like Trump, the Biden administration too is not buying the Pakistani argument that the road to peace in Kabul passes through Kashmir and rejects the hypothesis that the Kashmir issue and the Afghan problem are inter-related. India, in turn, has convinced the White House that the Kashmir issue is a bilateral conflict between India and Pakistan.

If the US asserts power to settle the long-standing dispute

of Kashmir, it seriously risks cooling relations with India, which it can ill afford. India is needed for a long-term and a bigger role. This explains why the US is reluctant to speak out against the human rights violations in Kashmir. The US will be unable to defeat the Taliban without help from Pakistan. And prolonged silence on the part of the White House on Kashmir would rupture Prime Minister Khan's new-found motivation to extend enhanced cooperation in getting the Taliban to ink a deal with the Afghan government for political settlement of Afghanistan. Every action to strengthen on one side annoys the other side. It is a vicious trap the US President walked into. The US foreign policy is largely dominated by its efforts to push back against what it views as a China threat. And India, with its similar rivalry with China, is perceived by Washington as the perfect and natural ally to help pursue that goal. Hence, Washington would desist from needling India on Kashmir, but at the same time not allow an open licence in Afghanistan.

In the meantime, everyone is looking at the newly elected US President Biden. As of now, he has maintained a much annoying silence on this prickly issue. He has neither chided Pakistan nor supported India on Afghanistan after assuming power. His silence has been extended on the vexed issue of Kashmir too in the fear of annoying one at the expense of the other. He can ill afford the silence for long. In every likelihood, President Biden would revise the timeline of US troop withdrawal without altering the basic structure of the peace deal. This will peeve the Taliban, but they will not lose out on anything even if the US abandons the peace deal. Hence, they are not much bothered about the new US policy, if any regarding Afghanistan. The Taliban dialogue with the Afghan government is almost broken, with no party showing up real intent and urge to conclude the peace deal.

The relationship between Pakistan and Afghanistan is on the downturn, and continues to slip in the recent months. Afghanistan is bleeding with the onslaught of Pakistan-enabled Taliban even with the on-again, off-again peace negotiations. The casualty and the destruction are unprecedented in the war-strife history of Afghanistan. The Taliban are dismembering the various districts and provinces of Afghanistan and making the civilian government weak. The writ of the Ghani government is openly challenged. The Ghani government is increasingly seeing an Islamabad footprint in all of these.

These developments have turned not only the Afghan government, but also the civilian populace against Islamabad. The rising border tension is a new addition to the long list of woes in the troubled bilateral relationship. Pakistan is unilaterally installing a robust fence along most of the frontier and believes it would address mutual security concerns.[130] This is seriously contested by Kabul, as the Durand Line has been disputed and remains unsettled. The border dispute between Afghanistan and Pakistan has flared up significantly in recent years, with frequent skirmishes and gun battles between the two forces leading to death of soldiers on both sides. The growing border tension and consequent killing may turn the Durand Line into a hotbed of border conflict, like the LOC between India and Pakistan, in Kashmir. These complex sets of issues have evoked anti-Pakistan sentiment within Afghanistan. The flare up of anti-Pakistan emotion has only strengthened pro-India sentiments among Afghans. It was reported that Afghans wildly celebrated the Balakot air strikes by the Indian

---

[130]Gul, Ayaz, 'Pakistan's Fencing of Afghan Border Remains Source of Mutual Tensions,' VOA, 15 October 2018, https://www.voanews.com/south-central-asia/pakistans-fencing-afghan-border-remains-source-mutual-tensions, accessed 21 June 2021.

Air Force through social media. When Afghanistan–Pakistan relationship is at its lowest ebb, India must step up its role in the Afghanistan peace process.

Pakistan is also facing the heat with its rising unpopularity in Afghanistan. And it has no option, beyond the Taliban, to resurrect its falling image. The economy is in the throes of a collapse and its key international allies have either maintained silence over Kashmir or defected in support of India. There is an increasing international pressure on Islamabad to break its ties with the Taliban and other terrorist networks spreading unrest in Afghanistan. Pakistan is already in the grey list of FATF, a watchdog of an inter-governmental body mandated to combat money laundering and terrorist financing. China is holding its slippage from 'grey' to 'black' for the time being.

India may not be a primary player in Afghanistan. It is not secondary either. India has got the ability to influence the calculus of Afghanistan. There is too much at stake and New Delhi should become more proactively involved and not be shy of even shoring up military engagement with Afghanistan. The outgoing US President Trump said in his last phase of presidential career that India should also be fighting against terrorism in Afghanistan—Pakistan should be fighting more—and not just the US that is '7,000 miles away'.[131] There are various ways of doing it, even without sending boots to the conflict-ridden country.

The Minister of External Affairs, S. Jaishankar said, 'For India, the priority is a stable and plural Afghanistan and the defeat of the Taliban. This would ensure that the region is

---

[131]The Associated Press, 'Trump dismisses U.S. stakes in Syria: "We're 7,000 miles away", *Arkansas Democrat Gazette,* 16 October 2019, https://www.arkansasonline.com/news/2019/oct/16/trump-says-us-troops-largely-out-syria-region/, accessed 21 June 2021.

not a hotbed for terrorism and is instead a conduit to Central Asia.'[132] Between India and Pakistan, the soft power of the great game has clearly played out in favour of India, making it wildly popular among Afghans in the race of earning civilian goodwill. But Pakistan has unquestionably kept India behind them in the strategic race to gain dominance and extend influence in Afghanistan, in both the pre- and post-peace process era. But the strategic slippage should not become permanent and a standard template of regional politics. It is time for India to get even. This is important not only because India's interests are involved, but also because the hopes and aspirations of ordinary Afghans cannot be trampled to satisfy the evil agenda of any single power. New Delhi should make it clear that India can win the strategic race too.

---

[132]Haider, Kamran, 'India, Pakistan battle for influence over Afghanistan,' *Mint*, 21 November 2016, https://www.livemint.com/Politics/mDs3mqjXCQs E3lD1ZrQDCP/India-Pakistan-battle-for-influence-over-Afghanistan.html, accessed 21 June 2021.

Acknowledgements

In the year 2005, when I first stepped on Afghan land, I was mesmerized by its rugged beauty and old-world charm. I soaked myself in its picturesque settings and the fantastic camaraderie, along with an unflinching commitment to make governance assuage the plights of Afghan citizens. Afghanistan was vibrant and there was abundant hope and optimism. My quest for a New Afghanistan turned into my first literary endeavour too! My first book *In Search of a New Afghanistan* was released in July 2012. Years rolled by and I found myself standing on the threshold of 2019, with myriad questions. What have we achieved in Afghanistan? Why am I being engulfed with a mixed feeling of hope and despair? In my quest to delve deeper into the root of the crisis that Afghanistan was facing, I unravelled quite a few knots while others still remain.

However, in this quest, first and foremost, I am deeply indebted to all my Afghan colleagues, friends and confidants, whose names I cannot reveal, but they continue to hold a special place in my heart. My deep gratitude to all of them. May they remain protected by the Almighty God.

Anindita Kali, my wife, who urged me to write the book, was my encouragement as well as critique as she read through my draft. A big Thank You to her! My ever-inquisitive son Ishaan too calls for appreciation for never getting tired of peppering me with questions about Afghanistan.

My special thanks to few close friends who made me believe that I was not meant to be a one-book wonder. I am grateful to Jehanara Wasi, my editor friend, for editing my book at the first level.

I am also grateful to my publishers, Rupa Publications, and its editorial team, with whom I went back and forth to give the book its final shape. Thank you for believing in the book and making it see the light of day.

Abbreviations

ADB	Asian Development Bank
ANA	Afghan National Army
ANASTU	Afghan National Agriculture Sciences and Technology University
ANSF	Afghan National Security Forces
ARVN	Army of the Republic of Vietnam
BRI	Belt and Road Initiative
BRO	Border Roads Organization
CAR	Central Asian Republics
CDC	Community Development Council
CIA	Central Intelligence Agency
CPEC	China–Pakistan Economic Corridor
CPI	Corruption Perception Index
DFID	Department for International Development
FATA	Federally Administered Tribal Areas
FATF	Financial Action Task Force
FDI	Foreign Direct Investment
GDP	Gross Domestic Product
GPS	Global Positioning System
HoA-IP	Heart of Asia-Istanbul Process

IARCSC	Independent Administrative Reform and Civil Service Commission
IDLG	Independent Directorate of Local Governance
IMF	International Monetary Fund
INGO	International Non-Governmental Organization
ISAF	International Security Assistance Force
ISI	Inter-services Intelligence
MADRAC	Micro Finance Agency for Development and Rehabilitation of Afghan Communities
MAIL	Ministry for Agriculture, Irrigation and Livestock
MISFA	Microfinance Investment Support Facility for Afghanistan
MoD	Ministry of Defence
MoE	Ministry of Education
MoPH	Ministry of Public Health
MoWA	Ministry of Women's Affairs
MRRD	Ministry for Rural Reconstruction and Development
MSP	Minimum Support Price
NABDP	National Area Based Development Programme
NATO	North Atlantic Treaty Organization
NDS	National Directorate of Security
NGO	Non-governmental Organization
NSP	National Solidarity Programme
NUG	National Unity Government
NWFP	North West Frontier Province
PMO	Prime Minister's Office
PoK	Pakistan-occupied Kashmir
PRT	Provincial Reconstruction Team
PTI	Pakistan Tehreek-e-Insaf
QCG	Quadrilateral Coordination Group
RAW	Research and Analysis Wing

SAARC	South Asian Association for Regional Cooperation
SIGAR	Special Inspector General for Afghanistan Reconstruction
TAPI	Turkmenistan, Afghanistan, Pakistan and India gas pipe line
TTP	Tehrik-e Taliban Pakistan
UAE	United Arab Emirates
UK	United Kingdom
UN	United Nations
UNAMA	United Nations Assistance Mission for Afghanistan
UNDP	United Nations Development Programme
UNHAS	United Nations Humanitarian Airline Services
UNODC	United Nations Office on Drugs and Crime
USA	United States of America
USAID	United States Agency for International Development
VAT	Value-added tax
WB	World Bank
WJP	World Justice Project
WoT	War on Terror

Glossary

Afwa: Political pardon.

Al Jazeera: An international English news channel, with headquarters in Doha, Qatar. Initially launched as an Arabic news and current affairs satellite TV channel with the same name.

al-Qaeda: An international terrorist organization network comprising loosely affiliated cells that carry out attacks and bombings in the attempt to disrupt the economies and influence of western nations and advance Islamic fundamentalism. The group is held responsible for the 9/11 terror attack on the World Trade Centre, US.

Bonn Conference: After Operation Enduring Freedom in which the Taliban government was toppled in Afghanistan, in December 2001, the German city of Bonn hosted a conference of Afghan leaders at Hotel Petersberg, to choose the leader of an Afghan Interim Authority—widely known as the Bonn Conference.

Burqa: A loose black or light blue robe, worn by Muslim women, especially, in Afghanistan, that covers the body from head to toe.

Haqqani: A Taliban-affiliated insurgent group, currently based in North Waziristan, Pakistan. The network is led by the father and son duo of (the late) Maulvi Jalaluddin Haqqani and Sirajuddin Haqqani. According to US military commanders, the network is the most notorious faction of the Taliban and considered one of the biggest threats to Afghanistan. The network is known for attacking Indian interests in Afghanistan, including the Indian embassy.

Hijab: A headscarf worn by Muslim women, sometimes a veil, that covers the face, except for the eyes.

Jihad: An Islamic, which means religious duty of Muslims. Muslims use the word in a religious context to refer to three types of struggles: An internal struggle to maintain moral and virtuous life, the struggle for spreading and defending Islam, or the struggle against injustice. However, with the passage of time, the Islamic fundamentalists used the term to mobilize Muslim youths to fight western and Indian interests, in the name of freedom from injustice.

Jirgas: Local consultation meetings.

Loya Jirga: Grand council or grand assembly of elders.

Madrasa: A school, where mostly Islamic studies take place.

Mujahideen: A person engaged in jihad is called a Mujahid; the plural is Mujahideen. However, in Afghanistan, Mujahideen is referred as a military force of Muslim guerrilla warriors who fought Soviet occupation in Afghanistan.

Sharia: Code of conduct or religious law of Islam.

SIGAR: Special Inspector General for Afghanistan Reconstruction (SIGAR) is the US government's leading oversight authority on Afghanistan reconstruction.

Taliban: Islamist militia group that ruled large parts of

Afghanistan from September 1996 onwards. Although in control of Afghanistan's capital (Kabul) and most of the country for five years, the Taliban's Islamic Emirate of Afghanistan gained diplomatic recognition from only three states—Pakistan, Saudi Arabia and the UAE. After the attacks of 11 September 2001, the Taliban regime was overthrown by Operation Enduring Freedom. The Taliban mostly fled to neighbouring Pakistan, where they regrouped as an insurgency movement to fight the democratic Islamic Republic of Afghanistan (established in late 2001) and the NATO-led International Security Assistance Force (ISAF).

Soviet Occupation: The Soviet war in Afghanistan was a nine-year conflict involving the Soviet Union supporting the Marxist Government of Afghanistan, against the Afghan Mujahideen and foreign 'Arab-Afghan' volunteer. The initial Soviet deployment of the 40th Army in Afghanistan began on 24 December 1979 and the final troop withdrawal ended on 15 February 1989.

Afghan Warlord: A warlord is a person with power who has both military (mostly private), and civil control over a certain region in Afghanistan.

ISAF: ISAF is a NATO-led security mission in Afghanistan established by the United Nation Security Council on 20 December 2001 by Resolution 1386, as envisaged by the Bonn agreement. It is engaged in the war in Afghanistan. ISAF is engaged in intensive combat operations against Taliban and al-Qaeda militants in Afghanistan.

Mullah: It is generally used to refer to a Muslim man, educated in Islamic theology and sacred law.

Bibliography

Chapter 1: Poppy: The Axis of All Evils
1. McCoy, Alfred W. 'How the heroin trade explains the US-UK failure in Afghanistan', *The Guardian*, 9 January 2018.
2. 'How the US military's opium war was lost', BBC News, 25 April 2019.
3. 'Afghanistan opium survey, 2001, 2002, 2004, 2007, 2010, 2012, 2014, 2016, 2017, 2018, 2019', UNODC.
4. PTI, 'Record-high opium production in Afghanistan creates multiple challenges for the region and beyond', *The Economic Times*, 22 May 2018.
5. Hennigan, W.J., 'The US sent its most advanced fighter jets to blow up cheap opium labs. Now its cancelling the programme', *Time*, 21 February 2019.
6. Whitlock, Craig, 'Overwhelmed by Opium', *The Washington Post*, 9 December 2019.
7. Felbab-Brown, Vanda, 'Afghanistan's Opium Production Is Through the Roof-Why Washington Shouldn't Overreact', Brookings, 21 November 2017.
8. Standish, Reid, 'This is What 12 Years of Failed Drug Policy Looks Like in Afghanistan', *Foreign Policy*, 27 June 2014.
9. Byrd, William A., 'Responding to Afghanistan's Opium Economy Challenge: Lessons and Policy Implications from a

Development Perspective', World Bank, March 2008.

10. 'US Bombing of Drug Labs in Afghanistan Is Just Counterproductive to Fighting the Taliban, Qayoom Soroush', *Just Security*, 6 September 2018.

11. Peters, Gretchen, 'How Opium Profits the Taliban', USIP, 2 August 2009.

12. Ahmad, Azam, 'Tasked with Combatting Opium, Afghan Officials Profit from it', *The New York Times*, 15 February 2016.

13. 'Counternarcotic: Lessons from the US Experience in Afghanistan', SIGAR, 19 June 2018.

14. Rahmaty, Sohrab, 'A Solution for Afghanistan's Opium Crisis?' *The Diplomat*, 2 December 2014.

15. Peterson, Elizabeth, 'Two Sides of the Same Coin: The Link Between Illicit Opium Production and Security in Afghanistan', *Washington University Journal of Law and Policy*, January 2007.

16. Walters, P. John, and Murray W. David, 'Kill All the Poppies', *Foreign Policy*, 22 November 2017.

17. Nissenbaum, Dion, 'Months of US Strikes Have Failed to Curtail Taliban's Opium Trade', *The Wall Street Journal*, 8 August 2018.

18. 'The Big Question: Why is Opium Production Rising in Afghanistan, and Can It Be Stopped?' *The Independent UK*, 14 October 2008.

Chapter 2: On-Again, Off-Again Peace Process

1. Khan, Behroz, and Faisal Shakeel, 'Which Way is the Afghan Peace Process Headed?' *Herald*, 16 April 2019.

2. Baker, Peter, Mujib Mashal, and Michael Crowley, 'How Trump's Plan to Secretly Meet with the Taliban Came Together and Fell Apart', *The New York Times*, 10 September 2019.

3. Warden, Scott, 'US-Taliban Talks Make 'Significant Progress':

What's Next?' *USIP*, 31 January 2019.

4. Glinski, Stefanie, 'Afghanistan Wants Peace, But Not Like This', *Foreign Policy*, 12 September 2019.

5. Mashal, Mujib, 'US and Taliban Agrees in Principle to a Peace Framework, Envoy Says', *The New York Times*, 28 January 2019.

6. Shams, Shamil, and Masood Saifullah, 'Afghan War-What to Expect from the US-Taliban', 27 August 2019, dw.com.

7. 'Getting the Afghan Peace Process Back on Track', crisigroup. org, 2 October 2019.

8. Akbari, Zahir Mohammad, 'Pessimisms and Optimisms About Progress of Peace Process', *Outlook Express*, 29 January 2019.

9. Bellhaus, Rebecca, and Saeed Shah, 'Trump Offers to Mediate Kashmir, But India Demurs', *The Wall Street Journal*, 22 July 2019.

10. PTI, 'Imran Khan, Trump Discusses Afghan Peace Process, Kashmir During Telephonic Conversation' *The Economic Times*, 22 November 2019.

11. Qazi, Shareena, 'Trump Cancels Taliban Talks: What Does it Mean for Afghanistan', *Al Jazeera*, 8 September 2019.

12. Tisdall, Simon, 'The US and Afghanistan: Can't Win the War, Can't Stop It, Can't Leave', *The Guardian*, 1 May 2018.

13. Ahmadi, Belquis, 'Afghan talks, no women, no peace', *USIP*, 1 March 2019.

14. 'Why is There a War in Afghanistan? The Short, Medium and Long Story', *BBC News*, 8 September 2019.

15. 'Afghan Peace Process', *Wikipedia*.

16. Salahuddin, Sayed, 'Kabul Expects US to Share Peace Deal Details', *The Arab news*, 24 August 2019.

17. Khan, Ismail, 'Taliban, US Agree on Troop Pullout Time Frame', *The Dawn*, 24 August 2019.

18. Walsh, Johnny, 'What the United States Gets Wrong About Peace Talks', *Foreign Policy*, 18 October 2019.

19. Hussain, Zahid, 'Exiting Afghanistan,' *The Dawn*, 4 September 2019.
20. 'The US War in Afghanistan,' cfr.org, 1999-2019.

Chapter 3: The Flailing and the Failing State

1. Chaudhuri, Shubham, 'Lesson from a Decade of Progress and Loss,' World Bank Blogs, 17 October 2018.
2. Malikyar, 'Helena Is This the Death of Democracy in Afghanistan?' *Al Jazeera*, 23 September 2014.
3. 'Afghanistan's Economic Growth Improves Slightly in 2019 Amid Challenges,' 26 September 2019, www.adb.org.
4. 'Afghanistan's Addiction to Foreign Aid, Mohammad Shamim,' *The Diplomat*, 19 May 2016.
5. Farzam, Reza, and Rustam Ali Seerat, 'The Failure of Foreign Aid in Afghanistan,' *The Diplomat*, 18 October 2016.
6. Lyon, David, *Politics without Parties: Afghanistan's Long Road to Democracy*, Online Publication, 29 January 2019.
7. Haidary Mohammad Shoaib, 'By Numbers, is Afghanistan's Democracy at Risk?' *Asia Foundation*, 15 August 2018.
8. Torfeh, Massoumeh, 'Why is Democracy Failing in Afghanistan?' *TRT World*, 30 October 2018.
9. Wakil, Mirwais, 'Why the US Democratic Project Failed in Afghanistan?' *The National Interest*, 21 April 2019.
10. Akbari, Mohammad Zahir, 'What are the Falling Factors of Democracy in Afghanistan,' *Daily Outlook Afghanistan*, 4 August 2019.
11. Matisson, John, 'How the West Failed Afghan Democracy,' *Financial Times*, 3 December 2010.
12. Bandow, Doug, 'The Nation Building Experiment that Failed: Time for the US to Leave Afghanistan,' forbes.com, 1 March 2017.
13. Edwards, Lucy Morgan, *State-Building in Afghanistan: A Case Showing Limits*, Cambridge University Press, 8 March 2011.

14. Witter, Jeffrey S., 'What Went Wrong: Why the US's State-Building Efforts Failed in the War in Afghanistan', digitialcommons@macalester.edu, 26 April 2016.
15. Starc, Katza, 'Limits of Internationalized State Building: The Stabilization of Post 2001 Afghanistan', The Bartlet Development Planning Unit (Working Paper No. 148).
16. 'The Doctrine of Failure in Afghanistan: Rethinking State Building and Punitive Expedition', IDGA Editor, idga.org, 7 December 2013.
17. Weijer, Frauke de, 'A Capable State in Afghanistan', Centre for International Development, Harvard University, 2013.

Chapter 4: The March of the US Follies

1. Gibbons-Neff, Thomas, 'The Army's Failure to Train and Equip Troops in Afghanistan', *The New York Times*, 9 July 2019.
2. Miller, Paul D., 'Critics Should Stop Declaring Defeat in Afghanistan', *Foreign Policy*, 12 April 2019.
3. Glaser, John, and John Mueller, 'Overcoming Inertia: Why It's Time to End the War in Afghanistan', *cato.org*, 13 August 2019.
4. DePetris, Daniel R., 'Why America Doesn't Want to Admit that it Failed in Afghanistan', *The National Interest.org*, 3 September 2019.
5. Bacevich, Andrew J., 'Op-Ed: Brutal Truths About Our Failure in Afghanistan are Being Drowned Out by Fake News', *Los Angeles Times*, 3 May 2019.
6. Barndollar, Gil, 'Op-Ed: The Options for US Withdrawal in Afghanistan? Either a Bad Deal or No Deal at All', *Los Angeles Times*, 29 August 2019.
7. 'Trump Risks Turning a Chance for Success into a Shameful Failure', Editorial View, *The Washington Post*, 19 August 2019.
8. Walt, Stephen M., 'We Lost the War. Get Over It', *Foreign*

Policy, 11 September 2019.

9. Anderson, Ben, 'The War in Afghanistan Is Far from Finished,' *Vice News*, 10 January 2015.

10. Walt, Stephen M., 'We Lost the War. Get Over It,' *Foreign Policy*, 11 September 2019.

11. Golby, Gim, and Peter Feaver 'Will Americans Call Afghanistan a Victory?' *The Atlantic*, 17 August 2019.

12. 'War in Afghanistan (2001-present),' *Wikipedia*.

13. 'United States Military Casualties in the War in Afghanistan,' *Wikipedia*.

14. Zakaria, Fareed, 'The US Needs to End the War with Afghanistan without Losing the Peace,' *The Washington Post*, 2 August 2009.

15. Bacevich, Andrew J., 'Want to Know What's Next for Afghanistan? Ask Vietnam,' *The Nation*, 11 September 2019.

16. 'The US War in Afghanistan, A Time Line,' cfr.org, ND.

Chapter 5: The UK's Helmand Misadventure

1. Lyon, David, 'What have British Troops Achieved in Afghanistan?' BBC News, 26 October 2014.

2. 'More British Troops are Being Sent to Afghanistan-to Appease Trump,' *The Guardian*, 13 August 2018.

3. 'Afghanistan: Britain Got Almost Everything Wrong and Should Admit its Failure,' *The Telegraph*, UK, 4 August 2014.

4. Grey, Stephen, 'Helmand: Anatomy of a Disaster,' *Foreign Policy*, 15 June 2010.

5. 'The Fall of Helmand,' *Al Jazeera*, 23 February 2017.

6. 'Operation Herrick, '*Wikipedia*.

7. McCoy, Alfred W., 'How the Heroin Trade Explains the UK-US Failure in Afghanistan,' *The Guardian*, 9 January 2018.

8. Farmer, Ben, 'Wars in Iraq and Afghanistan Were a Failure Costing £29,' *The Telegraph*, 28 May 2014.

9. Nineham, Chris, 'Afghanistan: Why Britain's Longest Modern War is a Failure,' *Counterfire*, 27 October 2014.

10. Moylan, Danielle, and Colin Freeman, 'Afghan District Where 106 British Troops Dies is All Set to Fall to the Taliban Again,' The *Telegraph*, 21 December 2015.

11. Glaser, John, and John Mueller, 'Overcoming Inertia: Why it is Time to End the War in Afghanistan,' CATO Institute, 13 August 2019.

12. 'Why Afghanistan is More Dangerous Than Ever,' BBC News, 14 September 2018.

13. Walt, Stephen M., 'We Lost the War in Afghanistan. Get Over It,' *Foreign Policy*, 11 September 2019.

14. 'WikiLeaks Cables Expose Afghan Contempt for British Military,' *The Guardian*, 2 December 2010.

Chapter 6: Indo-Pak Proxy Battle

1. Pant, Harsh V., 'India's Changing Afghan Policy: Regional and Global Implication,' US Army War College, Strategic Studies Institute, 14 July 2013.

2. Agarwal, Ravi, and Kathryn Salam, 'Why the Failed US-Taliban Talks Represent a Victory for India,' *Foreign Policy*, 10 September 2019.

3. Pant, Harsh V., 'India's Dilemma in Afghanistan,' Observer Research Foundation, 2 August 2019.

4. Shome, Pranav Kumar, 'Is India's Influence in Afghanistan Declining?' globalsecurityreview.com, 8 August 2019.

5. Jaison, Carl, 'Russian Taliban Bonhomie: And Opportunity for India,' southasianvoices.org, 26 September 2019.

6. 'India's Diplomatic Presence in Afghanistan Worsens Pakistani Fears of Encirclement: US Congressional Report,' 6 November 2019.

7. Akhter, Naseema, and Arif Hussain Malik, 'India's Involvement in Afghanistan: An Analytical Perspective of Current Interest and Future Prospects,' researchgate.net, December 2016.

8. 'Afghanistan-Pakistan Relations,' *Wikipedia*.

9. Hanauer, Larry, and Peter Chalk, 'India's and Pakistan's Strategy in Afghanistan: Implication of United States and the Region,' rand.org, 8 August 2012.

10. Pant, Harsh V., and Avinash Paliwal, 'India's Afghan Dilemma is Tougher Than Ever,' *Foreign Policy*, 19 February 2019.

11. 'India Pakistan Battle for Influence Over Afghanistan,' *Live Mint*, 21 November 2016.

12. 'India's Afghanistan Policy Should Rapidly Adapt to the Evolving Reality,' *The EconomicTimes*, 2 September 2019.

13. Saif, Khan Shadi, 'Afghanistan Fears Spillover of India-Pakistan Tensions,' *The Defence Post*, 28 February 2019.

14. Kumar, Ruchi, 'Afghans are Cheering for an Indian Win,' *Hikmat Noori*, 28 February 2019.

15. Jacinto, Leela, 'The Treacherous Fault Line Between Kashmir and the Afghan Peace Negotiations,' france24.com, 2 March 2019.

16. PTI, 'Pakistan Efforts to link Kashmir with Afghan Peace Process is "Reckless and Irresponsible": Afghanistan,' *The Economic Times*, 19 August 2019.

17. Aaamir, Aadnan, 'Trump Bets on Pakistan to Deliver Peace in Afghanistan,' *The Interpreter*, 7 August 2019.

Index